RUNNER

LIZZY HAWKER
RUNNER

A SHORT STORY ABOUT A LONG RUN

Aurum
Press

First published in Great Britain
2015 by Aurum Press Ltd
74—77 White Lion Street
Islington
London N1 9PF
www.aurumpress.co.uk

Maps © Alex Treadway

A catalogue record for this book is available from the British Library.

ISBN 978 1 78131 147 9
ebook ISBN 978 1 78131 467 8

1 3 5 7 9 10 8 6 4 2
2015 2017 2019 2018 2016

Typeset by SX Composing DTP, Rayleigh, Essex
Printed and bound by CPI Group (UK) Ltd, Croydon, CR0 4YY

This is for you.

Contents

Prologue

There are many reasons why a book is written. Sometimes to teach, sometimes to inform, sometimes to impart knowledge, sometimes to persuade, sometimes to convince, sometimes to entertain, sometimes to amuse. I don't pretend to have any such ambitions.

This book is simply the telling of a story.

Running a long way has been part of my story, as has writing these words. And as you read these words, this story becomes part of your story too. There are common threads in everyone's story. Whether or not you have ever, or will ever, run a long way.

The concept for this book was originally to write a semi-fictional account of a fictional race, an idea born after reading *The Rider* by Tim Krabbé, a gift from Simon Turnbull, the journalist who interviewed me after the 2006 100km World Championships. The fictional race eventually took shape as the 2005 Ultra-Trail du Mont-Blanc and the anonymous runner became my 29-year-old self.

The story then evolved to encompass both my journey through life to even reach the start line and where it takes me beyond the finish line. It goes beyond just competing and far deeper than just running. It is an exploration of what running has come to mean for me, and what it (or something else) can give to you. It is the story of my *long run* – a journey of discovery, of exploration, of rediscovery and realisation. A myriad of stories tied together with the tenuous threads of a miscellaneous assortment of thoughts.

This is my story, and I can only tell it as it is for me. The people who are part of my story will remember things differently and from their perspective because it is part of their story too. I hope I do justice to the truth as I know it.

This is not a how-to-manual. Neither is it a this-is-what-I-did and this-is-how-I-did-it. It is simply the telling of a story in the hope that it encourages you to go more deeply into your own story, to make your own opportunities and to have the courage to see where they might lead you.

So what was the race where this story starts? The Ultra-Trail du Mont-Blanc. It has now evolved to become a race of over 100 miles, climbing and descending over 9,500m, following the high mountain trails encircling Mont Blanc through France, Italy and Switzerland.

The church square at the centre of Chamonix. Where the race starts is where the race ends. There is no destination, the journey is all that matters.

But it is a long way.

Have you ever been curious to know how someone can run such a long way? Have you ever wondered what must go through their mind and emotions, what they must think about and feel for all those hours?

Whether you race or not, whether you run or not, you are also on a journey. This is your story too.

Come on, come with me, the race is about to start. The mountains are waiting for us.

> *We shall not cease from exploration*
> *And the end of all our exploring*
> *Will be to arrive where we started*
> *And know the place for the first time*
>
> T.S. Eliot, *Four Quartets*[1]

Part I

A Journey of Discovery

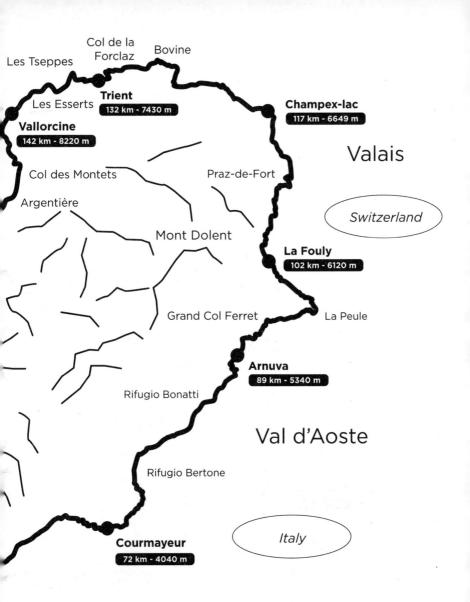

Les Tseppes

Col de la Forclaz

Bovine

Les Esserts

Trient
132 km - 7430 m

Champex-lac
117 km - 6649 m

Vallorcine
142 km - 8220 m

Valais

Col des Montets

Praz-de-Fort

Argentière

Switzerland

Mont Dolent

La Fouly
102 km - 6120 m

Grand Col Ferret

La Peule

Arnuva
89 km - 5340 m

Rifugio Bonatti

Val d'Aoste

Rifugio Bertone

Italy

Courmayeur
72 km - 4040 m

Chapter One

The start line. The beginning of anything.
You, your journey and where it will take you.
Poised in the space between the known and the unknown.
Infinite possibility.

I'm standing here scared witless and surrounded by a sea of people. The centre of Chamonix, the Triangle de l'Amitié Square to be more exact, and it is shortly before 6.30 p.m. on a Friday evening in late August. Most people at home will be packing up to leave work with the anticipation of a long-awaited bank holiday weekend ahead. Maybe the queues will be starting on the roads. The trains will be in their normal chaos. No doubt there is rain forecast.

I am a world away from that bank holiday fervour. I am a world away from anything I have ever done before. But some things are the same everywhere. Rain, for example.

It woke me last night with its persistent pattering on my tent. I scarcely slept in the end. When day broke it revealed one of those grey, damp, misty dawns that leaves you wondering if a world exists beyond those low-lying clouds. I didn't think there was any chance they would lift, but things change quickly in the mountains. A few hours later and it could even have been considered hot, so much so that the shade from the trees by my tent was more than welcome. And now? Well, it's dry at least, thank goodness. And really quite warm. And the skies are clear for the moment.

I feel tired though. I had barely any sleep last night, and there has been no chance to nap today, I'm too on edge and nervous for that. Ahead of me now is the prospect of forty-six hours on my feet, running if I'm lucky. Well, there will be time to sleep afterwards.

I am on the start line of the Ultra-Trail du Mont-Blanc. It is the third edition of this race and ahead of us is a long journey around Mont Blanc, which at 4,810m is the highest mountain in the Alps and Western Europe. Starting in Chamonix, the old alpine village which remains an eminent centre of alpinism, we will pass through Italy and Switzerland before reaching back over the border into France to arrive back here where we start.

Months ago now, I read an article about this race. Until then I didn't even realise that there were races like this. The idea of it caught my imagination and the thought of taking part slowly took a hold over me. I'm not even sure now what the pull was – perhaps it was as simple as the irresistible allure of making a long journey on foot through a beautiful alpine landscape. Or perhaps it was a curiosity to challenge myself in a way that I had never been challenged before. By March I had formed a plan. I was due to finish my PhD by the summer, so I reasoned with myself that if I registered for the race, then it would be a great excuse to plan a couple of weeks in the Alps to do some climbing. The race would be the last bit of fun before heading back to the UK to start my new job.

So I am here, standing in this church square in the centre of Chamonix.

Waiting for the start.

The minutes are ticking by. The people around me are unsettled. We are not quite sure how to fill these moments until the race starts at 7 p.m. Everything has been done that can be done. Race numbers have been collected and pinned on T-shirts. Kit has been checked. We have given in our drop bags for the support points in Courmayeur and Champex. Or at least most people have. I'm not entirely sure what most people have sent in those bulging bags of extras. But my miscellaneous assortment of kit is a little bit sparse. The only spares I have are a clean pair of socks and a clean T-shirt. The only shoes I have are on my feet, and still relatively new. Bought in a sale, they were a random purchase made just before leaving the UK, my choice governed by economics rather than performance. A friend had suggested that trail shoes could be a good idea for a race that would be on mountain paths. I'd not really thought about it. I've left a change of clothes in another bag that stays here in Chamonix to await my hopeful return. What else is there to do?

There is an all-pervading sense of restlessness. We are penned into this square sandwiched by the church, a few cafés and the huge number of people lining the street to see us off. There is no escape, not even the chance of a final bolt to the loo. No. Nothing to distract from the challenge ahead.

So what is ahead? I don't really have any idea. I feel like I'm in some sort of a dream. It has just struck me that in all honesty I have no concept of what I'm about to do. I have nothing to gauge it against, no yardstick to mark it by: 155km around Mont Blanc with 8,500m of ascent and descent,[1] it sounds quite impressive when you put it like that. That kind of distance is like running from Southampton to London, and *then* doing a marathon – and running that far with an ascent the equivalent of climbing to the summit of Everest from sea level and back down again. It is almost too difficult to conceive.

So what am I doing here? I love the mountains, and I love running. But something like this? Whatever made me think that this could be something I could do? What persuaded me to enter? Forty-six hours. That is the time limit they give us to get body and mind back to Chamonix. I have absolutely no idea if it is a realistic goal for me. Or if it is just a pie in the sky dream.

But sometimes you have to make those pies in the sky. Sometimes you have to dream.

It's simple really. Isn't it? All I have to do is run. Run until they tell me to stop, and then stop. I'm just not quite sure yet where that will be. A good friend once gave me some advice, a quote from Lewis Carroll's *Alice in Wonderland*: "'Begin at the beginning,' the King said, very gravely, "and go on till you come to the end: then stop.'" It will be my mantra for the race. To begin. To go on. And then to stop.

In my wildest dreams I hope I might make it back to Chamonix and the finish line. Logic and reason tell me I am far more likely to be stopped at some checkpoint for not making the cut-off time. No point in worrying about it now. There is nothing I can do. For now I just need to focus on starting. The rest will follow. It is inevitable.

I have found a step to sit on, in front of the church. The mass of people shifts and moves around me. People are talking, some are fiddling with their rucksacks, others are staring up at the sky. Already we are marked somehow, set aside from the spectators lining the street. It is a strange feeling. It is different to anything I have ever experienced before.

I have a feeling of complete anonymity. I know absolutely nobody here; my friends left the campsite last night and must now be driving back home to the UK. I don't know anyone else running. I don't know anyone at all in Chamonix. No one really knows I'm here. Sure, my parents do and I must have told a handful of friends that I was running a race at the end of my time in the Alps. But it won't really mean anything to them. It's strange, this feeling of anonymity. It seems to envelop me, not leading to a sense of loneliness as you might imagine, but rather an absolute freedom. Even in the controlled environment of a race there is this incredible feeling of freedom. And the race hasn't even started yet.

Not yet. But the minutes are ticking by. My stomach turns over.

Most of these other runners seem to look like they know what they are doing. With their skin-tight Lycra, tiny rucksacks and small, fit-looking figures they look like they know what they are in for. If looks count for anything then I won't even make it out of town.

I completed my PhD thesis this summer and still have that student mentality of spending as little money as possible and then only on essentials. Kit has to last until it wears away. A combination of my ignorance, inexperience and parsimony have resulted in my having absolutely no idea even of what to wear. Running a hundred miles, or at least some part of, must surely require something that is comfortable and that can serve whether it is hot or cold. What on earth will running through the night at over 2,000m altitude be like? The best solution I could devise was to resort to my ancient and trusted Helly Hansens. But I feel like I'm the only one standing (or sitting) here in holey long johns (thermals). And the rucksack was a bit of a conundrum. I don't really have one that you can run with, only my large mountain sack. My friends lent me one before they left yesterday. Somehow I'll figure out how I can get it back to them – they saved my day. It is a bit big though. The waist strap can't cinch tight enough to fit properly. Not to worry, at least it means I can fit in all the obligatory kit: one to two litres of water, two headtorches with batteries, survival blanket, bandage, passport, waterproof jacket.[2] How on earth do people manage with those tiny packs?

But time is passing. I bring my attention back to the moment. There is a faint hum of nervous chatter from some. Others are diving deep into themselves, eyes shut, steely focused faces. It makes me edgy, all too aware of my absolute ignorance of what really lies ahead. The calm before the storm.

Race start is imminent. I stare at the mountains towering so far above us, and feel incredibly small. I have an overwhelming sense of my insignificance. What is it that I am doing? Whatever pain, doubt, hope, joy that I feel in the hours ahead, who will care, who will even know? At the same time it is as though the world is before us and full of infinite possibility.

❖ ❖ ❖

The Ultra-Trail du Mont-Blanc encircles Mont Blanc, making a journey of over 100 miles, crossing numerous high passes on tough alpine trails. The race itself is a festival of exploration, endurance, sport, community and sharing – pulling runners, volunteers, communities and supporters into an experience that goes far beyond the race itself.

The Tibetan word *kora* means circumambulation or revolution. It is both a type of pilgrimage and a meditative practice in the Tibetan Buddhist tradition. Typically it is a circumambulation around a sacred site, as part of a pilgrimage or celebration or ritual, and very often that sacred site is a revered mountain, the journey to which requires an arduous trek over long distances, crossing a number of high passes and through difficult terrain.

I didn't realise during that first race in 2005, but for me this is what the Ultra-Trail du Mont-Blanc embodies. It is a celebration, a pilgrimage, a circumambulation – it is a *kora* for those who choose.

On reflection, much of my running has become a meditative practice and much of it has been in the form of a kora. Running in circles has taken me on some incredible journeys, sometimes smaller, sometimes larger: 400m on a track; 1km loops on the road; 100 miles around the 4,000m mountains of Mont Blanc, Monte Rosa and the Matterhorn; over 200km around the 8,000m Manaslu.

A pilgrimage is often associated with a physical journey, but it is also a search for moral or spiritual significance. It is also therefore the metaphorical journey into our own beliefs, the journey we make into a deeper understanding of ourselves, others and the world that we are living in. Life itself is a pilgrimage.

Running has become for me one of the ways I explore life – making a physical journey to make a journey within.

In Robert Pirsig's novel, *Zen and the Art of Motorcycle Maintenance: an Inquiry into Values*, he writes, 'In a car you're always in a compartment . . . You're a passive observer and it is all moving by you boringly in a frame. On a [motor] cycle the frame is gone. You're completely in contact with it all. You're *in* the scene, not just watching it anymore, and the sense of presence is overwhelming.'[3]

This is something of what running does for me. When I'm running there is no longer anything between me and my surroundings – my feet are in a rhythmical contact with the earth, I'm breathing the air, I'm looking, I'm listening – it is a sensually intimate relationship. And the more at one I am with my environment, the more I am pulled into the present.

This is when the physical journey of my run takes me on a journey deeper into myself and into the experience of life.

Running may not always be the way in which I do this, it may not ever be the way that you do this. What is important is finding a way that lets us keep exploring, experiencing, searching, sharing, living – whatever it is that lets us be fully present in the moment with an innocent trust that the world is before us and full of infinite possibility.

The Ultra-Trail du Mont-Blanc holds a special position in the world of long-distance mountain running. It has a beautiful story. It started very simply with a group of friends wondering if it was possible to run the Tour de Mont Blanc.

The Tour de Mont Blanc is one of the classic long-distance walking paths in the Alps, one of the most popular in Europe. Linking together a series of ancient pathways used by hunters, herdsmen and traders, it encircles the Mont Blanc massif, the highest in Western Europe. There are many different variations but most walkers will take seven to ten days. Depending on the variation it covers between 150 and 200 kilometres and between 7,500 and 12,650 metres elevation.

In August 1978 Jacky Duc and Christian Roussel were the first to try running a tour of Mont Blanc nonstop. They made the journey in 25 hours 50 minutes. In 1980 the first woman, Edith Couhé, completed the journey in 28 hours 2 minutes. Years later Michel Poletti and his friends also had the dream, born of a mad enthusiasm, to see if it was possible for them to run the route in one stage. They had no more ambition than simply to do the journey and to share it. Then the idea came to create a one-stage race, keeping as much as possible to high alpine trails.

The UTMB, with Michel and his wife Catherine as race directors, started in 2003 with 718 runners from 19 countries, and the support of 250 volunteers. In testing conditions, just sixty-seven runners finished. The race has evolved over the years and in 2014 included five different races with a total of 7,500 entrants from 77 countries, supported by 2,000 volunteers. The level of organisation is phenomenal and the numbers are simply staggering – 150,000 route markers (made by volunteers), 3,000kg cheese, 9,000 bananas, 9,700 litres of soup, 55,000 biscuits . . .

There weren't so many trail running enthusiasts when the UTMB began, but now the sport has grown exponentially, and is continuing to develop worldwide. It is in continual evolution and from 2015 will finally be recognised as an athletic discipline by the International Association of Athletics Federations (IAAF).

Despite the increase in the numbers of runners taking part, the UTMB hopes to keep the human values which motivated it from the beginning – simply to 'offer an extraordinary, authentic and respectful journey' and to share those values and passion with all the participants – runners, volunteers, partners and communities.

❖　❖　❖

A stillness falls over us.

The final briefing is given, words are spoken, but I cannot take them in. A brief silence and the haunting strains of Vangelis's 'Conquest of Paradise' fill the final moments. The music stirs my apprehensions into a curious hopefulness that I can make it back to Chamonix on my own two feet. And then we start to move. I'm carried from my position on the church steps by this surge of people around me, we pass under the arch marking the start, and this is it. We have begun. The road curves and people are lining the way before us. So many people. The entire town seems to have entered into the spirit of things. It is unlike anything I have ever experienced before.

Leaving the festivities, we make a slow jog along the road out of Chamonix until the point where we are directed onto the wooded trail down the valley towards Les Houches. Now the trees stand witness to our effort, just as those crowds had as they lined the street. We are moving slowly, barely running, too many of us too close together, jostling for space. I tread carefully, trying to avoid people with poles. I haven't seen this before, people running with poles. Several times I am nearly tripped up. It frustrates me.

I try to set the frustration aside, and I ease into the rhythm of this gentle pace. After the long day of waiting it is good just to be moving. The evening air is cool enough to balance out the heat from our as yet quiet exertion. I stop worrying. No point now wasting energy wondering what I could or should have done better to train, to prepare. This is it. We are running. That is all. We just have to keep running.

Onwards along this forest track, hugging the side of the valley, never too high, never too low, it leads us on a rolling descent. Finally we emerge – people are waiting there to applaud us across the river and up the road into Les Houches. It looks like drinks are laid out for us on those tables in front of the church. But we haven't been going long, no one really stops, and so I continue on this wave that has been carrying me forward.

The light starts to fade as we begin the first ascent. I turn back, high above the valley floor now, and the sky is streaked with pink alpenglow from the setting sun. The beauty makes me shiver with an odd delight. The irrepressible rhythm of nature stands proudly aloof, it cares nothing for our preoccupations, for our concerns, for what is happening in our small world. The sun will set tonight, and it will rise tomorrow. This certainty puts things in perspective, it gives me a reassuring confidence that whatever I am feeling and enduring through the night, the world will keep turning. This innate grace in nature is somehow a comforting distraction.

I said we were running. But it is only here, after two or more hours, that the crowd of us thins enough for me to actually feel like I am really running. We climb higher, the crowd thins out more, the enormity of the journey ahead already starting to test our bodies and minds.

That fading light wanes and darkness falls. The beauty of the sky as the sun was setting has gone. Moving into the darkness of the falling night, I'm enveloped by its inky blackness. It is like a blanket shielding me from the reality of the race, the incredulity of our journey. It lets me hide in obscurity, in anonymity. I'm just one of these shadows moving forward through the night. No one to observe how I am running, no one to look at how slowly I am going. No judgement. There is still that incredible feeling of freedom.

The field has thinned out even more. It is a relief to be able to move more freely now, to allow the terrain to dictate my pace rather than the stream of runners ahead of me. I am surprised by the support here, it is night now but people have left the comfort of their chalets to stand outside and cheer, to ring cowbells, to encourage. It is humbling to think that they are there just for us. The sporadic bursts of noise contrast starkly with the thick silence of the night, the long empty stretches in between where the only accompaniment to my movement is the sound of my breath and the crunch of my footsteps. Hands on knees, I climb to the first col, Col de Voza.

I begin finally to settle in to my journey. I allow myself to think, I let my mind wander as I try to comprehend what it is I'm doing.

This first descent is long. I have no idea of where I am now. This is new territory for me – literally and metaphorically – geographically, physically, mentally, emotionally. And this is just the beginning. I have no idea how I will cope, whether I will have to struggle with body and mind, or whether it will come easily. I have no idea how the hours ahead will be, what it will be like to run through this night and into the next. I have no idea where or when the end will come. But I have to let go of all of that. I cannot worry about what I don't know. It seems a pointless waste of energy, and the body and mind are going to need all the energy that they can muster. I realise that I have to surrender into the effort, into the experience. I have to let feet and legs carry me forward guided by the trail beneath my feet, buoyed by the magnificence of the shadowy mountains.

Emerging from the darkness of the woods, I see lights, hear voices. There seems to be some kind of a party going on. Les Contamines is making merry as it encourages us through. I pause. We've been running for hours already. I'm sure I'm supposed to need something to eat, something to drink? I pass up and down in front of the laden tables. I don't feel like much at all. But I'm curious to see what they provide. It is a veritable feast, a generous buffet of all kinds of food. I stuff some bread and cheese in my rucksack pockets. Just in case, for later. I start to move, and hesitate. Surely it will be getting colder up high. I decide to be cautious, easier to change here, now, under the light of this lamp-post, than with cold hands sometime later. And I'm in no hurry after all. I'm buried somewhere in the middle of the pack (position 504, had I known), so many people ahead, so many people behind. So no, I'm in no hurry.

I exchange T-shirt for well-worn thermal. No more excuses to delay, the night is waiting. It doesn't take too long to reach the end of the valley, Notre Dames de la Gorge. It's dark here in this forest, but there are more people, more lights. The trail leads steeply upwards, cobbled stones underfoot. It is almost electric, this feeling here, people are again lining our way, this time with fire torches; the flames dance before my eyes. Their enthusiasm boosts my spirits. We have come this far already. What more do I need to do other than simply to keep moving slowly forwards?

Chapter Two

Stillness is what creates love. Movement is what creates life.
To be still and still moving – this is everything.

Do Hyun Choe

Moving into the stillness of the night. To be still within our moving, is this all we have to do? I take my time here, sometimes running, sometimes walking. I don't really feel any pressure to push harder. We emerge from the forest and penetrating deep into this valley the trail flattens out. Indistinct in the darkness the shape of the landscape impresses itself upon me by the feel of the trail beneath my feet and the shadowy ridges etched against the night sky. I reach the alp at La Balme, the lights and caring welcome from the volunteers a cheerful digression from the silence of the dark trail. A small drink and then I'm pulled away and onwards by thought of the miles yet to go. I have no idea yet if I have any hope of making all the cut-off times. I'm carrying the road book[1] in my rucksack but don't really want to dig in to get it out and check the timings. So far, so good. I'll just carry on and hope that my carrying on is good enough.

The climb here is long enough to focus my attention and effort. I'm passing people, though. I fall into conversation with another woman, Maria. We keep each other company for the last stretch of this ascent to the 2,329m Col du Bonhomme. The air is colder here, but being high up above the valley lifts my spirits; it is hard to make out in the dark, but here I have the sense of being in a real alpine environment. This is where I like to be. The trail leads us off on a gentle ascent, the terrain much rockier underfoot now and needing some agility. It is fun. Maria seems surprised that I can move so effortlessly when most of the runners around us are slowing down. I've explained to her that I've never done a race like this before, but love being in the mountains. We talk for a while and then she urges me onwards, saying I should keep moving, her knee will slow her on the descent soon to come.

We meet again on the podium during the prize-giving. She had won her age group, but was astounded to know I had won the race having been so far back in the field at the point we were running together. We stayed in touch, have since shared many runs and ski tours together, and she became a good friend.

I reach the Croix du Bonhomme; I pause and crouch to the side off the trail, needing to pee. Some of the other runners around shout with mirth, 'C'est une fille.' I smile and reply, 'Oui, je suis une fille.' Yes, guys, we do have to crouch. But I realise the source of their mirth is the fact of me being a woman rather than the fact that I too need to pee. They hadn't realised this small figure moving upwards through the darkness with them was a girl. I realise that, Maria aside, perhaps there aren't too many women around in this part of the pack. I'm not sure if that is because most are ahead, or because most are behind us, or simply because there aren't that many women running.

Winding downwards. Steeply downwards. There are a myriad of small paths, it is impossible to know which is the easiest underfoot, the most direct, the quickest. But then, it's OK. I'm in no hurry. I look down onto the lights from the headtorches of people ahead of me far below. It is an awesome sight. But it looks a long way down (over 1,000m in fact).

Finally I realise that the valley floor is drawing closer, we are on a gently zigzagging track now, and there are lights below us, voices, the sound of merriment and partying. I take my time, but still it doesn't take long to reach the lights. We are channelled into this refreshment point at Les Chapieux by an avenue of candle torches. It is simply magical. The lights guide us into a long marquee with long trestle tables laden with a generous array of food and drink. It's not exactly a gourmet meal, but it looks like a feast to me almost fifty kilometres into the race and in the depths of night (shortly before 2 a.m.). I eat a little, drink a little and leave the tent, here discovering the reason for all the voices. This whole place is having a party. It looks like they're having a lot of fun. There is a momentary temptation to stay, to share the jollity, to linger there with the lights, the warmth from the burning fire, the promise of more substantial food and drink. The temptation is momentary only, though. My world is the dark night waiting on the other side of this conviviality. More candle torches lead me back out into the darkness, and the sounds of the revelling fade behind me.

I start up a single-track road, my feet beating a gentle rhythm on the tarmac. I fall into pace with a man for a time. He seems to be impressed that I am still running, and seems sure that I must be well placed within the women's field (position 242 overall at this point). Well for sure, we'd come a long way, but I'd taken it easy, I hadn't run with any real intensity, so I was still moving easily. Perhaps it is the unfamiliarity and strangeness of a race like this, and the novelty of moving through the inky darkness of the night, but I am actually really enjoying it. Honestly, enjoying it.

It is here, in the depths of the night, in a place I have never been before, tired but excited, that I really start to register the immensity of the landscape I am passing through. The rising road leads me deeper into the valley and I gain height with every step. I sense rather than see the valley opening and widening out, I sense rather than see the power and beauty of the cirque of mountains high above me. It makes a deep impression on me; it is here I realise what a privilege it is to be running through this environment, what a privilege it is simply to be out in the mountains on such a night. Under the cover of darkness, I can feel the beauty rather than see it. There is no other way to describe it. It is a place that I know I want to return to with the luxury of time.

I have returned since, in training, countless times, but nothing quite matches the beauty of that first night, not even in the clear light of day. Perhaps it also had something to do with the unexpectedness of having reached that far, somewhere between 50 and 60km, and mostly in darkness; perhaps it was something to do with the anticipation of the journey yet to come; but that first night had an indescribable beauty that – there at least – has yet to be replicated.

There is a small collection of huts at La Ville des Glaciers and our route leaves the single-track road and crosses the river to join the trail leading up to the Col de la Seigne. The climb is slow in these dead hours of early morning. There are always lights ahead of me, pinpricks of reassurance that I'm not alone in making a strange effort this night. We are alone and yet together, each locked in our own individual experience, but sharing the same common goal to make it through the journey and back to Chamonix on our own two feet. Knowing that others are doing exactly as I am helps to make some sense of being out on these high alpine trails in the depths of this night. I pass people, the trail is smooth beneath my feet and the climb is a steadily flowing effort rather than a tiring struggle. I pass more people (almost a hundred people, I find later, on this 11km section between Les Chapieux and the Col de la Seigne). I stop thinking. I surrender into that almost curious stillness reached when you are in the middle of an uncommon physical effort. And we are still only just over a third of the way through.

The gradient of the mountainside beneath my feet eases and I see a larger glow of light ahead on the horizon. I can make out the col lying ahead of me now, a saddle between the mountain ridges etched against the night sky. I reach the glow of light and realise it is a checkpoint, a tent with some staunch volunteers defying the cold. I have kept moving, my thin thermal top is enough to keep me comfortable, but seeing them wrapped up in bundles of fleece and duvet layers makes me realise how cold it is up here. We are at 2,516 m, not so high, but high enough. We'll only cross one pass higher in the rest of this wild journey back to Chamonix. There is no food here, they simply check my number. The effort of the climb over, I feel the chill as I pause and I quickly run off, descending easily on the winding trail. Moving swiftly downwards I lose the wind that had whipped across the pass. In less than half an hour I reach the Refuge Elisabetta and take a moment there to drink something warm.

From here it is short work descending to the Lac des Combal. This is a peculiar landscape in the darkness. The unexpected flatness takes me unawares – should I run, should I walk? Sandwiched between the terminal tongue of the Miage glacier and its outlet in the Val Vény, once the glacier acted as a natural dam by partially blocking the bed of the Doire de Vény, but now this is an alpine meadow akin to the mountain steppes of the much higher Tibetan plateau. Soon crossed, our trail leads away from the descending outlet, and upwards towards the Arête du Mont Favre. We are in those dead hours of the night now; somehow it is always darkest just before dawn. It's hard to keep my focus, and I fight the tiredness, the urge to shut my eyes. I know these dead hours so well from months of night-watches working onboard ship. Strange to think that my work at sea could have been curiously valuable training simply for this.

Dawn finally emerges from the remnants of those hardest hours just before light. It breaks my reverie. As light floods the sky I am filled with emotion. The night has passed. The beauty of a new day brings hope. Whatever hardship, whatever challenge the day ahead is to bring, it is there to be lived – to be alive is everything, there is infinite possibility.

I am reminded of a quote from Bram Stoker's Dracula: 'No man knows till he has suffered from the night how sweet and dear to his heart and eye the morning can be.' It is true, there is an undeniable sweetness to the coming of morning when you have been awake through the entire night. As the sun rises in the sky and colours flush the clouds above me I realise I can trick myself a little. If a new day has dawned then surely I can delude myself into thinking I must have slept somewhere along the way, so really I should be as good as starting afresh, on untired legs and with a burning eagerness to keep moving forwards. It sort of works. Until I fall flat on my face, stumbling with tired-ness. A knee graze only, I bounce back up and continue rolling down this beautifully runnable descent.

I falter into the next checkpoint, Maison Vieille on the Col Chécrouit, with the effervescent host Giacomo waiting to greet us. I don't stop, sure that Courmayeur must be close now. Sure enough, less than thirty minutes later, after losing height rapidly on the twisting descent, I reach the old alpine village and the checkpoint housed in the local sports centre. Wow. I didn't think I'd make it this far.

It is just after 6.30 a.m. I have arrived in time for breakfast you could say, almost civilised. But somehow the soullessness of the large sports centre is disconcerting. I miss the intimacy of the mountain checkpoints. It is a maze in this place. I manage to find some food, something to drink, but I'm feeling good and I don't really want to linger here unnecessarily. Someone points me to one large room, there are mattresses laid out and blankets at the ready. But I don't need to sleep! Another person points me to another room with a red cross on the door. I peer inside, but I don't need a physio or a massage. I just want to leave this warren of rooms and empty corridors and get myself back out onto the waiting road. I am finally pointed to the exit and, frustrated by the waste of time, I present my number to be checked. They hesitate as they check the records and I'm taken aback when they assure me that I'm only the second woman to pass through. How on earth? What could have happened to all the other women in the race? I can't quite make sense of it.

❖   ❖   ❖

Where does anything start?

A child. A journey. A mountain. A dream.

Where did running start for me? For sure, we all run as children, but somehow it became something that was so much more than a simple pastime. It became part of my everyday. It became my normal.

Why did running become part of the fabric of my life and how was it that I found myself on that start line at the end of August in 2005? I ask the questions. I'm not sure I know the answers. And no one else can give them to me. But what I do know is that somewhere deep in the imagination, emotions and wonder of a young child a seed was sown. This seed was the beginning of a lifelong love of the mountains. And it is that love of the mountains together with an innate endurance and stubbornness that seems to have made me what I am now, an endurance athlete.

The selectivity and unreliability of memory and the distance of time mean that it can be difficult to differentiate one moment and one impression from the experiences that come later. But if the root of my endurance can be traced back to anywhere, then it is to my first experience of Zermatt and its mountains at the age of six. The seeds must have been there in me even earlier, but this was the point of a realisation, a recognition of a love, the birth of a passion, even an instinctive feeling of who I was, even if at that point I had no idea how that would be expressed.

On that first visit to the mountains I had no idea of where it was I was going. I had absolutely no expectations beyond the excitement of making a journey to a new place. It was a simple family holiday to Europe and its Alps, a first time for all of us – my parents, my older sister and brother, and my two-year-old younger brother. Family summer holidays had until that point been to the beautiful bay of St Brelades on the island of Jersey. My parents were both from London's East End – we had no link into the world of exploration or mountaineering and I'd been fed no stories of mountains and their legends, of mountaineers and their explorations. I knew none of the rich history of endeavour. It was an alien world to me, one completely different to the London suburbia in which I was growing up.

But something struck a chord inside the heart and mind of that six-year-old child.

We lived in Upminster on the outskirts of London. It is suburbia, the last station on the green line (the District line of the Tube). Organising a family of six onto a flight and then a long train journey from Geneva to Zermatt must have been a feat in itself. I have a vague sense now of the excitement of making a long journey to somewhere new. The unknown lay ahead.

Stepping off the train and emerging into the Bahnhof Platz was arriving in a different world. There was a cold sharpness to the air on that dark April night, and a distinctive smell I still cannot define, but that continues to greet me every time I arrive. The village is car-free with guests transported in small electric taxis, in horse-drawn sleighs, or else on foot. That caught my imagination – never having shared the love of cars of my (engineer-to-be) brothers. It was Easter time, a warm Easter, and night-time cold was tempered by the warmth of the sunny days. Here even the sunshine had a different quality to England – a harsh intensity magnified by the reflection off the snowy meadows. Too young to join my father and older siblings, I tried skiing in a class group on a gentle meadow in the village. An individualist even then, I balked at the constraints of the group tuition.

The Matterhorn, of course, is visible in all its glory right from the village, so its beauty and immensity impressed itself on my young mind right from the beginning. But we also took the train up to Gornergrat (3,135m) and here the panorama opens out – 4,000m summits in every direction, crevassed glaciers, rocky faces. Coming from the bleakness of suburban outer London, rows and rows of houses punctuated by car-filled roads, this was a wild and enticing landscape that somehow gave a promise of a world to explore. Days were spent outside in the elements, nights sharing a meal together. My favourite evening was spent in a typically Wallisian restaurant,[2] cosy and warm from the burning fire, with a toasted cheese sandwich that came wrapped in a serviette, needing careful unpeeling to avoid less edible additions. I was content tucked away in that warm corner after a day spent outside, with my bread and cheese, and my book. Simple pleasures. I was never without a book even at that age – the words on the page giving a window into other lives, other stories – for a while absorbed in the world those words conjured up; for me their story was my story too.

The memories themselves are becoming hazy and vague to me. But some things stand out in sharp relief. The feeling of being 'home'. The absolute certainty.

I cried on the train down the valley as we started the long journey back to London. This had only been a holiday, but these weren't the tears of a petulant child wanting more time to play before the inevitable return to school. These tears were quieter, they were raw, they were a recognition of some deep emotion within the heart of a child. As though our leaving was not in fact simply a leaving, but the loss of something precious.

I cried in that way just once again. Exactly thirty years later, this time leaving Kathmandu, recognising the depth of the love I was feeling, unknown and unexpressed as it was. I had absolutely no idea what would happen, if or how this love would be manifested, returned or not. It was just there again: that feeling of absolute certainty, that this would be an important part of my life, again that sense that this was 'home'. Only now I loved not only with the wonder and curiosity of a child, but with the heart and soul of a woman.

Leaving Zermatt that first time I had no idea if or how I would ever return; I was a child, my movements and opportunities dependent on family decisions. But I knew then that the mountains, or more precisely what the mountains represented for me – beauty, challenge, exploration, the world – was where I would be drawn to – the stage on which part of my life would be played out.

Back in the greyness of suburban London I realised a distinct difference between myself and my parents and siblings. While having had a wonderful holiday, that is what it remained for them, a holiday. Despite my youth, this had been something so much more for me, something that would have to be realised in some way.

The others settled back into routine, into school and work, but I was missing something. Something had changed, the concept of where I belonged was shifting. Life fell back into the pattern of school, playing with friends and whatever else it was that we did then, but I had a sense that I was just biding my time.

I was waiting.

It's hard now to think back to a time when I wasn't running. But when we are children it is nothing more and nothing less than simply what we do. From birth we are developing muscle strength and coordination, and our movement progresses to rolling, sitting, crawling, until that moment arrives when we have gained sufficient confidence and balance to take those first teetering steps. As that confidence and balance grows, the teeter evolves into a toddle, and the toddle into a run. We become nimble on our feet.

We sprint with little hesitation. We play. We run around. We play, we run, we run, we play. It is spontaneous, it is an expression of what we are feeling – excitement, apprehension, mirth, dismay. It is instinctive and impulsive.

We run on the hard tarmac of the school playground, the softer grass of the playing field; we feel the unevenness of the pavement on the way home, the firm give of the sand along the line of breaking waves. Our run is a happy burst of enthusiasm, a fearful scamper back to the familiar.

But life happens and we all too often seem to forget all of what we once knew. We either don't run, or if we do then running has become an 'exercise', something that either we are told to do, or we tell ourselves to do. Something that is measured in terms of value and benefit, rather than being an expression of feeling.

But sometimes, in spite of our forgetfulness, a thread holds us fast to what we once knew so well, and that tenuous connection keeps us running through the years of growing up until we arrive in adult life knowing what it is still to run. Carefree no longer, but we still remember something of that feeling we had as a child, when the act of running was full of wonder, curiosity. When it was simply a being there in the moment with an innocent trust that the world was before us and full of infinite possibility.

The earliest photos I can find of me running show a sturdy, pigtailed six-year-old in gym shorts and plimsolls on a school playing field in the early summer, soon after that first visit to the mountains. I can't remember what it felt like. But the photos show even then a certain focus within my carefree happiness. Not first and not last. It was just what happened on those early summer sports days.

We returned again that summer to Zermatt, and started to make some easy mountain hikes on those now snow-free trails. With a two-year-old brother in tow they would only have been easy walks, but perhaps now more than in the snowy village of Easter-time I would have put together the enjoyment of physical movement with the allure of the mountainous landscape surrounding me. The contrast between the pastoral landscape of the lower trails on which we hiked and played and the harsh beauty of the lofty summits towering above intrigued me.

We returned, and we returned again. Sometimes summer, sometimes winter. And this love of a mountainscape became deeply ingrained. But still there was that feeling of waiting for something.

Chapter Three

*Climb if you will, but remember that courage and
strength are nought without prudence, and that a momentary
negligence may destroy the happiness of a lifetime.
Do nothing in haste; look well to each step; and from
the beginning think what may be the end.*

Edward Whymper, *Scrambles Amongst the Alps*

I head back out into the early morning, my feet beating time
again on tarmac for a while, through the old village, through
the newer parts of the town, through the church square and
upwards again. The narrow road leads further into a small valley and eventually becomes a trail that will take me up towards
the Rifugio Bertone high above the Italian Val Ferret, according
to my studies of the maps and road book, that is. I start to
get excited. We had been camping further up in the Val Ferret
just a few days ago. With too much rain and our route out of
condition, we had aborted our climb and retreated from the
mountain hut back to the campsite. I had instead run up onto
some of the trails traversing high above the valley. Perhaps I
would recognise it a little. I sort of hoped it might be drier than
a few days ago. The trails then had turned into unrecognisable

rivulets of mud and cow shit; we had escaped lightly given the landslides in other parts of the Alps, but it would be so much nicer running on dried-out trails.

Suddenly my preoccupations with the probable condition of the trails were thrown aside – what was it they had said in Courmayeur? How could I be the second woman in a race of 2,000 (or thereabouts) people? I wrestled with myself as to what exactly the implications of this were. I hadn't really come to race, I thought my challenge was just to see if completing something like this in the time given was even a possibility for me. What to do now? Should I continue relaxed and easy as before, or should I try to work harder? I couldn't really decide. It felt a strange position to be in. But then, as the effort of the climb refocused my concentration, I realised it was almost irrelevant – there was a long, long way to go, we were still only something over halfway through.

Past the Rifugio Bertone the trail traverses, cutting through the hillside far above the valley floor. It's a real delight to finally be able to stretch the legs out and break into more of a run, tired as I am. We are on the backside of the Mont Blanc massif now, and across the valley the Grandes Jorasses rise up in an impressive collection of summits along a one-kilometre ridge. It is strikingly complex. I make my own more modest way along the length of the Val Ferret, passing the Rifugio Bonatti, the end of the valley getting ever closer. I'm enjoying this, and I'm almost disappointed when the trail plummets downwards in steep zigzags towards the valley floor. Partway down it leads through some low scrubby trees and shrubbery, so I'm suddenly upon two runners before I realise. Hearing my footsteps, they pull aside to let me pass. I do, saying 'Merci beaucoup', only realising when I am already some footsteps beyond them that one was a woman. Was she the leader? Had I just overtaken her? Minutes later I reach the checkpoint at Arnuva and pause to take a drink and stuff some food in my rucksack pockets. The two runners arrive behind me; it is indeed the woman that had been in first position, and her husband (Simone and Marc Kayser, I discover later). He notices the British flag on my race number and asks how I can run in the mountains if I am from England. Goaded by the unintended insult, I head out of the checkpoint and decide to see if I can make it up the big (nearly 800m) ascent to the Grand Col Ferret before they do. It is the highest point of the race and the border between Italy and Switzerland. It would sort of be nice if I could be the first woman into Switzerland, I think to myself.

It is a great climb and, gaining height fairly quickly, some of the zigzags give a view back the way we have come, the entire length of the Val Ferret and Val Veny, all the way to Col de la Seigne at the head of the latter. It is well over six hours now since I stood on the top of that windy col. It feels another world away.

I think back to the start line in Chamonix. It feels like several days ago rather than just fifteen hours or so. Time has taken on a whole new meaning. I draw my attention back to the trail right here beneath my feet. I have work to do if I want to try to keep ahead of that pair until the col above us. It is the first time in the entire race that I really try to put some work in.

My effort is rewarded. I reach the 2,490m col, elated to be at the highest point of the race. There is no sign of the woman or her man behind me. It surprises me, I had been sure that they would be all out to catch me, and almost certain they would. What to do now? I'd focused my effort on reaching this border point as the first woman, I hadn't thought beyond that. I can't linger here though, waiting for them to arrive. The trails are there in front of me, waiting. I decide to see if I can make it to the next checkpoint before they catch me, that would also be good, then I can take things from there. The descent off the col is beautifully runnable, it feels something akin to flying, almost effortless. It puts a smile on my face, and I let myself just enjoy the feeling.

I'm soon upon the next checkpoint, an alp, La Peule. There are cows up here, plenty of cows up here, surely they can offer me some milk. I ask, and happily down a mugful after the long night of milkless tea and coffee. I notice another runner with a British flag on his number. As I run past him and out of the aid station he shouts some words to the effect of 'you go, girl'. It buoys my spirits.

The runner was Jez Bragg, a talented ultrarunner who has since become a good friend and a fellow athlete on the global team of The North Face – it was also his first UTMB. Jez later described to me the struggle he was going through at the point I ran past him; he was feeling somewhat overawed by the most epic of challenges he had at that point faced, and was dealing with a deep sense of loneliness, partly because of his extreme fatigue and partly because his lack of language skills prevented him sharing the journey with those around him – there weren't so many foreign entries in those early years of the event. He noted my uniquely British look – no sparkly high-tech kit, just a simple running outfit and shoes which 'didn't look too suited to running'; they were pretty hefty trail shoes. He remembers my slight build, but also, he says, my 'look of steely determination that you wouldn't find more powerful anywhere'. He recalls me overtaking him in a flash as I left the aid station, and he muttered those words of encouragement in recognition of something very special happening. He says now that his instincts were right: 'A British win, of course, but also the start of a quite remarkable endurance running career for Lizzy Hawker.'

❖　❖　❖

The running (and the reading) continued through school and into university. I was running every day by then, and had been for a long time. But somehow it never even crossed my mind that I could join a club, or race, run with or for the university. Barring a few novice weekends with the climbing club, social life of any kind seemed to be subsumed into a haze of survival. Studying Natural Sciences at Cambridge wasn't the easiest of choices, as I found out when I got there. Certainly reading about physics seemed a lot more fun than learning the nuts and bolts. After a year the physics was dropped, the maths was continued, and I dabbled with the history and philosophy of science and various biologies. All hours seemed to be taken up by the one objective of just keeping my head above water. It was an interesting time.

My introspection was, for a while, broken by the allure of the rowing boat. But being fairly lightweight my ambitions were curtailed to bow in a second boat. I enjoyed the camaraderie, the early mornings, the sunrise on the river, the rhythm of a boat moving well, only to be simultaneously frustrated by the dependence on seven others plus cox to turn up at the boathouse in the early morning, my lack of strength, and my feelings of unease during evening social obligations.

After years of feeling competent in the things that I chose to focus on and managing to ignore what I didn't want to deal with, I was faced with total inadequacy in too many respects. Running was easy: there were no demands, no expectations.

Absorbed in revision for finals, there was one book that reminded me of the world that was waiting; it was the book that kept me sane. *Clear Waters Rising* by Nick Crane tells the story of his walk along the chain of mountains which stretches across Europe from Cape Finisterre to Istanbul. Alone, despite being newly married, his was an extraordinarily simple journey, but it became an exploration of the last mountain wildernesses in Europe and the people that he met. It reminded me of how little we really need. But what really captured my imagination was that you could, yes, just walk out of the door and keep going. Without fuss or fanfare.

I had no real idea at that point what shape I wanted my path through life to take, other than not to fall into what could be expected or easy. Around the time of my finals I saw a year's job at the British Antarctic Survey (BAS) advertised on the zoology department notice board. This solved the immediate problem of what to do – I could stay in Cambridge for a year longer (the BAS headquarters being on the outskirts of the city).

A summer came between university and BAS, bringing with it an opportunity to explore that waiting world. A poor substitute for the remarkable journey that Nick Crane had undertaken, I devised my own small version of adventure and returned to Zermatt alone. I took to walking long distances every day, finding an irresistible appeal in starting early and finishing late, living on picnics of bread and tomatoes. My time was my own. No one was watching me. No one was judging me.

The trails I knew already from family holidays I made my own, and I trod new ones. I spent the money that my grandmother had left me on a guided ascent of the Matterhorn (and preparation climbs on the Riffelhorn and Pollux). I went with a local Zermatter, a friend of friends. My grandmother didn't have much money to leave, but that £500 felt like a fortune. Sure, I could have done better things with it, but climbing the Matterhorn felt like an investment in the future. I hope she would have approved. She never left the UK and lived her life in the East End of London – I'd have taken her there to the mountains if I could.

I was happy. Immersed in that mountain landscape life had an irresistible simplicity. I thrived on it. On our preparatory ascent of Pollux our guide asked me if my ancestors had been among the British that had made the mountains around Zermatt their second home. Some chance! They would have been working to make ends meet back in London. But I seemed to be able to move about in the mountains with a distinct kind of ease; it begged explanation. Somehow, despite the lack of history, I felt I belonged, there in the mountains.

The time came to make my attempt to climb the Matterhorn. After days of frugality I treated myself to untold luxury as I left the village – apfelstrudel with vanilla sauce, just in case I didn't make it back. Any number of thoughts run through your head as an inexperienced novice. I spent the night in the 3,260m Hörnlihütte at the very foot of the Hörnli ridge. It was a place I had walked to many times, but spending the night there I felt close to the history that had gone before. The 4,478m Matterhorn is not the highest mountain in the Alps, or even in Switzerland, but it is undeniably iconic; ask any child to draw you a picture of a mountain, and it will look something like that familiar pyramidal shape. It was one of the last great alpine peaks to be climbed, and its tragic first ascent in 1865 by Edward Whymper and his companions marked the end of the golden age of alpinism.

I slept but little, nervous and already anticipating the 4 a.m. start. The route was easier than I had feared. I remember it more as a scramble than a climb, and with a local who knows the route it is almost simple. We were the second party to the summit that day. It was better than any party; it had been a glorious experience. I sat there on the summit at 8 a.m., kicking my heels over Italy, wondering what lay ahead, what other heights I would reach, literal and metaphorical. We made a swift descent and by 11 a.m. we were drinking a beer back in the hut. There we parted, my guide and I. It had been something very special. I ran myself down the trails to Zermatt; time was of the essence, I had a train to catch to meet family that evening. They had no idea what I had been doing. I couldn't miss that last train connection.

And so, maybe, there it started, a frugal life filled with buses and trains to reach the places where I could find a beautiful freedom on foot. And all the while being a little economical with the truth of what I was doing, hoping to avoid causing unnecessary worry or concern to family.

I began full-time work at BAS, and it was then that I really started to go to the hills more. Weekend climbing trips away with Antarctic veterans escaping the flatness of the Cambridge landscape and the tedium of weekdays in front of the computer.

And still I was running every day.

My passion for the polar regions was really an extension of my passion for the mountains. Those with whom I was working must have been amused by my youthful fascination and yearning simply to go South. My job entailed analysing results from data loggers put onto fur seals breeding on South Georgia, the island made famous by

Shackleton in his epic story of survival, *South*.[1] As the seals went about their normal daily diving behaviour, the loggers collected temperature and salinity data from the waters about South Georgia. This data could then be used to build up a picture of the physical oceanography, which when related back to the biology gives a representation of the ocean ecosystem and its dynamics.

Important stuff, but I have to admit I found more inspiration in Shackleton's story than in the data I was working on. His third expedition to the Antarctic aimed to cross the continent from coast to coast, via the South Pole. Early in 1915 their ship the *Endurance* became trapped in pack ice deep in the Weddell Sea before any shore parties were even landed. The ship was eventually crushed and the team camped on the sea ice for months before finally launching the lifeboats and eventually reaching Elephant Island. With five of his crew members, Shackleton then crossed 1,300km of ocean to reach South Georgia, making an epic journey across the mountainous island to reach the whaling station with its promise of help from the outside world. The final members of the expedition were rescued in August 1916. It is an incredible story of survival, particularly given their utter reliance on themselves for fifteen months or so. Their survival depended on their resilience to cope with the situations that developed.

I should have known that a year-long post at BAS, based in Cambridge as it was, would only whet my longing to experience the polar regions (north or south). The office was an environment in which the unusual was the normal. It was a fascinating place to be working.

The opportunity to go South finally came when a PhD student had to pull out of a research cruise and it was suggested that I could take that place. There were just two weeks until the long military flight to the Falklands via Ascension Island. With approval to put my job on hold for the two months, my decision to go was obvious. A blur of preparations ensued, including a visit to the doctor's surgery for the requisite vaccinations. Working at BAS with the constant flow of departures to and arrivals from the South, you start to become a little bit blasé; it is after all what is normal. But sitting there in that surgery, trying to explain just where it was I was going, I realised how very far from normal it was. There can't be so many science research facilities with a large warehouse where you're issued with all kinds of exciting kit – from overalls and the humble fleece through to moleskin trousers, large and cumbersome but warm work jackets and any number of pairs of gloves. I wasn't entirely sure what I was getting myself into.

The day came to leave and, our gear packed into large upright duffels, we boarded the bus that would take us to Brize Norton. No ordinary trip, this would start with a suitably unordinary flight from the RAF base of Brize Norton in Oxfordshire to Stanley in the Falkland Islands via a refuelling stop on Ascension Island. This was my first experience of a military flight, and each detail bemused me; security checks on entrance to the base, food and drink coupons for a fairly uninteresting meal and a nine-hour flight to Ascension Island looked after by uniformed personnel rather than regular stewards and stewardesses. The 45-minute stopover on that tropical island was simply to refuel. As we were escorted off the plane and across the short distance of tarmac to the small wired compound, the humid heat was like a wave washing over us, a wave that didn't subside.

Mark, my mentor and boss for the duration of the cruise and now my good friend, initiated me into the tradition of drinking a small can of beer to mark the shifting worlds. We had crossed the line (equator) during that flight; I later heard stories and decided that if I ever did it by ship, I would, as tradition dictated, shave my head. That particular challenge still awaits.

After a second nine-hour flight our arrival on the Falklands was as unusual as our departure from Brize Norton. It was a long and bumpy ride on an untarmacked road from the RAF base to Stanley, the capital. On an island with a population of about 3,000 people, Stanley with its 2,000 residents was a veritable metropolis.

Someone had told me that if I had the chance I should first go South the slow way, the old way, by ship. When you shift worlds slowly and take time to travel to a place you somehow realise and appreciate the distance and disparity so much more.

I was lucky that this is how it happened for me. We made our way by ship across the infamous Drake Passage, the 800km-wide passage between the southern tip of South America at Cape Horn and the South Shetland Islands of Antarctica. It is the shortest crossing from Antarctica to the rest of the world's land and has notoriously rough waters. I learned the necessities of tying everything down to survive the forty-degree rolls; I learned how to sleep wedged into the pillow space of my bunk; and I learned to adopt a bent-knee stance, allowing a slight sway to compensate any movement of the ship beneath me. I crossed Drake Passage in wild conditions, but later I crossed again in an utter calm. This was far more disconcerting, discomfortingly eerie, as though the ocean was gathering energy for some terrible storm.

It wasn't easy being captive onboard ship for so many weeks at a time, although the newness of the experience gave me distraction. There are only so many laps of the monkey island (the deck above the navigating bridge of the ship) that you can do. We kept the same watch as the ship's officers and seamen – four hours on, eight hours off, two shifts per day.[2] A ship works twenty-four hours round the clock, and so did we. It meant sleeping in scraps too, learning to nap in odd corners of the day, and learning to live quietly so as not to disturb cabin mates on different shifts.

We were onboard RRS *James Clark Ross*, an ice-strengthened 100m-long Royal Research Ship fully equipped for science. She can carry up to thirty-one scientists, and about twenty-five crew members. We were a full ship that time, taking supplies down to Rothera, one of the UK bases on the Antarctic Peninsula. The aim of the cruise was to investigate and describe the response of the ocean ecosystem to climate variability, climate change and commercial exploitation. I was working as a physical oceanographer and collecting data about the temperature, salinity and currents of the waters we were passing through.

The days were a mixture of blue skies with bright sunshine and grey sea fog. During the latter the greyness of the sea would merge with the greyness of the sky, giving a perturbing feeling of claustrophobia despite the empty distance to the 360-degree horizon. There was a small gym on the ship, but it was a sad substitute for running and required a determined fight against the tedium. On later cruises I would take to skipping on deck.

We had logistical obligations in addition to our research programme, which made for welcome distractions. We made a call to King Edward Point on South Georgia; I stood by Shackleton's windswept grave, walked across a beach of elephant seals and stood under the 3.5m wingspan of a stuffed albatross in the island's museum. I lifted endless boxes offloading cargo at Port Lockroy and Rothera. We changed the CTD³ cable on the ship, winding it up and down the deck in a blizzard, and were rewarded with a half-day holiday. That holiday allowed me the opportunity for a small excursion off the Rothera base, high up onto an over-looking ridge. I was overawed by the sight, the immensity of the landscape. We were disturbed by a sound resembling that of an avalanche. Casting my gaze around the cirque of mountains, I could see no signs and it rumbled on and on. Finally looking down into the bay on the far side of the ridge I saw the explanation. An iceberg was calving off the glacier. It was an unbelievable and unforgettable sight.

I developed a new passion for being at sea. I counted it once: eighteen months of my life were spent working onboard ship at sea – that is a long time. There is something exceptional about being able to see as far as the horizon in every direction – no land, no other ship. If you can ignore the fact that you are on a ship and that you cannot avoid the constant lights and noise, then there is nothing but you, the sea and the sky. It gives a certain peace. I often wished we could stop the ship, turn off the generators, turn off the lights and drift for a while, just listening to the silence.

Going South was a pivotal experience. I can remember sighting my first iceberg from the monkey island, the air cold now on my face and carrying the unmistakable smell of winter. The Antarctic blew my mind. It is a place of immensity, harsh contrasts and a stark beauty. It is a place that belongs to no one, and so to us all. Strong connections were made, deep and lasting friendships.

The Antarctic is in fact the only continent without a native population. The Antarctic Treaty, in force since 1961, has frozen all claims of sovereignty and has set the Antarctic aside as a scientific preserve, establishing freedom of scientific investigation and banning all military activity. It is a diplomatic expression of the operational and scientific cooperation that has been achieved 'on the ice'.

Twelve months later, the year-long job complete, I was kept on with some kind of temporary understanding, some more data analysis work and another research cruise. We were supposed to be at sea for Christmas (and for the turn of the millennium). However, the ship got stuck in the ice for a month and all plans for the season had to be changed. Frustrating on the one hand, it was also a perfect demonstration of our utter powerlessness in the face of nature. It reinforced the importance of learning patience and cultivating a resilient equanimity, which would later be fundamental to my efforts as an athlete, just as they are for all of us in the physical, mental and emotional challenges that life throws at us.

So the festive season was spent volunteering in Cambridge, learning new things and being totally humbled by the courage with which people face difficult situations. Finally at sea, we had our own shorter experience of days drifting icebound and learning the meaning of mallemaroking (the carousing of seamen on an icebound ship). Unlike my first cruise, this time I was on twelve-hour shifts, the night shift at that. I learned to dread the dead hours between 02:00 and 04:00, and to love the informality of twelve hours working with good friends, eating in the seamen's galley rather than the officers' mess, and lugging endless cups of tea around the ship. We used to take turns making each other drinks and then carry them back to the lab in a biscuit box on a string. It could be swung around and overhead as we navigated the narrow stairwell without spilling so much as a drop. On this and later cruises I became used to working through the 'coming off' night-watch at the end of the cruise, so learning to work double days and deal with sleep deprivation as well as the re-socialisation. Coming back into 'days' the ship seemed to suddenly multiply in personnel, and I would realise that there could be people onboard I hadn't seen the entire time at sea.

These long night shifts and the switches in and out were, I think, great training for the long races that would come later. Little did I know it at the time. They taught me how to go without sleep for prolonged periods of time, all the while dealing with the nausea of being at sea. I got used to dealing with the tiredness. It is somewhat inevitable when you're standing twelve-hour shifts, and the constant rocking motion onboard ship only adds to the fatigue. All great endurance training.

And back on land, I was still running.

Chapter Four

And I tell you, if you have the desire for knowledge
and the power to give it physical expression, go out and explore.

Apsley Cherry-Garrard, *The Worst Journey in the World*

Somewhere further along the trail I realise that I've made it to the next checkpoint and still the woman and her man haven't caught me. Now what? I decide just to keep on running the best that I can, taking it checkpoint by checkpoint. I could make it a game to see how many checkpoints I could pass through before they do catch me. The trail here leads along the Swiss Val Ferret, a long runnable descent, first through the village of La Fouly, then through the smaller village of Praz de Fort, before the ascent up to Champex Lac. It is about a half-marathon from the Grand Col Ferret to Champex, but it takes me quite some hours.

I'm relieved when I reach the quiet lake of Champex. I'm hungry and tired; it's time for a rest. There are alpine horns playing here, the four players in traditional dress standing side by side, marking our arrival in the village. The sight and sound of this welcome brings tears to my eyes. I hadn't even thought I would reach this far, let alone arrive as the first woman. It is almost overwhelming. Whatever happens from here, this is something to remember. I try to swallow my emotion and focus on the immediate concerns of finding the checkpoint with its promise of something to eat. I look in vain for signs of the checkpoint as I run along the lakeside. Surely there must be some mistake, I was certain there should be a refreshment point here. I ask but nobody seems to know, but then they wouldn't, not being part of the race. I keep moving forwards and finally, a couple of kilometres beyond the village, I stumble into a large marquee in a clearing in the forest. It is the checkpoint.

Should I stay, or should I go?

This big marquee is one of the major checkpoints, and people seem to be taking their time. But I'm not entirely sure if there's anything more I need to do. Everyone has been very kind. Someone even walked me over to the table laden with food, insistent that I should avail myself of what is being offered. I've eaten a yoghurt and a piece of blueberry pie. It looks home-made; it would be rude to refuse. People seem to be occupied with changing clothes, eating, drinking, talking to family and friends; some are lying down with their eyes shut. But I have nothing to change into, no one was here waiting for me of course, and, remarkably, I don't feel tired enough to need a lie-down. Not yet, at least. I sit for a while. It seems to be the done thing. The men who arrived before me are still here, the ones that arrived with me and after me are lingering. It feels almost churlish to rush out, the volunteers have gone to so much effort for us. I glance at my watch and I'm shocked to realise I've been here for more than half an hour; it's surprising how time can slip away when you're doing nothing very much. Enough is enough, it's time to get myself moving again.

I leave, and head onwards into the heat of the afternoon. A few that had been ahead of me are now behind me. I don't get very far before the motion of running juggles the food around and I'm overcome by the need to empty out. The forest thankfully gives me some cover, I take a few minutes and someone passes. Then there is no one. I jog-trot up the gently inclined track leading ever deeper into the valley. The track comes to an end, giving way to a trail that climbs upwards, steadily winding between the trees and boulders. I'm alone here. I think back to the stream of runners in front and behind me during those early miles. I'm ahead of most of them now (all but twenty-six or so, it turns out). It is a strange thought. I wonder how they are faring; if bodies and minds are holding up, if it is quite what they were expecting, if they are having fun.

I start to ask myself the same questions. The body seems to still be in good working order, perhaps more tired now than at the start, but curiously comfortable. There is still a long way to go, so it's just as well I still have some effort left to give. And my mind is calm. I'm still expecting to be caught, I am unable to rid myself of the feeling of being chased. But I have in a strange way almost disconnected from that. I am taking it section by section, checkpoint by checkpoint. Is it what I was expecting? Hard to know what that was. In some way it is far beyond everything that I was hoping for. It is, quite simply, an awesome mountain journey. And that is what I love to make. My journeys are not usually this far or so fast all in one stage, it has to be said, but still, this is just a natural extension of my wanderings in the hills and those long mountain days. A fairly extreme extension, admittedly. From the way things are going I know now that at least I should be able to make the cut-off times. I just have to keep myself moving forwards. And the question of whether I'm having fun? Well, I am happy to be here. And I'm full of wonder at having made it this far, whatever happens now. So yes, I think I am having fun.

There must be a long way to go yet, though. The clouds above me are swirling. But the way is clear and easy to follow.

No need to think. I can just focus on moving ever forwards. The trail crosses a few rivulets, not yet rivers but something more than streams, still carrying water from these past days of rain. Steep zigzags now and they draw my focus inwards. Hands on knees again. One step at a time. The trail gains height quickly and I'm subsumed into the swirling mists. I hear strains of music from above. I can't understand where it's coming from. It is unearthly. Beautiful. But unearthly. I feel in full possession of my senses, so how can I be hearing music? I keep moving. There must be some explanation, but for now it is simply a beautiful accompaniment to my movement, the thread that is pulling me upwards.

I climb higher, the zigs and the zags finally reach their conclusion and here lies the explanation for those haunting sounds. A man is standing there, playing a French horn. It is an almost unreal spectacle. From whatever direction he approached it would have taken him hours to reach here. I can't help wondering how long he will have the patience to stay. I'm thankful to pass before he has left.

I try to pick up my pace into a steady jog as the trail gently pulls me around the mountainside. The music becomes fainter behind me and then I am alone again, any views of the Rhone valley far below obscured by the clouds. The path keeps curving round ahead of me, until at last an alp hut looms ahead and the hanging cloud dissipates. There are people, and a table waiting under a small covering; it is the next checkpoint. I've been longing for a milky cup of tea or coffee since night fell last night. There's been plenty of tea and coffee to be had but, apart from that mugful at La Peule, no milk. I wonder if it's worth trying here. I ask, and the answer is yes, I almost can't believe my luck. I'm handed a cup and, full of anticipation, I take a sip. The taste is a crushing disappointment and for the first time a wave of nausea rises. Bouillon, meat bouillon, with milk. It is a most unlikely combination and almost too much for my vegetarian stomach. I move onwards, not waiting for a second cup of something more palatable. It's cool now, the drink was more for comfort than necessity. After spending so long in Champex, deluded into that false sense of security, I'm feeling some pressure now. I'm sure the woman behind me must be fast approaching. I've held her off for hours, but for how much longer? I have to keep moving forwards, putting in as much effort as I can. So I run on, trusting that the nausea will pass.

The trail reaches its zenith and a small gate marks the start of the descent. A glance behind me reveals no sight of the woman yet, or her man. I start downwards, the pull of gravity easing my effort, but the focus demanded by trying to move quickly all the while avoiding the rocks and the roots requires just as much energy. It is a glorious descent, there is no other way to describe it, the speed welcome after the long climb; the trail is smooth enough to really run, but there are more than enough of those rocks and roots to focus the attention and keep me right there in the moment. Eventually the roar of traffic grows louder and the trail momentarily collides with the real world as it crosses the Col de la Forclaz. The speed of the cars passing is a little disconcerting, and there are people standing here, waiting to cheer and encourage. The support is so welcome, but the sudden reminder of a world beyond the race is a bewildering contrast to the solitude above. I'm almost glad when the trail leads me away. My escape is short-lived, with the swift descent to the valley floor cutting through the winding road a couple of times, and then the sleepy village of Trient is suddenly no longer lying below me. Schoolchildren are manning the refreshment point in the church square, they wait eager to hand me food and drink. They are so excited, I feed off their energy. The welcome that they give me is humbling. They want to touch my hands in congratulation, they shout cries of 'bon courage' to wish me well with the rest of my race. Their shouts remind me that I am the first woman and finally it starts to dawn on me that the lady behind might, possibly, not catch me. I realise that somewhere along the way I ran myself into a race. It is no longer just a challenge to try to keep ahead of the cut-off times, it is no longer even just a game of trying to stay ahead until the next checkpoint. No. Now I am here to race.

It is the last big ascent now. I was here a few days ago, on a long meandering walk-run. It feels good to have familiar ground under my feet again. I know how the trail will lead me upwards through the forest, I know how the valley floor will drop away, I know where the angle will ease as I climb higher. I put the effort in, the legs knowing now where to push and where to ease up, and then this 700m climb is over, the trail curves around the mountainside and finally I have turned through this huge circle that our feet are etching on these trails around Mont Blanc. The trail traverses along the valley some way, and then I am heading downwards towards France. Somewhere here in this descent the threatening clouds let loose, and the rain starts pouring down. I cross back from Switzerland into France on some indeterminate tuft of grass and then I'm on the large ski track leading downwards to Vallorcine. I ran this those few days ago, needing to reach the last train back to Chamonix. So, I know I can run this now. It should be easy to pick up the pace but the rocks under already battered feet make that difficult. I move as steadily as I can, nearly catching the man ahead of me.

I don't want to linger long at the checkpoint, not even to stop and change a layer. The people here are wonderful, they are excited for me. They would do anything they can to help. But that is just it. The support is tremendous, but I have to finish this on my own, under my own effort, just as I started.

There is a slight incline now as I run towards the Col de Montets. At this stage of a long run the ups and the downs seem to take care of themselves. But it is running these flatter sections that is hard. The incline is gentle enough to demand to be run. I feel like I should be able to keep a good pace, but on now tired legs I have to fight the fatigue just to keep moving. And there is a cameraman in front of me, asking questions. I feel rude, but I cannot talk, I pull all my focus into moving onwards and upwards, and then again I am alone.

It is just me and the effort demanded of me.

❖ ❖ ❖

After a few years of trying, I was finally successful in receiving a place in the lottery for the 2000 London Marathon. I'm not entirely sure now why I wanted to do it, other than it seemed like something I should try, once at least. The aforementioned research cruise was a challenge, curtailing any serious hopes of training until our return six weeks before race day, but a colleague, Andy, also had a place so there was some interested amusement at work as to who would be first. I don't honestly remember much about 'training', just the attempt to fit in a few long runs usually achieved by looking at the Ordnance Survey map, picking a route that looked possible and setting off. Once, maybe twice, I made it from Cambridge to Ely, along the river where possible, and back by train, only to get teased at work and asked whether I even realised that a return ticket doesn't usually cost too much more than a single.

Memories of race day are hazy too, except for the relief of finding the right start (divided up into colour blocks as they were then), the queues for the Portaloos and the almost nauseous feeling from the smells of breakfasts cooking in the pubs along the route. Afterwards, where did I go, how did I get home? I can't be sure, but what does stay with me is the knowledge that the marathon was something I enjoyed running. I revelled in the novel opportunity to run through the streets of London with the traffic (for once) stopped. There was a peculiar strangeness to running with so many people but there was a wonderful sense of camaraderie and immense support from the crowds.

My time was nothing special, 3:40 and change; there were just minutes between Andy and I which made for good coffee-break conversation, but still it was merely ordinary. Not first and not last. Just as it had always been.

What changed? Nothing and everything.

Somewhere I saw an advert for a ski-mountaineering course in the Alps offering the opportunity to learn about crevasse rescue and avalanche danger and how to ski uphill with skins.[1] I had long since stopped skiing. I wanted to leave behind the crowds, the queues and the dependence on machinery. I like to think now that it was purely environmental concern, not wanting to contribute to the scar that the lift systems leave on the mountains. I had seen it in all too many places in the summer months. But perhaps it was more personal than that, simply an aversion to being in the mountains with large numbers of people. The cost: personal, financial, environmental. So for many years I had avoided the snow that I loved. But this was a chance to learn how to travel in the mountains on my own terms, under my own steam. Somehow I scrambled together enough savings to go. The course was run under the auspices of the Eagle Ski Club, and led by mountain guide Rob Collister. Getting to know him was a huge privilege, and I developed a deep respect for his opinions and his experience. I liked his phi-losophy and humble approach[2] – they shaped much of how I try to travel in the mountains. He epitomises the concept of travelling lightly, quite literally in the respect of carrying nothing but the bare necessities, but also in trying to have minimal impact, and holding in deep respect both his com-panions and the land through which he travelled.

Perhaps Rob listened to my dreams, or simply observed my morning runs on icy roads before our course day offi-cially started. Whatever it was, something made him suggest that if I liked running and I liked mountains, then at some point perhaps I should try a marathon in the hills rather than the city. This simple suggestion encouraged me to go to the hills I loved and enter the Snowdonia Marathon, a challenging loop around Snowdon, the highest mountain in Wales. I was humbled by the thought of running on hilly roads, I was drenched even before the start, but more than anything I was enthused. Daunted by the sight of that first climb up Llanberis Pass, when it came to it I learned that actually it was doable, it was 'OK', I seemed to make ground on the people around me and after the effort of the climb I could then savour coasting down towards Llyn Gwynant. Of course, there was a point when things felt tough, but the mountains provided distraction enough. I can't find the results now, the online records don't seem to stretch that far back. But I was still not first and not last.

I returned for a few years until, without any real inten-tion, I won the Ladies' category – perhaps surprising myself as much as anyone else. It was a precursor of what was to come. It was the start of things changing.

Naturally, the suggestion then came that perhaps I should try running *on* the hills, rather than just around them. And so I did, for several years trying the Welsh 1,000m Peaks Race. My only problem was that I had absolutely no experience at running in the fells (a requirement for the fell running category). So the only way (for me) to take part in the race was to be in the mountaineer's class. This was a different kettle of fish, running in long trousers, heavy boots (yes, my size 38 had to weigh the same as a size 43, so substantial walking boots for me, trail shoes for those blessed with large feet) and a full rucksack. And I had to be able to navigate, since much of the race was off-trail and clear weather more likely to be a dim hope than a reality. I can't remember my first result – again, the online results don't go that far back. What I do remember is peeing before the start behind a hedge, crouching in a patch of nettles and being rewarded by some significant stings for my efforts, and then later staring in awe at the real fell runners that passed with such ease. I made friends with a lovely man from South Wales, and his partner. We met at the race year after year, until the year finally came when by some quirk of fate I actually won. The mountaineer's class, still, of course. But I won outright (male and female), and was henceforth forbidden from re-entry. They were the rules: if I tried it again, it would have to be in the backwaters of the real fell running class (a daunting prospect that I haven't yet returned to attempt). There are rarely prizes of note in these fell running races and minor road marathons but, over the years, my efforts in Snowdonia earned me an assortment of watercolours of those beautiful hills. It was a place I had come to make my own. A decade later they still wait for a wall to be hung on.

Between these early races came my first experience of the place that had for so long held an utterly compelling

fascination for me: the Himalaya. It was probably irrelevant to my as yet nonexistent career as runner, but
absolutely fundamental in my life as an endurance athlete.
Just as I had done before first going to the Antarctic, I
managed to again get permission to put life on hold, this
time in the form of official leave from my PhD at the
National Oceanography Centre in Southampton. Life had
again shifted with the objective of earning my passage back
South. My ambition was to be in the position of applying
for a permanent job at BAS should one come up.

I was living a simple life, shifting from rented room to
bedsit to rented room. Minimal income excused me from
buying into some of the expected norms such as getting a
foot on the housing ladder. It is something that now I'm
glad to have resisted, life having swept me along to some
unexpected places. I may change my mind when retirement
is forced upon me and I resort to life under canvas on some
remote alp or a distant cave in Mustang, a wild and wonderful corner of northern-central Nepal. Would that be so bad?

Anyway, yes, I resisted many norms. I passed my driving
test and decided that actually driving was extraneous to
requirements (a decision precipitated in part by the restric-
tions on students in Cambridge to having a car). Really, it
was just so much simpler to do without. Relying on my
bicycle and the train were much easier, apart from the
times I would return to the station and find my bike stolen,
or until the expensive lottery of train tickets in the UK
became too much to handle.

Still, even now, and older, I have few of the attachments
that have become normal in much of the world. I have no
house, no car, just one bicycle in Kathmandu and a laptop
that travels the world with me.

* * *

The Himalaya then; my opportunity came in the guise of an Eagle Ski Club expedition led by Rob to the 6,387m Kalanag, deep in the Garhwal Himalaya in the northern reaches of India. It is one of the major peaks in the Bandarpunch (meaning tail of the monkey) mountains, close to the Ruinsara valley. Its summit was first reached in 1955 by John Gibson, an English teacher at the Doon School in Dehra Dun.

Apart from my work at sea, I had never been outside Europe (save for a childhood holiday to the US and the 'wilderness' of urban California). I had never done anything remotely like this and with just two seasons of touring I was still a relative novice on my uphill skis. I had never really travelled, what experience did I think I had? To my hesitant delight, I was accepted on the expedition. I can't be sure now what preparations I made. My housemates in Southampton were concerned for me at the thought of the rigours of a month's exertion and the discomfort of expedition life. I couldn't wait to try it. I was lent a rucksack large enough to swallow up my sleeping bag and a hotchpotch of clothing, and eventually the tent, stove, fuel and food. There was a lot to carry.

I remember now a spring evening in the garden of my PhD supervisor and his partner, both good friends, unpacking a parcel that I'd ordered. Unable to figure out the intricacies of leg zips and braces, we had resorted to a bottle of wine. That winter, my first in Southampton, had been wet and tough. I'd treated myself to woodwork lessons as some kind of consolation, and strangely they were to contribute to my expedition planning. After a battle with damp wood and dovetail joints, I eventually emerged with a good-sized chest, with a lid that most definitely shut. I still have it now. It followed me around the country from its Southampton birthplace, serving as a chair and a table when I had neither, but its first function was as my escape repository. As I gradually collected together all I would need for the expedition, everything was thrown inside my chest until the day came when packing could no longer be avoided. It gave me a vague sense of organisation then and for many adventures to come.

Kalanag is not a virgin summit. It is not even a particularly high summit, when considered in the context of the great mountains deep within the Himalaya, and neither was our route that technical or demanding. But ours was the first ascent (to the best of our knowledge) to be made on ski, and a first is always something special.

It was my first taste of expedition life, my first long-awaited opportunity to go to the Himalaya and my first experience of India and the Asian subcontinent. In the preceding month I'd had the same feelings as when I first went South to work at sea in the Antarctic. Like then, I had absolutely no idea what to expect and I wondered if there would be that same intensity of experience and rawness of feeling. A first time imbues an intensity lost to us in our every day.

Our base camp was a two-day walk from the road-head. Local porters helped carry our loads to base camp, their return help requested for several weeks later. Then we were alone there in that vast valley system, self-sufficient and self-reliant. We had everything we needed. Our expedition was almost of another age – we had absolutely no communication with the outside world – no computer, no satellite phone, no GPS tracker – had anything happened it would have been that two-day walk from our base camp to the nearest village. We were utterly reliant on ourselves, and with the naivety of youth I loved it. This was it. This was our world. This kind of isolation can focus the mind and remind us of what is truly necessary, clarifying how we really feel about situations in our everyday life. It is not a running away as people may suppose – rather it is an embrace of life and what it means to live.

Risk can never be entirely mitigated in a mountain environment. Being there is a privilege rather than a right, but being there never entails a careless disregard for the sanctity of life. Instead it is somehow a need to know how precious it is in a deep and immediate way.

A minor peak in itself, reaching the summit of Kalanag opened up a new world to me. As its heights gave view to endless mountains extending further than the eye could see, so it gave a window into the realm of possibility and the realisation that long-harboured dreams could be made real.

There was a lot to deal with: the immersion in a completely different culture followed by total isolation in the highest mountains I had ever been to, the physical challenge, the return. It is not often that we get the chance to live so simply. Life was pared down to the essentials, absolutely necessary when you carry it all on your back, and worries are focused on survival, keeping warm, fed, safe. It concentrates the mind and sharpens the senses. It intensifies the feelings, leaving you right there inside the experience.

It wasn't all good. I had the first realisation that my physical strength could be hard for others to accept. It was disconcerting and upsetting; I was as yet only early in my discovery that I possessed an uncommon endurance. It's interesting now to note that this reaction was from the only other woman, my tent-mate. In the years since I have been met with plenty of bemusement for being a small person running extremely long distances, or for my strange ability to be able to keep going for day after day after day in the mountains carrying loads that are a significant proportion of my body weight, or even just for the strength of my handshake. But men have only ever been generous with their respect.

I found the post-expedition return to Delhi hard. After the poor but sustainable life I had observed in the mountain villages, the sheer numbers of people on the streets of Delhi and its outskirts suffering abject poverty with a sense of utter hopelessness was difficult to comprehend. It put a disconcerting question in my mind – was our exploring just a selfish indulgence?

At the airport, despite being violently sick from food poisoning, I knew I would be back. I had no idea how or when, but I knew I would be. This had been my first experience of a prolonged period of time high up in the mountains, and I loved it. Returning to civilisation, it was the small things that struck me: the convenience of electricity rendering the keeping of a headtorch to hand unnecessary, the speed at which a kettle would boil water compared to heating a panful of snow with a small gas stove at altitude. These obvious (yet significant) contrasts both reinforce an appreciation for the convenience and ease of modern life and ignite a concern about just how easily we take luxuries for granted.

Perhaps this is one of the things that draws me back again and again to the mountains, to the wild places – taking as little as possible there with me. Stripping away those luxuries that I take for granted gives perspective. For me, gaining altitude and climbing high above the valley floor opens up my world. Quite literally, the higher I am the further to the horizon I can see. It puts things in context, reminding me of my insignificance, of just how big the world is and how small my place in it. And as the landscape opens up so too does my mental perspective – giving some perception into new realms of possibility.

It is utterly humbling. But it is also a source of great strength.

The hard thing is to hold on to what I learn there in those high and wild places – those fleeting glimpses of the truth of reality – and to live it when I am back in my everyday. That is the real challenge.

A year later, the summer of 2004, I was a year further into my PhD. And still running every day.

Southampton to Penrith is a long train journey north. It gave me time to contemplate what was ahead, not just a welcome weekend in the hills, but 42 Lakeland fells and 72 miles with 28,000 feet (just over 8,500m) of ascent in 24 hours. Being more or less a complete novice at running anything beyond marathon distance, what was I thinking? The Bob Graham Round (BGR) has a long and cherished history. My inexperience seemed deeply irreverent.

When 'men and mountains meet'[3] the spirit of challenge manifests itself in various ways. In the English Lake District walkers and runners have long been lured by the challenge of linking together the high mountains while covering great distances on the fells. The first recorded long-distance round was made in 1864 and the challenge slowly evolved to become what it is today; to run up and down 42 peaks in 24 hours, as first achieved by Bob Graham in 1932.

This remains the challenge, but the great and the good of fell running have made extended rounds with 77 peaks now the men's record, held by Mark Hartell, and 64 peaks the women's record, held by Nicky Spinks. Many incredibly talented runners have tested themselves – Joss Naylor, Mark McDermott, Jean Dawes, Ann Stentiford – the list goes on, but all who try are linked simply by the sheer delight of revelling in the freedom and beauty of the fells.

My friend Nick was organising the logistics for his American friend, Blaise. I had initially just been going to help out until Nick suggested I should also give it a shot. I felt an absurd guilt at my last-minute decision to join in. This was Blaise's attempt, and Nick had worked incredibly hard to set everything in place for him, local pacers, support, the lot. But I still couldn't quench my excitement at the thought of hours out on the fells and trying something that went far beyond anything I had ever tried before.

My only preparation had been fifty miles of far tamer ground on the South Downs Way, a long-distance footpath in southern England. I'd had a desperate urge for a long day away from the PhD writing, and with the vague notion of Nick's suggestion to join in the Bob Graham Round lying in the back of my mind, and a lack of time and money to go very far, I had put myself on the ten-minute £2.45 return train to Winchester one Saturday morning. My plan was simply to pick up the South Downs Way at its inception on the edge of town and then to keep running until hunger, tiredness or time forced me to retrace my steps for the homeward train. Hours later, alternately warmed by sunshine and drenched by torrential rain, I was back at Winchester station, mud- and blood-spattered to the bemusement of my fellow passengers. It was the furthest I had ever run.

It gave me an overwhelming sense of contentment. A contentment that a day spent on the computer just didn't seem to create. Science would say it was just the endorphins. It was, of course, but more than that also. It was the tiredness that comes from physically pushing for hours and the satisfaction that comes from knowing that you can. It was the simplicity of setting a goal and achieving it some hours later. It was the sense of possibility, the feeling of empowerment. That day, stopping for a swift break, sitting on a stile with the beauty of the countryside before me, I had an overwhelming feeling of how rich we are. The mountains, the woods, the fields, the trails, the wilderness. Nature is our birthright. No one can give it to us, no one can take it away from us. All we need to do is to make it our own. That is all we have to remember.

Arriving in Keswick, I stayed the night with a friend and turned up in a deserted car park at 7.30 a.m. on a Saturday in late July. With minutes to go until our agreed start time there were hurried greetings, introductions and instructions. I found myself standing on the steps of Moot Hall with Blaise, too late now to worry about if I'd given enough food or clothing to our support, too late now to worry about whether I should really be there. Things were unequal from the start. I had the unfair advantage of absolute naivety. With two pacers for each section, we inevitably separated. And then where we met our support at the road crossings I would sit and wait. Eventually, somewhere during that long day, Blaise decided to end his attempt. But everything was still in place, so with Nick's encouragement, we continued and all the effort was focused at trying to get me round and back to Moot Hall within the twenty-four hours. It didn't look promising: the weather had turned, and too much time had been lost with the waiting. But, as with anything, if you don't try then you will never know. I was carried on a wave of enthusiasm through that wild, wet and windy night, totally reliant on Nick and his heroic band of supporters and pacers. It was a joint enthusiasm to see if between us we could achieve this. We did. Just. There is an absolutely incredible generosity surrounding the Bob Graham Round. There are not many occasions on which people will turn out into the dark of night to run miles of rough fell to support a complete stranger in a questionable endeavour. It taught me a lot.

Looking back, what do I remember? Great company and good conversations; feeling strong; running wild; cup after cup of sweet tea; mists and stolen views; the utter generosity of those who came to pace; bemused hillwalkers; flapjacks; pouring rain; shivering; battling with hills of bracken; sips of hot tomato soup; the comfort of a dry change of clothes; night falling; running through the darkness; cheery welcoming voices; torchlit faces; encouragement; exposure; being drenched to the skin; ferocious winds; a grey and miserable dawn; tiredness; the feeling of having to push on; the wonder at still running after so many hours; gratitude; the feeling of being alive.

It was a long train journey back almost the length of the country, to Southampton on the southern coast. I took the sleeper, arriving in the early morning to an eight-kilometre cycle home with my heavy rucksack on my back. A quick change and I cycled across town to be at my desk in the National Oceanography Centre. It was almost as though the weekend hadn't happened.

Chapter Five

The finish line. The end of something.
You are where your journey has taken you.
An end begins what a beginning ends.

It is a jumbled story, but that is something of how I reached the point in my life that I found myself at by the March of 2005. I seemed to arrive there by dint of a peculiar mix of circumstances: some innate character traits (endurance, stubbornness, the need to work hard), some absolute certainties, a distinct disregard of many conventional motivations, and by putting myself in the position to take some unexpected and unusual opportunities. And so there I was, a restless PhD student living in Southampton with a habit of Antarctic cruises, mountains and running.

A chance reading of an article in a magazine given in a race bag held my attention. It was about the Ultra-Trail du Mont-Blanc. I don't remember the real impetus behind deciding to enter, but I did, hoping that it would give me the excuse for a climbing holiday in the Alps after finishing my PhD that summer. It was still early days in the life of the UTMB, the third edition, so there was as yet no rush for places, no accumulation of points required, no experience needed. It was just as well. I had none, not having ever raced in alpine terrain or beyond twenty miles off-road. That was the summer plans sorted. I just needed to finish the PhD.

Needing a distraction, I made a visit to friends in South Wales. They happened to be running a race; there seemed to be no reason not to join them. It was forty miles on a track in Barry. I had probably only ever run on the grass track on the school playing fields, and that for the 800m and 1500m, which equated to 'long distance' in those days. The furthest I had ever run while trying to hold any speed was a marathon. I had no strategy or intention other than to enjoy the day out. It was a blustery March day and the wind was sharp as it blew through the stands of the stadium.

It was an intimate field. All of perhaps 25 runners, and 25 patient timekeepers painstakingly counting the 161 laps of their allotted runner. Apprehensive? You could say that. But unlike in the mountains there was no danger of getting caught in an avalanche or falling into a crevasse. And there was no risk of getting lost. So in the grand scheme of things it had to be easy really, didn't it? All I had to do was run. So that is what I did. Courtesy of the meagre field and the leading lady having bigger fish to fry (needing only to run a certain distance to prove fitness for selection to a future race), I won.

The race wasn't quite the insignificant, local event that I had presumed and, bewildered by my victory, I was approached in that still-windy stadium by an England selector, there to observe the race fitness of that leading lady. He asked me if I'd be interested in representing England in the UK 100km Championships to be held during the Anglo-Celtic Plate 100km some weeks later. Nothing like that had ever crossed my mind. It couldn't have, I didn't even realise races like that existed. I thought about it. And

I said yes. Sometimes you have to take an unexpected opportunity, as you never know if it will come your way again. I had no expectation then that it would. So I decided that a visit to Ireland for a significantly long run while dressed up in the red and white colours of England was an experience worth trying. Once. I assumed.

A month later I found myself running laps around Phoenix Park in Dublin.

My training in the interim had been a twelve-day ski touring trip traversing a remote mountain range in north-east Turkey. While other runners would have been completing the last part of a focused training schedule and tapering off, I was enduring a penetrating cold and focusing on avoiding potential avalanche terrain as we made a traverse of the Kaçkar mountains rising above the coast of the Black Sea. My friend David, who was leading the trip, had been to the region once before but we were skiing into the unknown, working off two inches of a road map. Huge amounts of snow fell before and during our traverse so avoiding avalanche danger demanded constant awareness and caution. Making a traverse rather than attempting peaks from a fixed base necessitated the making and breaking of camp daily and with very low temperatures (-18°C or so) we never had the chance to properly dry out sleeping bags. It was a beautiful journey, but hard work with heavy packs since we were carrying tents, food and fuel. Not really the most restful of race preparations, but it was an incredibly rich experience. We were of course isolated in our small group during the traverse, but as we descended out of the mountains we experienced wonderful hospitality with numerous offerings of tea, and the mix of cultures was absolutely fascinating.

The subsequent clash of worlds was confusing. My Dublin flight was delayed, I missed the group dinner and I turned up at the table as last-minute preparations for the following day were being made. The stark contrast between the city of Dublin and the wilds of the Turkish mountains was mirrored by my abrupt arrival into the professional world of road racing with all its idiosyncrasies. No one had explained to me the ins and outs of a 100km race. No one had thought to tell me that I really should provide myself with an array of bottles labelled up for specific distances filled with luridly coloured sports drinks, together with similar provision of easily digestible food. Realising my anxiety on listening to the ongoing conversations, the team manager escorted me to the next-door 7-Eleven to buy provisions, and my roommate took pity on my ignorance and gave me some of her bottles.

The race began, and it ended. It was a long day in between (over eight hours). And I was, it has to be said, quite content not to ever have to run another lap of that park. Not first and not last. The comforting familiar. But somehow the next day, after a long walk with a friend to a high and windy hilltop on the outskirts of Dublin, having watched my male teammates negotiating even the stairs of our bed and breakfast with difficulty that morning, I realised that this might just be the start of something. My body and mind seemed to be able to cope with this kind of challenge.

I had a few months then of grappling with the final edits of my PhD, printing and defending my thesis, and applying for and getting a job at the British Antarctic Survey.

In between came a nearly snowless ski tour along the Swiss–Italian border with an almost distressing plunge through melted ice on the Lago del Sabbione. It still feels like the closest to death that I have knowingly come.

Avalanche danger in the late spring conditions had precluded us from taking the high route, and the hut guardian had assured us the ice across the dam was still safe. Far out from shore and ahead of the others the ice had suddenly given way beneath me. Time slowed, and I instinctively spread-eagled myself across the breaking ice. There was nothing really to bear my weight. Skis and poles were drifting in water; I somehow reached to them and threw them one by one across to firmer ice. The others threw me a rope, but I'm not so sure how much help they could actually offer, it was more psychological for all of us. I felt very alone. I slithered myself across the ice-melt until I too reached a firmer surface and, well spread out, we retraced our steps. Back at the hut the reality started to sink in. Stripped of my wet layers and sat by the stove to dry out, I realised it could have been a pretty serious situation. We talked to the guardian, but with the current avalanche conditions and the now suspect ice, our only option was to walk down and out of the valley, take a bus to Domodossola and rejoin our intended route before Monte Leone. It was an experience that again reinforced that need for a resilient equanimity and the willingness to adapt in the face of changing circumstances. Easier said than done.

At the end of our trip I bade farewell to my companions and with a few days to spare almost replicated our journey minus the glaciated sections. It was an adventure, scaring myself sometimes and with a night out sleeping on a pile of wood when the hut I was aiming for didn't have a winter room. At the end of my round trip back to Brig in the Rhone valley something had changed – I had realised that I could trust both body and mind to carry me through a long journey alone and on my two feet. It was liberating.

Some weeks later, after the oral defence of my thesis, I headed north, almost as far as I could go. A friend and I went to explore the Isle of Skye. We had but one glorious day on the Cuillin followed by days of getting to know the ridge in the mist and pouring rain. It is a place I would love to go back to.

Another alpine hike accompanied only by my bivy bag; some packing up of belongings; some goodbyes to good friends; and that was it. A train ticket, a heavy rucksack full of camping and climbing kit, a long journey through the tunnel and across France; and there I was, in Chamonix. And that is how it was that I found myself on that start line at the end of August in 2005. The world was before us and full of infinite possibility.

❖ ❖ ❖

Darkness. Dripping rain. The ever-weakening light from my headtorch bounces off the drops that fall in a steady stream in front of me. And behind me. And beside me. And above me. I have rivers running before my eyes. I can barely see the rocks and the twisted roots beneath my feet. The trees stand like sentries forbidding even an opening in the sky to offer relief to tired eyes. I feel like I've been running along this shelf of a path for hours now. It can't be that long, probably less than one hour, but I seem to have lost all track of time. The last refreshment post was in Argentière; this is it now, just me, the trail and those lights ahead of me, until we reach the end.

It was strange running through that village that has given a home to me and my brave little tent these last two weeks. A sloping meadow of a home. I had come to like it there, it had all I needed. It lay behind me now. Far behind me. How many hours would it be before I would be back there, sheltered at last from this incessant rain, warmly ensconced in my sleeping bag, and with the almost decadent possibility of making a brew on my little stove? A hot drink, what a treat that would be. With time to linger over it, savour every mouthful, warm my hands. For too long now I have been relying on a snatched gulp here and there. Yes, a hot drink would be a treat. But a treat that is not to be mine, not for a while yet at least.

I thought I knew this trail, the Petit Balcon Sud. I'd run it several times in the light when it was dry underfoot and bathed me in the warmth of the sun. I'd even grown fond of it, nestling into the steep forests that seemed to go directly up from the town, carrying me above the bustle of life below. So what was this strangely unrecognisable, unforgiving, demonic monster of a trail? Twisting and turning, relentless ups and downs, it seems to be a never-ending path into the worst of all my tomorrows and yesterdays rolled into one. What kind of a hell is waiting for me?

I blindly follow those lights ahead of me, praying that the gods of torches and batteries will be forgiving and let me reach the end without needing to change said batteries, or dig into my rucksack for that second torch. I should, I know. But that would mean stopping a moment. And those lights in front of me would dwindle ever further into the distance. And the next woman, she must be close. She and her partner are running together. They know this race. They've known what to expect. Surely that knowledge has given them a power to gain on me from this uncertain lead that I've held. They could be right behind me now, hidden by those twists and turns, the darkness of this forest. Pausing isn't an option. I'm not a spent force quite yet. I'm moving. I just have to keep moving, carving a body-shaped hole through the wetness. 'No, don't stop to change the torch. Drink? You had some, that last point. Too cold, too wet to need anything now. Food, no, that can wait also. Just keep moving those legs, or rather let them keep moving forward carrying you through the darkness, over the rocks and roots.'

So it goes. On and on. And on.

But, wait. Isn't this vaguely familiar? Finally, finally, the monster recedes and the comforting familiar returns. It's that last left corner bending off the balcony path, a few steps more and a right turn onto the last stretch of trail. I know now just how the trail will fall away beneath my feet, I know the small stream that needs jumping, I know how the last 200 metres will steepen until gravity pulls me onwards and downwards. The flickering torchlights ahead of me draw away. But this is it, I've hit the road, there are lights. Streetlamps. I've made it back to Chamonix. I can scarcely realise that the end is so close. The tarmac is hard underfoot, an abrupt change, but, oh how welcome. It brings with it the knowledge that the finish line must be minutes away at most. Surely, surely I can't be caught now, or at least if I am I might have a chance if I can just open up my stride. I'm not sure I can handle a sprint finish, but having got this far, I'd give everything I have. A left turn, just metres to the main road now. And someone is standing there. Someone is going to guide me in.

There are more lights, of course, the cafés and restaurants will be open, people will be eating a late supper, or maybe drinking a beer. Oh, but look, there are people standing lining the sides of the road. It's just like it was at the start. Well, perhaps considerably more holes in the crowd, wet, dark . . . but . . . why are they all still here? I make the last turn, and then I see. The finish archway in the church square. People waiting. The sound of clapping reverberates in my ears. Then the penny drops. It is for me.

They want to see the first woman cross the line. I am that woman.

* * *

It is all a bit overwhelming. What am I supposed to be feeling? There are flashes from the waiting cameras. I'm kissed on both cheeks. Who is this lady who seems to be in control of everything here? It all feels a bit of a blur. Kind arms welcome me. I'm handed a finisher's gilet. I'm nudged towards a table full of food. A bottle of water is put into my hands.

It is the end. There is no need to keep running. There is nowhere left to go. I've reached the end.

I can't quite take it all in.

The first thing on my mind is to ask the question that has been worrying me ever since darkness fell: 'Is there any way of getting back to my campsite?' Strange to run all this way. One hundred miles, near enough, around the huge massif of Mont Blanc, through three different countries. And then to be asking how to get a few kilometres up the valley. But right now that seems to be my overriding concern. How to get back to the sleeping bag that is becoming ever more appealing with every passing minute. The Chamonix valley has a great public transport system. But by some decree it seems to be understood that people without wheels of their own don't need to travel after the hours of darkness. So the trains stop. The buses stop. And I've stopped. I don't much feel like a long and wet walk. Not now. Not now I've stopped. I probably could have raced another twenty kilometres if that is what it took to reach the finish line. But now that I've stopped I'm not sure I could find the motivation to start again, to go back out into the pouring rain. But the answer is yes. One of the finish-line volunteers would be able to drive me. Relief. One problem sorted. I'd expected to arrive at some point tomorrow, or not at all, so I had given no thought to the 'how' of getting back to that waiting sleeping bag.

Next dilemma – I'm handed a can of beer by an equally wet, muddy and tired-looking man with a smile as wide as the finishing archway. I have been toing and froing for the last few hours with these couple of guys. Sometimes they pulled away on the downhills, sometimes I caught them back on the uphills. So it went. But look, they have waited for me. They have waited to see if I would cross the finish line after them. To see if I would cross that line as the first woman. We have exchanged but few words. No names, even. But we have shared something special. Experiencing the last stages of a race like this together, where you are nearly done in, creates a bond, even among strangers, that is hard to replicate. It is a special moment to share. A moment that is ours. Now. And only now. I stretch my hand out, not entirely sure that the stomach is ready for a beer, but eager to try and to share this moment with them.

But, wait. An official-looking lady explains to me that I need to go for a drugs test. Oh, right. This is a first. Drugs? But what drugs? Did they mean the hit of caffeine I had been longing for in that still-illusive café latte, or this brief feeling of euphoria induced by the endorphins released after having run a long way? It had been a very long way. But yes, of course, yes. But, 'Can I drink a beer first? Could it help with the rehydration?' No. No, is the simple answer. Better to go with the lady directly. So I'm bundled away from the finish area, away from my racing companions, away from the beer, away from the table of food. I'm wet. I'm soaked. A scratchy blanket is put around me, I'm handed that bottle of water, and given a chair to sit on. The procedure is explained to me, I'm given some forms to sign. I have to check that numbers on the various labels match up, but I think I just nod blindly, my mind far beyond the recognition of multiple-digit numbers. My cold, wet hands can barely handle a pen, and the resultant scribble is nothing much like anything at all, let alone my signature, woefully simple as it is.

Surely it should take some time to rehydrate, but suddenly I have to ask if I can try already. It's been cold and wet, and I've been having the odd sips of fluids here and there. Have I? I feel I need to go. I'm escorted to the toilets, plastic bottle in hand. I'm more than a little disconcerted to realise that I'm not left alone, that I have to be watched. It's one thing crouching down in the dark of night part-shielded by the low-lying growth. But to be watched in a toilet cubicle? I'm not sure I really like that very much. But what to do? To my relief I can fill the bottle, but I'm even more disconcerted to realise that I can't stop there. I hand the bottle over, and thankfully I'm left in peace to finish the rest of my business.

Drugs testing over. I start to think of what I need to do next – collect bag, shower, hot drink – before I can at last head towards that waiting sleeping bag. I hear familiar voices. It takes me a moment to recognise them. It is the friends who had been staying in the campsite in Argentière. I had thought they would by now be somewhere in the middle of their long drive back to England, but they had stopped for a night in Chamonix. They had been eating dinner in one of the pavement cafés and heard the news that an Englishwoman had won the race. It was of course the longest of shots that it could be me, but they couldn't drive off without finding out. And they had found me. They wait patiently while I find the building where the left bags were deposited, and while I find the showers in the depths of the sports complex. Hot water. What a luxury. I stand there awhile as the sweat, the mud, the tiredness are washed away. Warmed by the heat of the water, I realise how chilled I had got. Dazed, I move only when surprised by a man also in search of the com-forting cascade of warmth. Communal showers? Had women not been provided for, or had I just not looked hard enough? Too tired to care, I scramble into my dry clothes.

And then that swimming-head sort of tiredness starts to hit. A hot chocolate later and I am ready for bed. But first I should phone my parents; I'd promised to call as soon as I finished the race. I'd run near enough 100 miles, climbed the height of Everest from sea level and back down again, and their sleepily dazed response was to simply suggest that I had better get some sleep. True enough.

Back at the campsite I stumble over to my tent, which was thankfully still standing, and – too tired to sort through bags – I just bury myself in my sleeping bag. Tomorrow will be another day.

Sleep is restless. But I am warm in my sleeping bag, dry, and still. Not running, not moving, thankfully still. Nothing more I need.

Wandering to the supermarket the following morning the reality hits me. People are still running through the village with kilometres yet to go before reaching the finish line. They look tired. No. They look more than tired. They look like the walking dead. Almost. Two long nights on their feet. That is tough. You can see the tiredness in their movement. You can see the exhaustion in their faces, in the staring look of their eyes. And still they aren't finished. They have my utmost respect.

Sitting back in my tent, I suddenly think to check the timing on the programme. I'd won. That meant I should be at the prize-giving? I've had 4 p.m. in my head for some reason. But, no. It is 2 p.m. I suddenly realise I have minutes to get to the train station. The bus and train situation is sparse on a Sunday. If I don't hurry I'll be running back to Chamonix to get to the prize-giving in time. And I'm not sure I feel much like running anywhere yet.

Unbeknown to me, my mother is now phoning the Tourist Office in Chamonix, uncertain if she heard me right last night.

She asks if she can find out how a friend has done in the UTMB. 'But of course,' says the kind lady at the end of the telephone, 'but what is her name?' Well aware how much I shy away from attention, my mother hesitates. 'I can only give you her result if you tell me her name,' the kind lady urges. 'Elizabeth Hawker,' my mother says. 'Lizzy Hawker,' the lady exclaims. 'Oh my god. She won.'

Wandering into Chamonix, throngs of people walking through the streets, eating and drinking, I start to feel eyes on me. It makes me feel a little awkward, just a little ill at ease and unsure of what is to come.

The ceremonies pass in a blur . . . leaving hazy memories of standing on stage with a sea of people filling the church square. Where it all started was where it all ended.

The following day I run gently on familiar trails.

What had changed? Everything and nothing.

A return train ticket, a heavy rucksack full of camping and climbing kit, a long journey across France and through the tunnel and there I was, back in London. The only indication of my journey around Mont Blanc, a piece of wood inscribed 'I ere Femme' holding four running figures sculpted in metal and a surprising embrace from two older ladies as I claimed my berth on the sleeper in St Gervais – they had seen my photo in the newspaper.

Part II
A Journey of Exploration

Everest Base Camp
5350 m

Lobuche
4950 m

Dingboche
4400 m

Tengboche
3800 m

Namche
3440 m

Lukla
2840 m

Jiri
1905 m

Junbesi

Taksindu La
3062 m

Lamjura La
3532 m

Chapter Six

It's not about the records, it's not about the medals.
It's not about winning the race or making the podium.
It's about the fears and the tears, the laughs and the smiles.
It's about the shared experiences and the raw emotions.

It is still night. The chirrup from my phone wakes me from a restless sleep. 'Best of luck! Sleep well. Hope you get some pictures and have a plastic sheet for protection! Hope you had some fun up there. See you Friday at x pm.' It is a text message from Rich. I'm buried in a sleeping bag and trying not to think too much about what the morning will bring. His message makes me smile; it is going to be OK.

I fall back into that restless sleep for a few more hours.

The chirrup of my phone again. This time it is the alarm clock. My stomach rolls over. I've done this before, twice now. But still, it is a great, huge, big challenge. I don't know yet if the weather will be kind, or if my body will hold up. Actually, no. I trust my body. I'm pretty sure it can handle what I'm going to ask of it. But the mountains, the weather and the conditions are out of my control.

Weather has indeed been forecast. It is why I had been in such a hurry to get here. I've broken all the rules in the book when it comes to acclimatisation. But I feel fine. I peer out of my tent. Billi's tent. She is away now acclimatising for her ascent of the 7,861m Nuptse and has been kind enough to let me borrow it in her absence. There is a smattering of snow. But it is a dusting only, nothing to stop me. The big dump will probably come tonight.

And tonight I will be far, far from here and about 3,000m lower. Hence Richard's remark about a plastic sheet – I am probably going to get a soaking. So where am I now? In a tent perched on the shifting glacial moraine of Everest Base Camp at an altitude of 5,364m. And I'm about to run back to Kathmandu for the third time. Bonkers.

❖ ❖ ❖

'Namaste, didi. Namaste.'

'Namaste': the salutation by which people greet each other, head bowed and hands held together at the heart, throughout the Nepalese Himalaya and many parts of Southeast Asia. The literal definition is 'the spirit within me recognises and honours the spirit within you'; a greeting imbued with feeling and a significance that goes far deeper than our perfunctory 'hello'. It is a humbling gesture recognising our common humanity, our fundamental and undeniable equality. 'Didi': the Nepalese word for older sister, a term of endearment or respect. Or just friendliness, which is enough in itself.

These are words that have threaded through all my experiences in Nepal and the Himalaya right from my first expedition to Kalanag in 2003. After that first experience I knew that I would return, I just didn't know how or why or when.

If Zermatt and its mountains were the point of a

realisation, a recognition of a love, the birth of a passion, then Nepal has been the place that has deepened that love and intensified that passion. It has been the place that has challenged me and given me solace. It has shaken me to the core and filled me to the brim with life. Nepal has become a place that holds my curiosity, my passion, my bewilderment, my wonder. It is the place where I lost my heart.

If the Ultra-Trail du Mont-Blanc and all that went before that led me to stand on that start line was a journey of discovery, then running from Everest Base Camp to Kathmandu and the athletic career that my three attempts spanned have been a journey of exploration.

My first UTMB opened a door into a new world. It led me into the world of competitive running – it was the bridge from running mostly for myself and dabbling in a few races to the realisation that there was a potential there I needed to explore. As an endurance athlete my exploration of competition has taken me to extremes – long running, shorter running, faster running, extreme altitude, flat asphalt, mountain trails – it is the variety that I loved. It took me to five wins at the UTMB, a gold medal at the 100km World Championships, a 24-hour world record with an outright win and reaching the overall podium at Spartathlon. But these races were the smallest part of the story. Competition has always been a side-effect of my running. My running has never merely been the tool that enabled me to compete. I've found a peculiar satisfaction in flouting convention. It may mean I never fully realise my potential. But it may also mean that the path is more interesting.

Nepal and the adventures it has held has never been a turning away from competition, and I have raced my heart out on its sky-high trails. But it has also been a continuation of the mountain explorations that came before. The competitive element of racing and the yearning for other challenges simply became intertwined and developed in parallel; two strands of the same thread, just different expressions of what running means for me – a way to explore.

Reading back through notes I had written during the summer of 2006, I realise there is one dream I'd had since the very beginning of my running career. A dream that rooted itself completely outside of competition, one born of pure, unadulterated challenge. In a list of thoughts, dreams and plans for the future, sandwiched between hopes of a faster marathon and 100km time, and a diverse assortment of classic races, I had written 'a solo or pair run in Himalaya – of the ilk of that by Crane brothers, or Helene Diamantides and Alison Wright'.

Sometime after reading Nick Crane's *Clear Waters Rising*, I had found a second-hand copy of *Running the Himalayas*. His cousins, Richard and Adrian, crossed the Himalaya from east to west (Darjeeling to Rawalpindi) in 101 days, with minimal support, 5–6kg packs, and a live-off-the-land approach.[1] The Nepal part of their crossing took just over forty-nine days, including three rest days, on a route that took them through the middle hills (with a diversion to Everest Base Camp and over the Thorung La). Their story captured my imagination with its simplicity. The thought of a journey like that scared and excited me in equal measure. How? Who with?

Some time after that reading, I became aware of the journey that Helene Diamantides and Alison Wright had made during the 1980s – setting a Fastest Known Time (FKT) running from Everest Base Camp back to Kathmandu.

The label is of no great significance; what impressed itself upon me was the pure adventure and the spirit in which they made their journey.

It was a combination of both of these journeys that prompted that entry in my list of dreams. And that dream has given me more than I can ever explain.

A crossing of Nepal[2] I have attempted; I had to abandon and the story comes later. But the journey from Everest Base Camp to Kathmandu is now something I know intimately. It is perhaps not over, even yet. There is some history behind this seemingly pointless endeavour.[3] In those early years before the road was laid from Kathmandu to Jiri and before any flights flew to Lukla, the only way to get a message out of the mountains was to send a runner. Literally. And that is what happened.

In Sorrel Wilby's book *Across the Top*, describing her journey with her husband Chris Ciantar across the Himalaya from Pakistan to Arunachal Pradesh in India, she relates a meeting with Sonam Girme in Namche Bazaar, a place that has become so familiar to me. He had signed on with the successful 1953 Everest Expedition as a mail runner, at the tender age of twelve. It was the toughest job 'off' the mountain, but the best paid.

'All night, all day we running,' he moaned, 'no torch, see; just lamp.' They worked pairs on a relay basis so that they could rest for a few days between each Kathmandu-to-Base-Camp or Base-Camp-to-Kathmandu marathon. The average 'low altitude porter' rate was then three rupees per day and the journey to Everest took one month; but if a two-man mail team covered the distance between the city road head and the mountain in just four days, they were paid two hundred rupees each per trip. If they took a more leisurely five days, the wage dropped to one hundred and fifty rupees. Sonam mimed how he felt after a run. He crawled away from the fire on his hands and knees and curled up into a foetal ball in the corner of the room. 'Oh, very big pain!' he laughed. 'I couldn't move or cry or eat anything for two, maybe three day.' But the money made it all worthwhile. [4]

Running from Everest Base Camp to Kathmandu is a long way. It is round about 320km give or take a few kilometres for getting-lost-or-taking-longer-short-cut variations. It is about double the distance of that loop around Mont Blanc. It is a journey I have made three times now. The first was an opportunity that I just couldn't refuse. The second, I was finishing a race in the Khumbu and it seemed as easy a way home as any. The third was pure curiosity, not so much the trying for a new record (no real need, since I held it already), but rather the trying to tease out the *why* of doing something like that. I didn't. I'm still trying to figure it out now.

❖ ❖ ❖

I lie flat on my back, stretched out on the floor of my new office. It has been a whirlwind of a few days since that train back from Chamonix deposited me back in London. Life has been shifted to Cambridge, a new office, a borrowed bed, a borrowed bike. And this morning I found my way on borrowed bike from borrowed bed to this office floor. A route that will become all too familiar until I find a longer-term room. Or will it be how it was when I was here before? Shifting from pillar to post between research cruises. I'm becoming so practised at the shifting that life can be packed up in a couple of hours.

I'm struggling with a dodgy stomach; my body is taking some time to readjust to being back in the flatlands, and my mind is too. The exertions of last weekend – the Ultra-Trail du Mont-Blanc – feel a world away. They are a world away. No way even to start to explain to people here really. What kind of conversation is that to be had over morning coffee?

And so the daily rhythm of cycling to work, work, coffee break, work, lunchtime run, work, tea break, work, cycle home, begins. A few times the location of home changes. The lunchtime run varies between a couple of different routes and is more for the freedom that comes with clocking out than for any real training. Sometimes the one run becomes two, either in the early morning light or the fading light of day. And so life settles into a fairly monastic routine.

I meet Sarah Rowell, put in touch by a friend of Rob Collister's. She had been a sub-2:30 marathoner who had competed in the first Women's Marathon to be held in the Olympic Games in 1984 and is also an inspiring mountain runner. Talking to her encourages me. It makes me realise that I have some potential that would be a waste to ignore. The world of competitive running is there waiting to be explored. Sarah later became a close friend and gave me invaluable advice and guidance for a few years, until my life shifted away from the UK. I learned a lot from her experience and she was incredibly generous with her encouragement.

I'm restless though. I realised before I finished my PhD that I didn't in fact want to be a research scientist for the rest of my life, and the more I experience of research the more I realise I just am not really 'cut out' to be a career scientist. Promotion and progress seem now to be entirely measured on publication record. I love the writing and collecting the data, but sometimes I find it hard to trust the numbers I throw out. Working in a team would be different and good fun. But the way it works now you have to feign a false confidence that I don't have. And the significance of my research seems to be buried somewhere far in the future. I'm longing to feel that what I do matters now.

I get a call one day. It is the lovely girl from The North Face who I met at the closing buffet dinner of the UTMB. They invite me to lunch at their European headquarters, in Italy, and want to offer me sponsorship. It comes as a bolt out of the blue – I'm just a mountain-loving, sea-going scientist playing at running. The UTMB had been my first mountain race. A mixture of my natural hesitancy, some misgivings about how they might want to use me, a few doubts as to what I could offer to them in return and a disbelief that I could actually be worth sponsoring, all serve to delay things. We finally agree that they will help me travel to some races in 2006. This was a relationship that was to develop over the coming years – with a growing mutual trust – until eventually they were supporting me with a stipend and I'd built up a reputation in the community that was of unequivocal value to them.

Somewhere in the middle of autumn I'm invited to a reunion dinner in the Lakes for the Bob Graham Round Club[5] (by dint of my almost-didn't-happen round in the summer of 2004). I meet Helene Diamantides, and talking together about her Himalayan adventures and her run from Everest Base Camp back to Kathmandu sows a seed in my mind. It is a world away from anything that I know or have experience of but could this be something that I could dare to try? I'm later interviewed by Mark Hartell, long-time record holder for the BGR, for his RunFurther[6] initiative to promote ultrarunning in the UK and in the email conversation that follows we realise that we both had hopes of trying that Everest Base Camp to Kathmandu challenge. The seed was starting to grow.

While I was feeling the draw of competition, the urge to explore the mountains in other ways was still strong, and spring plans had given me something to look forward to all winter. I'd saved up my leave and clocked up as much overtime as I could. 'We're going to Kyrgyzstan,' I said. 'To where?' was the inevitable reply. A landlocked nation of Central Asia, it is sandwiched between the proliferation of new independent republics that sprang up after the dissolution of the Soviet Union. Across the somewhat artificial national boundaries persist a complex fusion of ancient ethnic groups, creating a fascinating mix of cultures, beliefs and traditions. Its mountains had captured our curiosity – mine and that of some friends. The Ak-Shirak range of the majestic Tien Shan, to be more specific; first explored in 1857, they had since been only rarely visited. Devoid of habitation and subject to an inhospitable climate, they had been closed to travellers for most of the twentieth century.

The thought of an adventure had kept me going through the long winter of cycling to and from work, the desk-bound hours in the office, the miles of wet and windy running. I had run some races and had even won a few. I had run my second 100km road race, so now had the uncertain privilege of being UK 100km Champion. It had been a strange experience, running laps around a windy RAF base for over eight hours. It had taught me the restorative powers of a simple cup of sweet tea in the final throes of a long and cold race, but it felt so much easier than the laps of Phoenix Park in Dublin a year earlier – as an athlete I had improved and surely had the potential to improve further. It had also given me an experience of the rougher side of competition though, and I had learned the uncomfortable disparity between generous support and jealousy. My roommate had, I think, been expecting to win. So sharing a room that night was a little uncomfortable. It is the way things sometimes are.

The timing of our expedition was fortuitous (for me). I had my first experience of injury, iliotibial band syndrome, possibly the result of running for so many hours in one direction on a cambered road during that 100km race. Whatever the cause, the advice was to stop running. This was my first taste of quite literally being stopped in my tracks. I hated it. So the time on skis on glaciated terrain couldn't come soon enough – there I wouldn't be able to run even if I was able.

The last days before an expedition are always a haze of packing, repacking, weighing and re-weighing. Continually questioning, 'too much or too little?' This time was no different, but it was a good distraction. Pulks, tents, sleeping bags, stoves, food for eighteen days in the mountains, skis, skins, poles, transceivers, cameras. Everything had to be pared down to the pure essentials, I was mindful of having to carry or pull every kilogram, but those inevitably crucial items still had to be remembered.

We were ski-mountaineering (once we reached snow at least); making sky-high tracks in unknown territory. Our objective was to make a traverse of the Ak-Shirak range. During our journey in from city to mountains our young interpreter was full of enthusiasm for satiating our curiosity and teaching us about the history and culture of her country, a beautiful nation, now independent, but one still fraught with difficulties. Our truck rumbled across the plains to the lake of Ysyk-Köl. An incredibly beautiful expanse of water, the second largest alpine lake in the world, it is reminiscent of the sea until you recall it is at an altitude of 1,500m. This was our oasis of calm to leave from and return to. After a couple of hours of intense pulk creation (kiddies' sledges with various combinations of plumbing tubing, wire, duct tape and prusik cord to simulate traces), we enjoyed a feast of traditional Kyrgyz delicacies under the setting sun. The following day we (just) made it over the high passes despite the remnant snow cover, until on one descent our drivers decided to ignore the efforts of locals to direct us towards a safe passage and we became stuck in the only patch of remaining snow. Hours passed, our drivers being reluctant to accept suggestions or help, until salvation finally arrived in the guise of a minibus. Cigarettes, vodka and a little money changed hands and we were on our way into the border zone.

We lamented those lost hours. After being unceremoniously dumped by the 'roadside', the fall of darkness meant it was impossible to find the faint track leading up our approach valley. We made camp where we were and the following morning set the tone of the next few days. The valley was bare of snow so the easy approach hauling pulks that we had envisaged instead turned into days of double-carries and slow, frustrating progress. Eventually we found a safe point at which to access the frozen riverbed and followed our highway to heaven.

Making camp at the foot of Kyrgyzia (the highest peak in the range at 4,946m) we were awed by the beauty of the peaks around us, potentially all unclimbed. This was wilderness country, the extent of our isolation emphasised by the length of our approach. We reached seven modest summits and lived a simple life with a primitive routine: rising with the light, sleeping as darkness fell. They were days of exertion, skinning upwards, floating downwards by ski, making and breaking camp, stamping out space for tents, digging snow, melting water, eking out food and fuel, star gazing. I thrived on it.

The mountains tell their own story, but eventually we emerged down the Petrov glacier. The way out proved as challenging as the way in. Then, finally reaching the gold mine road, we were kindly escorted off the premises to our pickup point, an abandoned meteorological station, by security guards. We must have looked hungry, for they donated us a dozen bread rolls. To my intense disappointment all were meat, so while they were devoured by the others, I had to wait still longer to satisfy my longing for fresh bread.

Our journey had both the excitement of a long exploratory traverse and the satisfaction of attempting virgin summits. There was peace in the sweetness of those summit moments; poised momentarily between the tension, the struggle, the toil of the ascent, and concern for the descent yet to come. Yet even on those wild summits was evidence of environmental exploitation as we peered down into the Kumtor gold mine; the yellow plume of fumes, the boom of an explosion, the sight of the whole of a mountainside cut away, terraced, mauled, a constant hum from the mine workings.

There had been a wonderful contrast between companionship and solitude; we had worked together, we had relied on each other and yet there had been beautiful moments of being alone, skinning on ahead following our tracks from the previous day, weaving a safe route through the cavernous crevasses, beyond the reach of threatening seracs (columns or blocks of glacial ice) – solitude, contemplation, silence. I'd had a dawning realisation of the freedom we had to be there. I'd felt the simple delight in being alive.

But time in the high mountains is a privilege, not a right, we live there on borrowed time. I always realise this on the descent, on reaching the tree line and running water. We can actually only sustain ourselves in the lower altitudes where there is water to drink and the ability to make a fire. In the high mountains we can only travel and be grateful for the opportunity to be there. But that journeying through the high mountains, which demands an absolute presence in the moment, somehow connects me to a core of stillness deep within me. And that strength is what I draw on in my running and in my every day.

❖ ❖ ❖

I lie back in my sleeping bag for a minute, reluctant to leave its cocoon of warmth and safety. I have that familiar jumble of feelings – anticipation and apprehension, eagerness and reluctance. It is the same as before any race. But this isn't a race. There will be no route markings to follow, there is no official start or finish, there is nobody to race against. It is just me. So why am I making this long journey again?

It is April, I've been back in Nepal for a while now and during these spring weeks Richard and I have had evenings full of long conversation. One night talk turned to the concept of endurance, of going beyond what would generally be considered hard. I couldn't really give him a satisfactory answer as to the *why* of my running these long, long distances. We had started talking about my last run from Everest Base Camp to Kathmandu.

I wondered what it would be like to try it again, but this time to be asked questions while doing so, to try to tease out that *why* of doing something like this. And so the idea was born, I would attempt it again, Richard would come to support me at Jiri, and we would try to answer those questions.

A week or two had passed and I'd realised there was only a small window of opportunity before we had to leave for Mustang and the inaugural edition of Richard's race.[7] Time was getting short – if I was going to do this it would have to be now. Rushed plans were made, although continuing the tradition of a simple do-it-yourself approach to record breaking, not many plans had to be made. I would fly to Lukla, walk myself up to Everest Base Camp and run out to Jiri, where Richard would meet me with Upendra and we'd make our way back again to Kathmandu. Put like that it sounded simple. Could it be that easy?

I sit myself up and make my few preparations. There is not much to do. I put my contact lenses in, put my half-comb through my hair, and brush my teeth. I already slept in my running skapri and thermal so I just pull on my hat, fleece pants and big duvet jacket. I walked up here with the bare minimum but I'll run out with even less. I have a tiny pack which can hold everything I need – lightweight duvet jacket, lightweight waterproof jacket and bottoms, a hat, thin gloves, my water bottle, some food, my mobile phone, a spare thermal top, headtorch, my glasses and some rupees. That's it. I'll leave everything else here; Billi can bring it back to Kathmandu in a few weeks' time at the end of her expedition.

I walk over to the mess tent. When he heard that I was going to make another attempt at this, Russell Brice, the leader of Billi's expedition, kindly invited me to stay. I'd accepted eagerly – it's not often you get the chance to stay at Everest Base Camp – there are no lodges here for trekkers so unless you are part of an expedition there is no opportunity. I am hugely grateful to be here rather than staying in an icy lodge lower down in Gorak Shep. They have looked after me well, although Russell seemed disappointed last night when I refused the offer of fresh steak and instead asked for my usual abstemi- ous diet of tomato soup and chapati. Listening to their expedition stories helped calm my nerves, took my mind off what I was about to do and stopped me wondering if I was going to wake up with a thumping headache. I should have done, given my foolishly swift ascent to altitude. The recom- mended acclimatisation rate is to ascend 300–500m per day, with a rest day every four days. That would make it a six- to ten-day walk from Lukla to Everest Base Camp. I have done it in two. From leaving Kathmandu, which is at an altitude of 1,400m, I had one night at 3,440m in Namche Bazaar and one night at 4,620m in Dhugla, before arriving here at 5,364m yes- terday afternoon. My example is not to be followed! I feel fine though, no headache, and now I'll make it out before the snow comes. I know from experience that I usually acclimatise quickly, but even so it was pushing the envelope. It has been a gamble, but I'm lucky, it seems to have worked out. So far, so OK.

I'm up too early for breakfast but the kitchen staff are there waiting for me. I gulp down a few cups of sweet tea and mash some Weetabix in a bowl in place of the not-made-yet porridge. Russ and Ellen walk over with me to the stupa – in lieu of any start line this is my self-designated starting point. We take a few photos and I strip off my big jacket and fleece pants; Ellen will leave them back in Billi's tent for me. I'm wearing every scrap of clothing that I'm taking with me, it's probably about -10°C and I need to get moving now. Shivering, I give them a quick hug and they wish me luck. I'm happy they are here with me, it is good this time to have friends to witness the beginning.

This is it. My third long run out of the Khumbu.

Chapter Seven

To see a world in a grain of sand
And a Heaven in a wild flower
Hold Infinity in the palm of your hand
And Eternity in an hour

William Blake, *Auguries of Innocence*

I'm glad to be moving now. Just slowly at first here on the moraine, my feet skittering a little on the iced-over rocks. It is a beautifully clear morning. If the dump of snow comes tonight then it will be a different world up here. I'm thankful to have missed it, had it come already it would have put paid to any hope of making this journey in a faster time; breaking trail is slow, hard and painstaking work.

I feel a huge sense of relief now that I've started. It often feels like getting to the start line of a race is the hardest part. The training, of course, is one thing. But it is also the effort and hours spent on working out the logistics of bus, train, plane combinations, the searching for the cheapest tickets, and then the actually getting there, not to mention the butterfly stomach and the nerves. Once I'm on that start line my job is simple. All I need to do then is to run.

Same now. Only this time I really hadn't been sure that I was even going to get here. It was out of my control.

The weather had delayed flights into Lukla and I'd spent two long days in Tribhuvan airport waiting. On the third morning I said goodbye to Richard for the third time. This time it had to work out, I was running out of time with the approaching bad weather high up and our imminent departure to Mustang. Back in the airport my heart sank; flights were again delayed. This time the man working on the counter took pity on me as I sat there patiently whiling the time away. He had come to know me over the last days, and so when one seat on a helicopter became available he suggested me. Helicopter? The possibility hadn't crossed my mind. It would be a huge expense, over three times the cost of the flight, and what if I didn't even make the record? But, it could be the only option. My thoughts and emotions were in a tumult. I asked for ten minutes to decide. I sent Richard a text, needing an objective opinion from someone other than myself. 'Do it', was his advice, adding, 'money can always be found', and as to whether I made the record, 'irrelevant, it is the story that counts'.

I only had about forty minutes until the helicopter was scheduled to leave. All my money was in Richard's safe keeping, the other side of the city. The helicopter guy was so eager to fill the place that he offered to take me by motorbike to collect the money. It was the quickest journey I've ever made across the city, through the heat of the day already clad in my mountain-running clothes. Clutching tight hold, the going-fast-created-wind blowing my hair, I wondered what on earth I was doing. But Richard was right, it is the stories that matter, and even getting into the Khumbu was part of this story, part of the challenge.

He was there waiting at his gate, my bundle of money in his hand; I took what I needed and my extra duvet jacket too, worried about the bad forecast for the days ahead. A quick hug goodbye and that was it, if the helicopter flew, I would next see him in Jiri after thirty or more hours of running.

The helicopter did fly, it was a bumpy ride and rain had greeted me at Lukla. It was past four o'clock and most people were already finding a lodge for the night. But I had to make it directly to Namche Bazaar that night to start the acclimatisation process. So I had pushed on along those wet and slippy trails, through the falling darkness, and arrived in a wet and deserted Namche about four hours later. I'd picked a lodge at random, eaten something and tried to dry out as much as I could.

The next day I had pressed onwards and upwards along those trails I know so well. A few texts passed backwards and forwards between Richard and me. Our friend Alex Treadway had left days before, he was also headed to Everest Base Camp for a photographic assignment; we had planned to try to intercept each other, and document the beginnings of this adventure with some photos.[1] I was aiming to sleep at Dhugla (4,620m) that night but according to Richard, Alex with his far more sensible approach to acclimatisation was staying lower in Dingboche, so I had decided to pass through the village en route. It had been a cold afternoon with clouds hanging low. Arriving at the entrance to the village I'd started a systematic search of all the lodges; we were out of mobile reception so I was hoping to find Alex escaping the murky afternoon and enjoying a hot drink in the dining room. How else to find him? I'd started to worry that I would miss him – he could be sleeping or outside walking – and then on my opening the door to the dining room of one lodge Alex had looked up in almost startled surprise. I stopped for a chat and a few cups of hot lemon. The weather was too bad to try any photos then, so we had agreed to meet the next day. From there it would only take me a few hours to reach Everest Base Camp.

I was late meeting Alex – we hadn't been entirely specific about our meeting point – and the clouds were already rolling in. We had a twenty-minute window, and then any further efforts were rendered pointless. He promised to intercept me on my way back downwards. Billi too, she was heading down towards Lobuche and we had met in Gorak Shep as I worked my way up the trails towards Everest Base Camp.

It was only yesterday, but it feels like weeks ago already. Time has already taken on a whole new meaning. I find that in races also. Totally absorbed in the now, I lose all sense of the passage of time. Is that what Blake was talking about in his poem, to hold 'eternity in an hour'?

Anyway, despite all the uncertainties I'd made it into the Khumbu and up to Everest Base Camp. I'm running now, the journey has started and my job is to get myself back to Kathmandu in as short a time as possible. After all the effort it has taken to get here, now I'm just heading straight back. Bonkers.

❖ ❖ ❖

I'm a little bemused. A little tired. A little hesitant. I'm not sure quite what this is going to mean, but somehow I realise that this is significant. It is going to have implications for all that follows. I feel like I'm standing at the edge of all I've known.

I've just won a race: the 2006 Zermatt Marathon, with nearly 2,000m ascent. And I ran faster than I did that first London Marathon, despite the climb. It doesn't really seem credible. One year ago I was walking back to Zermatt after a climb of the 4,206m Alphubel, and I crossed the path of the marathon. People were running. They were already at the 30km mark, and they were still running, but running upwards. I can remember being in complete awe. I never imagined that just twelve months later, I would also try. Far less did I ever imagine that I could win a race like that. But I have.

And despite having won a few races this year, this feels different. Very different. It feels like this is serious. It is taking things to a new level.

I am sitting on the mountainside. The festivities are over, the prize-giving and the music finished. It felt strange to be there alone, no one to share the moments with (something I would get all too used to). I am walking down now from the finish at Riffelberg to Zermatt. There is still strength in my legs, and it seems a shame to waste the beauty of this late afternoon sitting on a train. Andrea, the race director, even handed me back a 100 CHF note for the registration fee I had paid. I don't think she had expected the winner to come from the pool of non-elite normal runners. I don't think anyone had. In this world of mountain marathon running I am a complete unknown. I sit here on a rock, staring across towards the Matterhorn, which had been pulling me ever closer during the race itself, and open up the envelope I had been given on the podium. I gulp. It is the equivalent of more than a month's wages, and for a few hours of work. It is a little overwhelming. As is the smell of the round of cheese in my rucksack (the 'natural' category prize). It will keep me going for the rest of the summer.

Weeks passed back at the desk in Cambridge. The round of cheese became gradually smaller.

And then, another alpine foray. This time to Davos for the Swiss Alpine K78, racing 78km on mountain trails. It was a region I knew from winter skiing but over fifteen years earlier; this time it would be my feet that would learn to know the bare trails. My parents were there for a holiday, I had only a few days, just the weekend. I had to get back to work.

Something provoked some anger in me. It doesn't happen often. But it stirred a determination, and a passion that stayed with me until I was standing on that start line both wanting and needing to fly. Friends had taken me to the start, their young son and his cousin woken early from sleep, and on the spur of the moment they decided to follow the start of the race rather than return straight home. I was a novice at this. Seventy-eight kilometres of mountain trails and I was running it as I would a marathon, carrying nothing, and without support to hand me food or drinks along the route. All I had was what I ran in and what I could grab from the refreshment points.

It was good to be running, I was happy to be able to focus in on the simple task of getting myself back to the finish line in the stadium of Davos as fast as possible. Nothing else mattered. Everything else could wait. Life was in suspension. I didn't see any other women. And, I did fly. It came easily to me that day. I seem to remember the effort being sustainable, never too much, but obviously never too little. I made the long ascent to the Kesch-Hütte as quick as the quickest men (I later found out), and the volunteers there at the checkpoint were bemused to see me take almost no food. I snatched perhaps just half a sweet roll, my naivety giving me the freedom to flout conventions, had I known what they even were. The weather turned as I ran the delightful panorama trail towards the Scaletta Pass, traversing high above the valley below. The coolness spurred me onwards. I reached the pass drenched and cold, it gave impetus to my descent – the quicker the descent, the sooner to be warmer. I had to pause to ask a hiker on the trail to do up my shoelace, my hands being too cold to deal with knots. Low in the valley I was surprised by cheers from my friends. Having heard that I was at the front of the race they had abandoned any idea of returning home, and hours after having been woken early from sleep those young boys were still smiling and cheering me onwards.

The valley out from Dürrboden is long. But eventually I hit the road, which meant only a kilometre or two to go. I kept up as high a pace as I could, certain the second woman must surely be closing in from behind. Then the moment came when the stadium was in sight, a few more strides and I was inside the gates, a few more steps and I was handed a wreath of olive leaves. I wasn't sure what to do with it, so ran with it in my hand round the curve and there it was – the finish line. Only four men had entered the stadium ahead of me. That record still stands.

It was a swift transition back to the flatlands. I was subsumed back into the routine of cycling to work, work, coffee break, work, lunchtime run, work, tea break, work, cycle home. Two weeks later I raced again, this time 50km on the road, in Gloucestershire. I'd been selected for the 100km World Championships but had to prove fitness. My performance and my record at the Swiss Alpine seemingly held no weight with British Athletics. It seemed almost an unnecessary effort to race simply for the point of proving fitness, but I had no choice. My initial intention was simply to run the distance in the accepted time to prove that fitness. But once the race began I could, of course, not let up. Not until I had set what was then a new UK record.

More weeks passed at work, back in the same routine. But by now it was hard to focus on the science when my heart was on the run. And that round of cheese was getting ever smaller, marking both the passage of the summer, and my initiation into the world of competitive running.

After my efforts in Zermatt at the beginning of the summer I'd received my first race invitation, an entry to the Jungfrau Marathon; the cost of travel would be covered and accommodation provided. It was a scary prospect to be one of the elite, but an offer not to be refused. The marathon is an awesome race, right to the foot of the Jungfrau, the Eiger and the Mönch. It claims to be the highlight of the mountain marathon circuit and is described as the 'New York Marathon' of the mountains. Its unique challenge is the near-flat first half requiring significant speed, followed by a 1,500m climb to Kleine Scheidegg demanding the skills of a mountain runner. This intimidating combination gives it an almost cult status among elite runners.

I kept to myself before the race. It's what I did, and still do. I was diffident and unsure of my place there. This keeping to myself is partly my instinctive introversion, partly the need to disconnect, partly the need to maintain clarity and preserve mental and physical energy. But it is also the way I am. Wary to get too close to people. For a long time I thought that my self-sufficiency was admirable. It, like everything else, is illusory. I found that out later.

A restless sleep and race day dawned. Its chill autumn morning gave way to the heat of a summer alpine day. Blue skies created a festival atmosphere for the spectators and supporters who were almost deafening in their applause as we passed through the mountain villages. I ran hard. But not hard enough. I'd picked up a cold racing in chilly, rainy North Wales the previous weekend; my warm-up race for this, which had turned into a 10km personal best. Was the cold still there, or was it simply that I was not good enough? Second place. Something that I should have been proud of then and there, I later learned.

But in my short experience of racing I had become used to leading from the front. Despite my anonymity, despite still being the unknown, it had quickly become what I expected of myself. I enjoyed everything about the race, but I can remember now the waking at night afterwards, questioning myself over and over again. What had I done wrong? What could I have done better? It was days before it wasn't the first thing I thought about when I woke up. It took time for me to feel the guilt less intensely. Other things keep me awake now.

I was now not just running, but racing. Having discovered there was more potential within me to explore, it would have been a waste not to pursue the possibilities. But with this shift came the weight of my own expectations. I wrestled with the peculiar combination of not believing what I had achieved and yet very quickly expecting nothing less and much more. I found it hard to possess those good performances and even harder to really give myself credit for them. It was as though those performances belonged to something much bigger, much greater than me, as if I was a passive participant in a drama where the script had already been written and I was simply playing the part that had been given to me. Whereas I keenly felt my second place at the Jungfrau Marathon to be *my* failure. I questioned whether I had done something wrong, whether I had misjudged what I needed to do before and during the race. So many factors play into a race performance. But this one I owned. I owned the failure. I had written the script and it was my fault.

One month later I was en route to South Korea for the 2006 100km World Championships as part of the Great Britain team. I had no leave left, and so was forced to make a special request to take more, unpaid. Just enough days to allow me to get to travel, prepare, race and return. Permission was given after consideration. It is sometimes disconcerting to remember that – ability, preparation and opportunity aside – what does and does not happen can so often be down to a technicality, a rule in a rule book, a refusal or a permission.

Gold. The reality didn't sink in while I was still in Korea, neither did it back at my desk on a grey October day when the heat of that distant land seemed just a hazy memory; it still hasn't now. It was a huge privilege to be representing Great Britain in a World Championship event, but as my first international competition it carried with it an almost daunting responsibility. We had just a few days there before the race to give us time to get over any jet lag and get used to the country, to bond as a team and to prepare ourselves mentally and physically for the long haul. This was a World Championships, it felt different to anything I had done before, there was a seriousness so far absent in my previous race preparations. I went walking in the local hills. I kept it quiet. We were supposed to be resting. But I needed the comforting familiar of being on my feet and out in nature.

In the pre-race listings I was ranked nineteenth, and mentally I was questioning whether I should even be there, racing in that talented field. That aside, I also knew that I was in good form, the best that I had probably yet been with respect to running. I knew I was ready to run as well as I could do and with the naivety of inexperience I thought that was enough. Enough to do what would be doing well for me, that is. I just had no concept of what 'doing well for me' could become. That is all.

The days passed slowly. I made some small runs in the park near where we were staying, I strode out on longer runs along convenient bike paths that on occasion turned into longer-than-intended runs when I didn't remember the landmarks I thought I'd noted. I was bemused by the practice of the local Koreans, out for their morning walks, to walk backwards. I noted to my teammates that I really would have lost the plot, or be hallucinating, if I saw people running backwards during the race. I listened to Vangelis's *Conquest of Paradise*, a piece of music that stirred up something deep inside me and made me shiver with anticipation, as it had done since hearing it on the start line of the Ultra-Trail du Mont-Blanc.

The night before the race I went out to the park that I had run around so many times by now, and drank a small beer sitting on a patch of grass. I sat for a while. I'm not sure it was a meditation, but it was certainly a thinking my way into the next day's race. It was a dive into the stillness deep inside.

After some hours of uneasy sleep, the start inevitably came. It is strange, the last afternoon, the last evening, the 'last supper', the last night, the last (restless) sleep, the last breakfast, before an important race. These everyday incidents take on a strange significance, as I suspect they would before an impending and expected death. It is as though the world will stop with the start of the race. And you are powerless to hold time in abeyance. The progression of time is inevitable. The start will come.

I shivered by the water's edge in my Great Britain vest in that darkness that comes before dawn. The moon was a golden orb in the sky. The emotions at having even got to the start line were almost overwhelming. It is the 'before' that is the hardest part. Once on the start line the job is simple. Simply to run. I decided there and then that all I could do was to run the best race I could – with my heart and soul, as well as my head and legs.

The race began . . . and I did just run. People ask how time passes in a long race, but it does. The running becomes almost a moving meditation, helping you through the times when you feel great and the times when you feel like you can't go on. There are moments of camaraderie with your supporters and fellow competitors, and moments of feeling entirely alone.

And yes, I don't joke, I did see some local Korean runners running backwards. And no, I wasn't actually hallucinating. I hadn't realised at that point that there is a 'backward running' movement. It is believed (by some) that it can balance the strain of normal running as the opposing movements cause muscles to fire differently. There are even 'backwards' races.

I ran what I felt was a comfortable pace out of the start, but was more than a bit disconcerted to find no other women ahead or around me. What did they know that I didn't? So I held back. A little. Until the second woman caught me and we ran together for the next 40km. From then I was alone.

There comes a point where you really do believe you will go the distance, but it's never over until it's over.

This was just my third 100km race, and I certainly needed more practice at how to eat and drink while running with intensity. Unlike my first 100km race, I did at least know that I should provide myself with sustenance. But my idea of this was limited to a bottle of Ribena brought from the UK, some squares of chocolate, and a few sandwiches from the breakfast table. I took on what I could. But it obviously wasn't enough and I started fading during that last 20km. I knew Monica Carlin, the Italian runner, was catching me, but I didn't look over my shoulder until about 200m from the finish line. She was there, fast approaching. I didn't know if I could keep things together and hold off her challenge, but I wasn't making it that far and not giving my all to find out.

So after just short of seven and a half hours of (fairly) fast running we had a sprint finish. I gave it everything. I ran. And the end came. Gold.

It was the only medal for Great Britain in senior athletics that year, as a journalist pointed out to me sometime later. And the only recognition was a reluctant letter from UK Athletics many, many months later.

Looking back, although I seemed to fall into the world of competitive sport, I had been training in the raw for years. Endurance had become for me a way of life rather than a sport. That mindset had always been there, right back to the days when even as a child I preferred to do things the hard way. One incident stays with me: back in Zermatt in winter, frustrated by the thought of wasting time queueing for a cable car, I walked down, skis over my shoulder, and beat the rest of the family back.

I'm not convinced I'm an athlete. Not in the conventional sense. Endurance is simply an innate character trait.

It is probably my greatest strength and will, no doubt, be my absolute downfall. Perhaps I'm inherently lazy. I read of the lengths that elite athletes go to cross-training when injured. I have had to spend hours on a treadmill in the depths of winter, but still fight every moment in a gym. I find it hard. But I would (and do) walk for hours across strange cities rather than take a taxi. Buses are a last resort. I would rather (and have done) struggle on crutches down flights of polished stairs and along hundreds of metres of dusty, potholed roads rather than ask someone to bring me a packet of milk. This is how I am. Is this independence? Or just a frustrating unwillingness to rely on anything other than my own body and mind?

By the end of the summer of 2006 I had reached the point where I could no longer compete anonymously and be a surprise, and for sure the expectations were high. But the expectations I have of myself are always greater. That is the way it is. It is an incredible feeling when the running is flowing. It is hard when injury or my mind stop me from doing what I know I can. But learning to ride out the rocks and the rolls is part of the journey. That is life. It is something I have learned to know intimately through the medium of running.

Chapter Eight

The only 'meaning' comes from the focus,
the attention, that we give.
Which is enough, perhaps, since it is somewhere
in that we find our 'flow'.

I stop trying to rationalise what I'm doing and just let myself enjoy the simple movement of running. All my apprehensions are melted away by the beauty of the morning. The skies are clear, early cloud has filled the valley below and the sun is hitting the summits of Nuptse, Pumori, Thamserku and Cholatse. I relish these first miles, emerging out of the shadows of these majestic summits into the early morning sunshine.

Finally warm again, I reach the group of lodges at Gorak Shep and crossing the ancient lake bed the sand is soft underfoot. People are already setting off to walk up Kala Patthar (5,550m). It lies on the south ridge of Pumori and affords the most accessible view of Everest from base camp to summit. Even their day packs are bigger than my tiny rucksack.

I make short work of the dusty trail through the boulders beyond and head downwards. It is easy ground here now and despite being at an altitude of around 5,000m I can keep a decent pace. It is pure delight, no other way to describe it; I savour the moments here. It strikes me that there can't be too many places in the world where it is possible to do this, to really run at this altitude! A few groups of trekkers are making their way slowly upwards, their steps heavy and measured. I startle them as I pass swiftly by. They look shocked. My rapidity evokes a mixture of doubt and incredulity.

Alex had promised to intercept me here at Lobuche to take some photos, but I catch no sight of him and hear no shout as I run through this strange little accumulation of lodges. Maybe I'm earlier than he's expecting, maybe he is eating breakfast, but I can't waste time to stop to try to find him. Disappointed, I run on downwards, wondering what has happened. And then I hear them calling. Alex and Billi are both there waiting for me on the pass with the cairns in memory of those who have died climbing Everest. It is somehow comforting to see them. It is as though having witnesses gives my long journey some kind of uncertain credibility.

I linger for ten or fifteen minutes for Alex to take some quick shots. I worry about Billi, who is having a hard time with acclimatisation; we hug goodbye, I tell Billi to look after herself and wish her well for her ascent; Alex I will see sooner back in Kathmandu. They tell me to run well, to keep safe and to not let Richard hold me up.

It's just a short descent to Dhugla now and Mr T, the owner of the lodge, is there waiting for me with that promised cup of tea. I happily ask for a second and he slips a Mars bar into my hand. I'll save it for later – I rarely eat them but it will be a treat to look forward to in the middle of the night. They are worth a lot at this altitude. Things that are cheap back in Kathmandu increase exponentially in price the higher up the trail you get, understandable when everything has to be carried up here by yak or by porter. But it makes me think twice about buying what isn't strictly necessary.

Time to head onwards. I know these beautiful trails of the Khumbu so well now. It feels like they are more familiar even than many of my alpine haunts. The memories of all the times I have trodden them before run through my head but they are absorbed into the sensations and feelings of 'Now', so my experience is somehow time past and time present merged into one. But isn't this how we are? Everything that came before had to happen for us to be the person we are now. And the greatest moments of clarity come when we look back and we realise that it was all necessary and all beautiful.

I pause in Namche to buy some outrageously priced cheese bread and eat it on the move. Some long way down that well-worn trail it starts to rain. Again. My heart sinks and questions go round and round in my head. Is it going to be the same story as last time, a long wet night? And if it is, will I make it through this time? Will I be strong enough to keep going for hours wet through (however good my lightweight waterproof, it is no match against a determined downpour). I stop briefly for a hot drink, and to think. But there is nothing to think about really, I know I will carry on just as long as I can. It is that innate stubbornness. Once I've decided to do something I will see it through to the bitter end. I'm not entirely sure where this really came from. Obstinacy, perhaps, and a wanting to do things differently. I remember as a child telling my car-mad brothers that I would never have one; thirty years later I am still carless. And I haven't eaten meat since the age of five when I realised its connection to animals, and decided it simply wasn't for me.

❖ ❖ ❖

Nepal and that run from Everest Base Camp back to Kathmandu – the seed was growing. Mark had by now put together plans for a combined mountain and run adventure in Nepal, and invited me to be a part of it. Scared and excited by the thought in equal measure, I couldn't decide if it was an idea I should ditch there and then or if it was a challenge I could conceivably hope to attempt. It just seemed so far beyond anything I knew.

Life continued apace as I tried to balance full-time work at BAS with serious racing. Unsure about a career in research I resigned, found part-time work at the British Oceanographic Data Centre in Liverpool, shifted location and was continuing to race. I wrestled with the contradictions between my working and racing lives. My part-time wage barely covered rent and my commute. It wasn't even keeping me in bread and cheese. I was spending far too much time travelling to get to races and there was a disconcertingly stark contrast between racing hard on alpine trails and walking back into that open-plan office for a day at the computer with my office mates still sitting at their desks, totally unaware of the places I had been. Thoughts of Nepal were thrust to the back of my mind.

But I couldn't ignore the opportunity that such an adventure would bring and, unable to resist the challenge and the pull of the mountains, I agreed to be part of the Everest Base Camp to Kathmandu attempt with Mark and Stephen Pyke (Spyke). I was flattered at their eagerness to have me join them, both had far more experience than me and held numerous records both on the British fells and further afield. Just weeks before departure I finally committed to join for the mountain part too. My decision inevitably precipitated a frenzy of activity and time passed in a haze of preparations.

Apart from everything else I had to figure out what needed to be done about my 'Whereabouts'. Since June

2007, some eight months after my win at the 100km World Championships, I had been on the IAAF's out-of-competition drugs testing list. The 100km hadn't long been recognised as a discipline by the IAAF, so in this regard it was a great step for ultra road-running. I was on a list of seventeen that included Paula Radcliffe, Mo Farah, Christine Ohuruogu, Dwain Chambers and Kelly Sotherton – the road and track elite of the UK in other words. It was the most recognition I'd ever had of my status as a world champion.

In reality it meant giving an hour slot (with an address) each and every day where I would be available to be tested. It had been hard enough at home. Generally I put the hour slot before needing to leave for work but, living alone, if I forgot and was in the shower and didn't hear the doorbell that would be a 'missed test', likewise if I popped out to get milk for morning coffee. I had never really considered how easy it might be to miss three tests. Thankfully I didn't, despite being so much on the road between the UK and miscellaneous locations in the Alps for races. But what would they make of six weeks in the Himalaya? I was an outlier in the world of the IAAF. My efforts at the 100km had me straddling the worlds of conventional track and road running with the Olympics as its pinnacle and the rather more eclectic world of longer distance trail and mountain running without so much as a governing body. I suspect the IAAF was used to rather more conventional athletes whose days rotated between training location one, two and three, rather than a part-time scientist with a habit of running long and longer distances in far-off mountains. I wrote to my contact at the Whereabouts office. The advice was simply to just give as much information as I could. So that is what I did. For every day my entry read 'location:

somewhere in the Khumbu, Nepal'. They didn't come to find me as far as I know.

And again I was throwing myself into the unknown. Ama Dablam is a stunningly beautiful mountain in the Khumbu. At an altitude of 6,837m it would be the highest that any of us had ever been to. Ama Dablam means 'mother's necklace', with the long ridges on each side like the arms of a mother (*ama*) protecting her child, and the hanging glacier resembling the traditional pendant, the *dablam*, worn by Sherpa women. First climbed in 1961 by a mixed UK, US, and New Zealand team, it is now a popular expedition peak. However, the benign and protecting image conjured up by its name is anything but in reality.

We were only attempting the normal route of the Southwest Ridge, but it is technical (although mostly fixed ropes) and exposed. It was waiting for us, that 'Matterhorn of the Himalayas' with its soaring ridges and steep faces.

I wasn't sure if I was more scared by the prospect of our climb or our long run. But I couldn't wait. Things get done as they inevitably do, life was finally packed up, and the door shut behind me.

Nepal reminded me a little of India from that first expedition four years earlier. But Kathmandu showed a much gentler chaos than Delhi. It was a riot of colour, smells, sights and sounds. I felt its draw, but I didn't learn to know it and love it then as I was to later. We, the esteemed Vic Saunders (our guide, a lovely man and now a great friend) and I, left soon for the mountains. Before we did we were interviewed by the wonderful Billi Bierling, journalist and now 8,000m climber, on behalf of the legendary Miss Hawley for her Expedition Archives.[1] Billi has since become a good friend and she confessed that she was very sceptical about the possibility of us completing both our mountain and our run. A 6,000m mountain is a challenge in itself.

The others – Mark, Spyke and two other friends – were en route already, they had left earlier to walk/run into the Khumbu via Jiri. They were making a recce for our run out. My late decision to commit meant I hadn't been able to leave work any earlier. I felt guilty, aware I'd be relying on their experience, their knowledge.

Om Mani Padme Hum, the omnipresent Buddhist mantra, engrained itself from the very beginning into my experience of Nepal. It represents the practice of generosity, ethics, patience, diligence, renunciation and wisdom. The Khumbu is populated by the Sherpa people, of Tibetan origin and Buddhist religion. The trails there are strewn with the evidence of their religion – chortens, prayer flags, prayer wheels, mani walls. The beautiful mantra is carved into stone and spun on those prayer wheels (clockwise to follow the direction of the movement of the sun across the sky) along every path.

Those high mountains of the Khumbu were home to us for that month. Its people welcomed us as we travelled lightly from lodge to lodge on our way in, exploring side valleys above the main village of Namche Bazaar. We acclimatised with a climb of Island Peak (6,198m) and wandering lesser-known paths we crossed the not so frequented Kongma La between Chhukung and Lobuche. We ran up to Gorak Shep and enjoyed the comfort of a simple cup of tea after a long day on foot with a cold mist to shroud our last hour of effort. We touched the north faces of Lhotse and Nuptse, those elegant towering giants. The world as we knew it fell away and we were subsumed by the empty spaces of the heights and the simple life in the mountain villages.

We reached our mountain already acclimatised and eager. We had our own base camp, sharing with Henry Todd, veteran climber and expedition leader, over a ridge hidden and away from the main 'city' of tents. A lodge has since been built there, but then it was just a summer grazing pasture. And the city has since become a circus with over 250 people passing through base camp in rotation each season, and less than 100 actually reaching the summit.

The climb was a learning, a game of patience, of control, of joy, of trust. A heart-rendingly beautiful ridge line for the inexperienced apprentice that I was, full of exposure. As we gained height and the views opened to give a different perspective on the landscape that had become so familiar, it gave me a window into the realm of possibility. And just as on Kalanag years before, I realised again that long-harboured dreams could be made real.

Our dream was to run back from the wildness of those mountain heights to the chaos of Kathmandu. Mid-morning on a late October day we arrived in the dusty heat of the Dasarath Stadium; weary, footsore, scratched and grimy we were greeted with smiles and garlands. We had set a new record. I cast my mind back over the previous seventy-four hours to another world. Arriving in the chaotic heat of the streets of Kathmandu felt a very long way from our start in the silence and peace of dawn at Everest Base Camp. It was an incredible contrast. And it had been an incredible journey.

A journey that almost didn't reach its conclusion.

It began in the chill of an autumnal dawn, clad in fleece and duvet jackets, on the rocky moraine of Everest Base Camp. We touched the flag of the first Thai Everest expedition just as the first tents were stirring. We logged our GPS, started our watches and set off to scramble across the glacial moraine. We had slept a chilly night at a lodge below in Gorak Shep, so we had already been on the move for ninety minutes fuelled simply by tea and tsampa (roasted barley flour) porridge. As we turned back towards the waiting descent my apprehensions were lifted by the morning's incredible beauty. With warmth on our limbs we soon discarded fleece and duvet layers and I took delight in moving (relatively) fast over terrain usually taken at a snail's pace. I was lucky: I was feeling good, and had evaded the hacking bronchitic coughs that plagued Mark and Spyke, a legacy from Ama Dablam whose summit Mark and I had reached just a few days earlier.

Welcome refreshment awaited us at Dhugla lodge, where our new friend Mr T (Tashi Tsering) had copious amounts of milky tea waiting for us as promised. Further down the trail the traffic started to increase considerably with countless yaks, porters and tourists to dodge before we reached Namche Bazaar. There Vic was waiting for us with a hug, hot tea, pastries and to relieve us of those now unnecessary layers of fleece and duvet.

All too soon (for me) we had left the high mountains and by nightfall we had passed the trail to the large village of Lukla and its tiny airstrip. Having lost the crowds we were now back to the real Nepal, with simple lodges and sharing the trail only with local porters carrying huge loads of everyday necessities. Onwards into the night. Moving through the darkness I followed Spyke and Mark up the steep ascent to the Taksindu La. I hung on to the rhythm they set, falling into their movement to distract myself from the tiredness. I can feel now the cool of the night air as we topped out. I remember the stupa and prayer flags, the shadows of the few simple lodges half-distinct through the low-lying cloud, the eerie quietness.

Dawn broke as we ran the trail leading to Junbesi. It gave me energy – when the light comes after running through the night I always manage to delude myself that somewhere along the way I must have slept. So with night passing, and a new day arriving, it is like starting over again. I couldn't trick my stomach though, hunger gnawed at me and the prospect of tsampa porridge and tea after a long night fuelled by just a few biscuits and a miscellaneous bar or two left from my stock of mountain food was all-consuming. But the undulating trail curving round to Junbesi was longer than Mark and Spyke remembered. We passed the lodge that gives the first (or last) view of Everest on the way in (or out), not stopping out of eagerness to reach the village; we did, finally, and stomachs were satiated.

For most of the journey we were more or less self-sufficient and, having discarded our warmer clothing at Namche, we carried the bare minimum, with just a little food, and some water. We used the lodges along the way to supplement our supplies and to take advantage of copious amounts of tea, tsampa porridge and chapatis as we needed. It was a do-it-yourself attempt at setting a new record.

The roller coaster of ascents and descents continued. A day passed and the second nightfall was rapidly encroaching as we reached Shivalaya beyond the Deurali Pass. We stopped to eat, and it was here that Mark made a reluctant decision to leave us at Jiri. The mountain had taken more out of him than he had anticipated and his reserves were drained. We hadn't really discussed the possibility, or at least we'd discussed it but I'd never really thought about the implications of not reaching Kathmandu together. In any case, from Shivalaya we had to reach Jiri and the road-head on our own two feet, and together. Thirty-six hours in and we had covered less than half the distance. What should have been an easy two hours turned into a complicated confusion between the old trail and the still-under-construction jeep track.

Hours later we stumbled into Jiri. Exhausted, Spyke broke it to me that he also was finished. Dejected, and surrounded by a pack of stray dogs, we talked things over. Mentally and physically I wanted to continue. But it wasn't so long after the Maoist unrest, I had little experience then of travelling within Nepal, and I would be a lone woman. The others confessed they wouldn't continue in my position. So that was it, a decision made by default. We stood there surrounded by those howling dogs and tried to make contact with our waiting friends. No message got through. Jiri at night, without its bustle of chatter and buses and tea shops and market stalls, seemed a seedy and unwelcoming place. Dejected, we wandered back the way we had come and headed for some buildings beyond a barbed-wire fence. By chance, luck or good fortune we found a deserted hayloft, and pulling on our very few extra layers we buried ourselves in the hay and tried to forget. A few cold hours later, stiff and despondent, I woke from a semi-doze into a new day.

Was that it? After all our effort?

Unsure of where we were or what our welcome would be, we decided to make a quick exit, over the barbed-wire fence and back up the road towards the bus park. As we walked onwards together, Spyke suddenly voiced his thoughts: 'Could we still have a chance?' Just a few hours of restless sleep had given him a new lease of life. Grabbing at straws, I leaped at the chance to continue. We had no idea if the record could still be within reach with so much time lost, but it was almost irrelevant, having got so far I just wanted to make it back to Kathmandu on my own two feet. Even now, I'm not entirely sure why. We snatched some cups of tea at the roadside and stuffed some battered bread in our sacks.

We left Mark to the fate of the buses. He would meet us some hours later at Mudhe, where we hoped our friends would still be waiting.

We headed out, the tarmac hard beneath our feet. We had no idea if we could make it, but it didn't matter. I was just glad to be moving and trying. Some miles went fast, some went slow. We lost hours on our off-road short cut between Kirantichap and Mudhe. This was a section Spyke and Mark had reconnoitred weeks before, but we descended to the river too soon and had to battle our way back up a vertical kilometre and navigate our way across numerous paddy fields (to the bemusement of the local ladies working), before finally finding a workable descent and the bridge that would lead to hours of toil to climb up to the small town of Mudhe.

Darkness had fallen on our third night by the time we reached Mark and our waiting friends. From running alone for so many hours it was strange to suddenly be greeted by so many welcoming faces. We were far behind our expected schedule, so our friends had hours to pass time with the villagers, and the local youth club was there in force waiting to cheer us on our way. From here our route followed the road and our friends were able to follow us in their hired vehicle. They took it in turns to run a mile or two with us, providing inane chatter to help pass the long and lonely night hours.

Hunger gnawed at me during those last few hours of the night. It was unrelenting. But we had eaten everything we had carried and everything our friends had brought with them. We passed innumerable roadside shacks, but to my intense disappointment all were in darkness, shut up and quiet. No one would be stirring until first light. Sunday eventually dawned somewhere on the long ascent to Dhulikel, and there finally we found some roti and chai (bread and tea).

From here we were on the final descent into Kathmandu. The roadside gradually got busier, noisier and smellier as we drew closer to the city outskirts. For long stretches we each reached the point where we withdrew somewhere deep within ourselves. No longer talking, no longer eating, no longer making eye contact as our friends passed us in their bus. We were locked into an unseeing stare, oblivious to anything except the need to keep moving forwards. We were lost deep within our effort.

By 8 a.m. we were on the city outskirts fighting our way through the gridlock of traffic. From out of nowhere (I am still no wiser) a police motorbike escort appeared and the traffic parted before us. Spyke and I were flanked now by Mark and our friends – it was just as well as by this point I had lost all instinct of self-preservation and in the interest of perpetual forward motion I would have ploughed directly through any bus or bike that came in my way. Finally our police escort careered across the road and through the oncoming traffic. Not knowing the city then, I hadn't realised how close we were. This was it. We were metres from the gates of the stadium. There was a small crowd waiting, Vic, some journalists and the president of the Nepal Olympic Association.

I thought it was over. But it is never over until it is over. Spyke and I were sent off on a lap of that almost empty stadium before they would finally let us reach the end of our journey. It is possibly the slowest 400m I have ever run. Possibly. And then weary, footsore, scratched and grimy, we were greeted with those smiles and garlands.

A few words with the journalists, a happy goodbye to our Nepali friends, and a reduced group of us was left. Spyke fell asleep in the bus on the short journey back to our hotel. I found a shower, my first in a month, and tried to scrub clean my decidedly filthy feet. That evening we enjoyed an Indian/ Nepali feast, although our eyes were still bigger than our shrunken stomachs and the next day I haunted the alley-ways of Thamel, raiding its bakeries for soft, fresh bread.

We met with Billi again and this time she interviewed the three of us. She has since told me how impressed she was that I, as the only woman, was the only person to finish both challenges – the mountain climb and the run. I hadn't really thought about it. And, because it was something we just did, the implications of what we had achieved didn't really sink in. It was just a nice adventure that we had.

Focus and attention, intention and effort. These are what bring dreams to reality, that allow us to do what it is we want or need to do. And they are what give what we want or need to do meaning.

On that long road back to Kathmandu:

For long stretches we each reached the point where we withdrew somewhere deep within ourselves. No longer talking, no longer eating, no longer making eye contact as our friends passed us in their bus. We were locked into an unseeing stare, oblivious to anything except the need to keep moving forwards. We were lost deep within our effort.

When we have something that absorbs all our effort, our attention, even if only for a time, it is then that we can touch that alluring but ephemeral feeling of flow.[2]

When we have curiosity, persistence and humility; when the heart, will and mind – and the challenge, preparation and performance – are in synchrony; it is then that we start to feel the magic. We feel it. We know it. In essence it is characterised by complete absorption in what is being done.

This concept has been experienced throughout history and across cultures. The teachings of Buddhism and Taoism speak of a state of mind known as the 'action of inaction' or 'doing without doing', and the Hindu texts on yoga such as the Bhagavad-Gita refer to a similar state.

Life is crying out for our presence. As Alan Watts so eloquently puts it: 'For the perfect accomplishment of any art, you must get this feeling of the eternal present into your bones – for it is the secret of proper timing. No rush. No dawdle. Just the sense of flowing with the course of events in the same way that you dance to music, neither trying to outpace it nor lagging behind. Hurrying and delaying are alike ways of trying to resist the present.'[3]

Life in its entirety is contained in this moment, now. But sometimes we need to go to extremes to recognise that here and now is always with us. The biggest obstacle, of course, is the striving. As long as we look for it we don't see. To feel the flow of life we have to be totally present in the now – it can only happen to us, we cannot force it.

Chapter Nine

I may not have gone where I intended to go,
but I think I have ended up where I needed to be.

Douglas Adams, *The Long Dark Teatime of the Soul*

The rain continues, the trails turning muddy underfoot. At the turn-off for Surkhe I stop for something to eat. Here the Jiri trail parts ways with the main trail to Lukla; I know that somewhere in the next hour I will lose mobile reception (until I reach the Lamjura Pass, somewhere in the middle of tomorrow), so I send Richard a text to let him know my progress. As I wait for my chapati, a reply comes back. He is having a hard time with work and unavoidable deadlines. The bus is booked, but he might have to return early or arrive late. My heart sinks again. Deeper this time. Would he still make it to Jiri? My mind leaps to extremes – I imagine the worst – what if he can't come at all – what if Upendra doesn't either? I know with their support this journey is possible. Without? I'm not sure I will make it. That last stage from Jiri is hard enough when you have friends supporting you – would I have the motivation to run that long road alone? Besides, I am looking forward to seeing him. I tell him to do whatever he needs to do. It will all be OK. The reply comes back that he will do an all-nighter, just as I am going to do.

I am on the trail again now, wet again, and the tiny chirrup of my phone is a comforting reminder that Richard is there and thinking about me. He bids me well, tells me to call from the landline of a lodge if I need him: 'Checking weather again now. Hope it improves. Nothing like pain dripping from nose! No slipping. Slow and steady. Good luck!' And then I run out of mobile coverage. I run through the night uncertain if he and Upendra will be waiting for me in Jiri. But it is irrelevant. I have now to get myself to Jiri whatever happens from there onwards.

The rain has dried up now and this time these lower trails are burned into my memory. I stop at a lodge for food somewhere about 9 p.m., they recognise me there, ask if I couldn't stop for the night, rest and carry on in the morning? Yes, couldn't I? The sky in the far distance beyond the lodge is sporadically lit up, indicating lightning and a big storm. Will I run into it, or will it move my way? Can't I stay there and sleep? Before the idea can take a hold of me I turf myself out of the comforting warmth of the lodge and back out onto the trail.

I'm still following the drainage of the Dudh Kosi river here. One of its tributaries, the Imja Khola, starts right up there on the Khumbu glacier where I started this morning, but those high mountains are far behind me now, I'm back to the hill country and the thicker air of lower altitudes.

It is a long, long night. But thankfully it stays dry and I forget my concerns about running into the storm. After Jubing Bridge I leave the river and my way crosses the grain of the land with a quick succession of passes. I know so well the relentless roller coaster of ascents and descents ahead. I lose my way on the ascent up to Taksindu La. Only temporarily, but I waste a good hour or two wandering in circles on tiny paths. It serves me right for thinking I know these trails well by now. Reaching the pass I berate myself for my careless mistake and with the effort of the climb over I feel the cool of the night air, just as with Mark and Spyke on that first attempt years earlier. I circle the stupa with its prayer flags strung out, there is an eerie quietness and the shadows of the few simple lodges are half-distinct through the low-lying cloud.

I make a steady descent through Ringmo to the river crossing below. Dawn breaks as I run the undulating trail that curves around to Junbesi. I breathe a sigh of relief – this time I've got through the night, it is just today to go, before nightfall I should reach Jiri, but will Richard and Upendra be there? I pause in the Everest View Lodge for tsampa porridge and tea again, the aged proprietor knowing me well by now. I sit on the bench outside while it is being prepared, looking back towards Everest. I've come a long way, but there is still so far to go. Why is it that I'm doing this? There is no race, the record is sort of irrelevant since I have it already twice over and I already know these trails. Granted, I always have a simple satisfaction in making a journey on my own two feet, by my own effort – this is just further in distance and in time. I have a curiosity to see how this time will be different from all the others, to see how my body holds up, how my mind reacts and how I deal with whatever happens. There is always an excitement in the unknown. And, anyway, I'm enjoying it. Perhaps that is enough.

The simple task of eating is a welcome respite from the running and the thinking. It is a generous bowl of tsampa and the tea is good. Then, there in the warmth of the morning sunshine, I disconnect for a moment from my journey and the knowledge of what is yet to come. I'm safe, I made it through the night and I know I'm feeling OK enough to reach Jiri. I have a strange and contradictory mixture of certainty and doubt. I have made this journey twice before now, and I ran these trails for training a few weeks ago. I know what it is I have to do. I know I can do it.

But still getting back to Kathmandu is a huge unknown question. With this kind of distance and this number of hours on my feet, my mind and body could throw anything at me. Every time is different. I'm scared and I'm excited.

❖ ❖ ❖

Time went on and life had again shifted. I had wrestled with the twin fascinations and frustrations of scientific research where the outcome of what I was doing could take years to be realised, and not necessarily by me. It brought me to a realisation that I needed to try to find a direction and focus where what I did had a more tangible and immediate effect. I didn't want to lose my scientific background but somehow to find a different way to use it. I was now living mostly in the Alps, a semi-nomadic life, piecing together a modest existence. My relationship with The North Face had developed and with mutual trust they now supported me with a stipend; this together with various writing assign-ments and work with the Laufschule Scuol[1] to offer running camps sustained me.

A chance email to Fränzi Gissler, who with her partner ran the Laufschule Scuol as part of their company Outdoor Engadin, had led to a still-evolving working collaboration and a deep friendship. Sometimes great things happen out of the blue. I lived with them for a while, the three of us in a tiny studio, leading snowshoe tours for them one winter. They always have a bed for me now.

That collaboration led to me sharing my running with others in a new way through various training camps, some-times based in Scuol, sometimes running hut-to-hut through the mountains in the Alps. I led UTMB preparation camps, Chamonix to Zermatt and Tour de Monte Rosa running tours – they were great times, with much learning and great friendships. But trying to balance racing, training, running camps and various other obligations was tough. One summer in particular I shifted from race to training stint to running camp to race to obligation to race without an empty day. It makes for a rich and interesting time but it is hard to sustain.

And so the years started to take on a rhythm of their own – a quiet hermit-like existence countering the pace of the racing season (which now extends year-round). I made sacrifices. We all do. Life is always a balancing act, we just have to work out what means the most to us and what we can do without. I sacrificed a full-time job and financial security for the flexibility I craved – to be able to race, to train and to have the freedom to choose how, when and where I worked. An athlete's life also demands sacrifice on a daily basis – long days at the laptop punctuated by training, eating, sleeping – no time (or inclination) to browse in the shops, to watch television – nights out were few and far between. The uncertainties of this kind of lifestyle were balanced by the simplicity and the richness of the experience. We make a choice. We always make a choice.

❖ ❖ ❖

It is August 2008 and I am here back in the Place du Triangle de l'Amitié, that old church square in the centre of Chamonix. I remember this place, oh how I remember this place. But it couldn't feel more different. I'm right at the front of the start line now, sitting on a baize green mat, rather than sitting on the church steps with a sea of runners in front of me as that first time. Beyond this baize green mat the road is empty. It seems to be waiting. Waiting to be filled with the 2,500 runners. And this time beyond the barriers there seem to be even more people lining the side of the street.

It is hard to say if I was more apprehensive that first time, or now. For sure then I had the fear of the unknown. This time I know what is ahead. I walked the route just two weeks ago over three long days. It reminded me that 160km is a long way. A very long way. And I'm standing here now with the winners of the two intervening years – who have both run so much faster than I did. This time I have my own expectations to live with and a tangle of questions. With a long summer of mountain races behind me have I already done too much? Will my legs be good? Will my mind stay strong? Will my feet be able to carry me the whole way back to Chamonix?

We stand here together and yet each alone. We are each alone with our own thoughts, our own hopes, expectations, fears and doubts. Grappling with the disparity between excitement and trepidation.

We start and I run. I keep running.

I don't see any other women. I am somewhere up at the front of the field.

It isn't always easy. Descending from the Grand Col Ferret kicks off the onset of tenosynovitis. The pain cripples me to what feels like almost a crawl by the time I leave Champex. But sometimes you can play with the edge, I've reached through to the other side of the pain, I'm running again and actually enjoying it again. I'm almost disappointed now to be making this final descent to hit the road for the final metres into town.

Again the crowds are waiting.

They want to see the first woman cross the line. I am that woman. Again. This is my second win.

People have asked me how and why I returned to the UTMB again and again. It was almost unintentional. But for a number of years the timing of other races and challenges still allowed me to be there in Chamonix at the end of August.

Life was too full ever to focus entirely on the race; I racked up huge distances above and beyond the requirements of training, often with training camps sandwiched between back-to-back races. But the UTMB still pulled me back year after year – perhaps partly the physical challenge (different every time) and that beautiful mountain journey – perhaps partly the shared passion, the shared dedication – and I was still waiting, there or elsewhere, for the race where I felt I had given everything I could.

For a long time it was enough for me just to run. But when that door opened into the world of competition I realised it would, for a while, hold my attention. My potential demanded an expression.

So why do I race? It is a question I have sometimes forgotten to ask myself until I've reached that point deep into a race when I start to wonder *why*, my attention adrift and my focus already lost.

Because yes, I've also had those races where I've stopped and I haven't finished. Physical pain I can and have run through – particularly from impact and trauma during a race. But if my head and my heart are elsewhere then no matter how fit the body, when my focus is lost, I've also lost the *why* of continuing.

Fear and excitement, anticipation and trepidation. Racing has the power to evoke a kaleidoscopic medley of emotions. Within the context of a race I can experience all extremes – passion, beauty, heartache, pain, tears and joy. This is part of its appeal. It reminds me of my fragility and my vulnerability. And yet I learn also to feel my strength and power.

As Carl Sagan said: 'We make our world significant by the courage of our questions and the depth of our answers.'[2] Racing and the training it demands force me to ask myself questions. To find the time, the discipline and the motivation to train I have to decide what among the myriad of obligations of daily life is most important to me. It cultivates self-awareness, I start to become more mindful.

Racing can give me a focus. It can give a direction to and motivation for my daily run. There is, of course, a time for everything. And racing will only ever be a part of my running. But sometimes I need what it is a race can give me – something to absorb my effort, my attention – moments where I am forced to step outside what is comfortable, time after time after time. I'm forced to focus on what I am feeling, on what I am enduring in the here and now, whether that is keeping warm in the cold, keeping cool in the heat, eating, drinking and looking after myself. Despite my physical effort, sometimes during a race I experience the moment where I am resting in stillness; I've stopped *doing* and I'm focused instead on *being*. And that is when I feel free.

But of course the race itself is the smallest part of the story. It is the journey that is important; the everyday, the day in, day out. Start and finish lines are just steps on that journey. The prize is not a position, or a time; instead the getting to know myself, the work and the training must be its own reward.

* * *

Albert Mummery, that eminent alpinist, described being in the mountains in this way: 'Above, in the clear air and searching sunlight, we are afoot with the quiet gods, and men can know each other and themselves for what they are.'[3]

'Is a long time ago now but this is to congratulate you on the very ascetically pleasing challenge that you completed', Richard, friend and housemate of Billi in Kathmandu, commented on my blog. He had just jogged back from Everest Base Camp to Jiri. Bad weather had stopped flights out of Lukla, but his run was also partly by choice as he was curious to see what it had been like for us: 'it was a beautiful run all in all.' It had been. In turn I was curious to know who this man was who had also found it so.

This was the Richard who was to become an integral part of my next two attempts. He is a passionate trail runner himself, the race director of some awesome single and multi-stage races,[4] and co-founded Trail Running Nepal,[5] an organisation which aims to develop the sport in Nepal, to encourage local participation and to offer support to Nepali trail running athletes.

Feeling I understood something of what Mummery was saying, weeks later back at the 2009 UTMB, I wrote in the days before, 'In many ways we will be alone up there in the clear air and searching sunlight. Alone in the sense that it is only us that can make our race. No one but ourselves. That is why in some ways the race is a metaphor for life. The hours ahead will bring us to know ourselves deeper, to know ourselves for what we are.'

I forgot the knowing 'each other' part. That was to come later.

I didn't know what the race was going to throw at me. Sodden feet led to a flapping blister the size of my heel. I was caught by my friend Krissy Moehl, winner of the very first edition of UTMB in 2003. I caught her back. We taped down the flapping skin for want of a better solution in the heat of the moment. Krissy passed me again and the rest of my race was like running on a bed of needles. I made the finish line, in second place and in pain, but I reached it.

As the years passed I developed my own training strategy for the UTMB. Sandwiched between my other races and leading training camps I would make one or two 'rounds' – two long days back to back, sleeping at the Bonatti hut. They learned to know me there, never minding when I turned up late in the evening and wanting to leave in the early morning. They always found me a bed. If I could do two back to back twelve-hour days then I knew I was coming into form. I learned to know every rock, every twist of the trail. I knew what effort I needed to put in where. I love the challenge of racing blind on an unknown route. But over the years I cultivated a level of intimacy with this trail that was special – such familiarity left space for me to explore it and myself in different ways.

I was still waiting to have *my* race at the UTMB but perhaps we never have the perfect race. Every race is unique with its own challenges and demands. Every race forces us to run with a little bit of pride and a lot of humility.

A few weeks later, after a whirlwind visit through the gritty energy of New York for the wedding of my younger brother, I was back in the Khumbu acclimatising for what would have been my first 8,000m summit, Cho Oyu. With a team of my fellow athletes from The North Face we had planned a multi-disciplined expedition – Simone Moro and Hervé Barmasse would attempt a new route, I would make the 'normal route' with Emilio Previtali who would then make a new snowboard descent. My descent would be the same way I had come (I hoped). Hervé and Emilio would cycle back to Kathmandu, while Simone and I would run. It was an ambitious hotchpotch of endeavours. I had been prepared for none of it working out – not reaching the summit due to bad weather, the cold, the altitude or sickness, or not having the strength to run back to Kathmandu after an 8,000m mountain.

The one thing I didn't prepare myself for was not even reaching our mountain.

The news reached us just after we had slept high on Island Peak (6,189m) as part of our acclimatisation. Way up there in the wilds of the Khumbu the concept of politics seemed very far away and somehow irrelevant. But it was the demonstration of political power by the Chinese that was to prevent us even reaching the base of our mountain. The border between Nepal and Tibet was shut. We had some days in our lodge in Chhukung, deliberating. I took myself off for a day's run to Everest Base Camp and back, desperately needing to do something for myself that wasn't governed by anyone else. Emilio remarked on the equanimity that long run had given me, he could read the change on my face. We continued deliberating, but the news coming to us was that the proposed date for the border to reopen was continually slipping back. Even if we made it to our mountain we would be out of time.

It was a frustrating twist since had we been able to cross the forbidden 5,806m Nangpa La we would have been a few days' walk away at most. It is a traditional trading route between Nepal and Tibet, but closed to foreigners, and in September 2006 Chinese border guards had opened fire on a group of Tibetan pilgrims attempting to leave Tibet, killing Kelsang Namtso, a seventeen-year-old nun, and injuring many others.

We were fit, well and acclimatised. I have to confess the thought of running back to Kathmandu had crossed my mind, but Simone, probably rightly, suggested we should keep solidarity in our disappointment. I can remember now that gently sloping descent from Chhukung as we walked out, the swathes of rough bracken, the familiar smell of juniper, and I wondered if, or how, I would ever return.

Simone and I met with Billi for a 'debrief' interview. I hoped to meet Richard then, as he had suggested in another comment on my blog, but we missed each other. I was back too early in Kathmandu and he was away running in Langtang.

The 2010 UTMB started under cloudy skies that quickly poured heavy rain. The downpour first abated and then set in determinedly. I reached St Gervais in the company of Scott Jurek and according to the iRunFar[6] race report I was just seven minutes behind Kilian Jornet, the race leader. By the time I reached Les Contamines (30km) the race was cancelled and barriers prevented us from heading onwards out of the checkpoint and upwards. There were distraught runners, outpourings of emotions and numerous rumours flying around of first a restart, then a later resumption of the race or permanent cancellation. Nobody really knew what was going on.

Back in Chamonix, my wet clothes strewn across the room in a vague attempt to let them dry out, I went to the finish line to see in the finishers of the CCC[7] and lingered, trying to make sense of any rumours. No sense was to be had and I was disorientated by the unexpectedness of being there at the start/finish archway in the church square just hours after the start of my own race. Finally back in my room in the early hours of the morning I fell into a restless sleep, but not before a chirrup of my mobile phone heralded a text message from the organisation. There would be a race – tomorrow morning from Courmayeur back to Chamonix on the UTMB route. Buses would leave from 6 a.m. to go through the tunnel. I scarcely slept and, still tired, found some breakfast and refilled my rucksack with the now still-damp obligatory kit. I wasn't quite sure what I was doing, but I'd sacrificed other race opportunities to be there, so I thought I should take whatever chance they gave us.

In Courmayeur there were bright skies and a festival atmosphere, if still a feeling of bewilderment at the turn of events. We laughed with each other on the start line, happy for the chance to race, but inside I was anxious. I had raced a hard 30km last night, I'd not had much sleep and barely anything to eat. Yet now I was standing on the start line of an 88km race – the shorter distance of which would inevitably precipitate a greater speed and intensity than I was right then prepared for – would I rise to the challenge? But as Alan Watts said, 'The only way to make sense out of change is to plunge into it, move with it and join the dance.'[8]

The race turned into a mudbath in places. Less of the running than a balanced skidding on some of the descents. It was fun, reminiscent of skiing, fairly quick work once I yielded to it and stopped resisting. Finally reaching beyond Vallorcine to the Col des Montets I was fully expecting an elevenish-kilometre valley run back to Chamonix. I'd misunderstood. Instead we were still to make the final 1,000m climb up to the Tête aux Vents. The checkpoint at Vallorcine was far behind me, I'd eaten just one biscuit expecting an easy run back to Chamonix, I was running on empty already. How to continue? But goaded by the motivation to keep ahead of any approaching woman (yes, I'd been warned the second-place woman was far behind, but you can easily lose significant time even on one ascent or descent if you are tiring) I made quick time to the top of the ascent and the rising trail that follows. I'd hoped to be there in the light, but our late morning start from Courmayeur meant that darkness fell somewhere on that ascent. Desperate not to be overtaken by a woman I made my quickest-yet traverse across to La Flégère, running scared from headlights I saw in the distance behind me, and made my quickest-yet descent through that dark forest despite the rocks and twisted roots.

According to iRunFar I 'smoked' the field on the Friday evening and again dominated on the Saturday. I had no idea. I just didn't see any other women. That was my third win.

Years and other adventures had intervened but eventually I returned to try the 100km again. The 2010 World Championships was hosted by Great Britain and held in Gibraltar, that tiny overseas territory at the southern end of the Iberian Peninsula at the entrance of the Mediterranean Sea. With an area of just six square kilometres it must have been the strangest location to decide to hold a 100km race.

This time had none of the sense of occasion of that first championship in Korea. Our athlete accommodation was on an out-of-service cruise ship. The thought of this had been giving me some cause for concern. After spending some eighteen months of my life at sea on a ship I knew how the smell of diesel is unavoidable. I dreaded trying to feel in great form, good enough to stand on the start line of a World Championship race, while dealing with the feeling of nausea those smells unavoidably invoke. Arriving on the ship my fears were confirmed, together with portholes that would of course not open (it has long been my habit to sleep with windows wide open), and psychedelic colours in the common areas – this was a cruise ship from the 1960s. We arrived as a team the afternoon before the race and went for a short jog together to shake out our legs after the flight. A line drawing of the race route had been provided but none of us thought a route recce very important, after all this was a World Championship race with simple, marked road loops. How wrong could we go?

The race started in the pre-dawn darkness right on the dockside just a few hundred metres from the ship. I'd just started to settle into a gentle rhythm when the pool of men running ahead of me suddenly stopped and stood still in the middle of the road. No one knew which way to go; the lead bike supposedly directing us had faltered. We made it up, pieced together a dogleg until we were on the 5km loop that would lead us through the rest of that 100km, which consisted of some tight twists and turns, a few inclines (small but trying in the later stages of a 100km road race), and some decidedly uneven surfaces in the docks. Partway through the race clipboard-holding officials diverted us onto a modified loop, before allowing us back onto the official route. We had gone wrong in our initial dogleg, so now the distance had to be made correct. It was just asking for trouble, and indeed the evening prize-giving was delayed for hours investigating claims from this and that team about whether some athletes had run extra distances. The reason for the debacle? The lead bike was ridden by the chief of police, who didn't think he needed to turn up to the planning meeting. It was farcical.

I led much of the race, but never felt the magic of 2006. About ten kilometres or so from the finish, both Ellie Greenwood (my outstanding GB team-mate) and Monica Carlin (from our 2006 sprint finish) passed me, and I rolled into a third place although just a couple of minutes slower than 2006.

Weeks later I received an email from Richard inviting me to run in the Annapurna 100, a 100km race on the foothills of the Annapurna range. It would be on 1 January 2011. I could think of no better way to start a year than to be back in Nepal and running. It was where I wanted to be, and I was sure there would be a way to make it happen.

Despite our best efforts, finding the cost of the flight seemed hopeless. Then I received a second invitation, this time to the inaugural Hong Kong 100 Ultra Trail[9] in the middle of January, and they would help with part of the cost of the flight. So that was it.

My preparations for my New Year challenge of back-to-back 100km races was characteristically unconventional. December saw me in San Francisco for The North Face Endurance Challenge 50-miler, with a disappointing second place and a disconcertingly bloody bruise on the back of my thigh (the consequence of racing hard on a niggle that manifested as a hamstring tear) that seemed to seep further down my leg with every hour of the transatlantic flight.

Ten days of rest and no running ensued, followed by a rushed build-up in training for the fast-approaching 100km races sandwiched into eighteen-hour days trying to finish a writing job for the Open University. And then, a few days after an uncelebrated working Christmas, the long and sleepless transcontinental flight transposed me from the icy, snowy winter of the Alps to the sunshine of Kathmandu.

I finally met Richard. And put in a probably incoherent appearance at the press conference organised at Summit Hotel. I'd been invited to stay there by Roger Henke, then manager and joint race director with Ramesh Bhattachan, and now a great friend. Apart from a short sightseeing run with Roger (and a cut knee) the next day was focused entirely on finishing the OU assignment sitting on the sunny terrace of the Summit, the clear winter days revealing the distant mountains in their full glory. A sleepless night (local festivities for the Gurung festival of Losar) and a day's bus journey later and we were in the lakeside town of Pokhara.

It was the fifth edition of the Annapurna 100 and I had the dubious honour of being both first and last as the only foreigner and woman to enter the 100km distance. It was a long day, but a great one. I must have been careless with hand-washing though (or touched one too many door handles) as the next day I relieved my stomach of its entire contents time after time after time, until finally I was retching air. I spent some hours cocooned in my sleeping bag until I could conjure up the strength to make my way weakly from the race hotel to a cheaper lakeside guest house. A day set me to rights and I put myself on the local bus to Besisahar. I made a swift five-day fastpack of the Annapurna Circuit. In the first few days of January it was bereft of the large numbers of trekkers that descend in the high season. It was wonderful; there was solitude, a time to think, and a time just to be in the moment. I saw just a handful of people, I stayed in empty lodges and ate in the kitchen with the family. I walked from freezing dawn to chilly dusk, it became almost a moving meditation. I was lucky, the snows hadn't yet fallen over the 5,416m Thorung La. I caught a beautiful sunrise on Poon Hill, and having slept in an empty lodge two hours' walk away, I saw no one until I crested the hill and found a horde of people drawn to the honeypot to await the coming dawn. Horrified by the sudden crowds, I watched the colours flood the sky, took a few photos and descended to a now much-needed breakfast in Ghorepani (where all those people had been staying). It was a long descent to Birethanti, now familiar from our race days before, and from there I found a local bus back to Pokhara, and the next day to Kathmandu.

These were small things, but I was finally starting to learn how to travel by myself in Nepal outside the cosseted, organised, accompanied tourist travel. Those days gave me wonderful images to remember, from the pastoral scenes of rural mountain villages, to the windswept solitude of the pass, to the wild landscapes of Mustang beyond, and back to sharing village life, crouched by the family fire. A final farewell dinner at the Summit, hugs goodbye (somehow sure I would see Richard and Roger again), and a short flight to Hong Kong. It was a whirlwind of contrasts from the wilds of the mountains, to the endearing chaos of Kathmandu, to the towering skyscrapers of modern Hong Kong. Confused by the stark contrast between cities I tried to heal my tendonitis (perhaps born of the long descent on stone steps between villages) in time to win the first individual 100km race to be held on Hong Kong soil. It was a nice way to start the year.

Chapter Ten

Our limits today may not be where they were yesterday,
or where we hope they will be tomorrow.
But it is today that counts.
And sometimes even in today we can go
beyond what we think is possible.

I pass through Junbesi, a beautiful Sherpa village with what is said to be the oldest monastery in the Solukhumbu region. I circle the stupa at the entrance to the village, and turn the prayer wheels; children are playing and we exchange some happy 'namastes'. Then it is the long ascent through pine forest up to the Lamjura La. Back in mobile coverage I send a quick text to Richard to let him know my progress. There is a comforting chirrup back. Richard is in a hired bus en route to Jiri, with Upendra, and with banana bread (I had been more specific with instructions than when Roger had supported me last time). He is coming! I wonder how his night had been, whether he managed to get what he needed done. I feel guilty at what I've asked him to do and the time I'm asking him to give up when his Mustang race is just days away, but selfishly I'm glad I have, it will be fun sharing the last part of the journey with him and Upendra.

Then another chirrup, 'Cappuccino in Jiri? Brought frother.' His message makes me smile, it is going to be OK.

How quickly can I reach that coffee? There is less snow on the pass than on my training jaunt a few weeks ago, but the descent to Kenja is as long and hard as ever. Non-runners can sometimes imagine the descents to be easy, but it is nearly 2,000m down and a rocky trail. On now tired legs the stones are torture for my already battered feet. I try to concentrate my energy and just focus on moving forwards.

I know these trails intimately now, there are no unrecognisable meanderings this time. I make the long haul up to Deurali and then the heavens open up as I run downwards towards Shivalaya. No sinking heart this time though, I can get soaked right through now, it doesn't matter, I'll be in Jiri in another few hours and Richard and Upendra will be waiting.

Another chirrup – they are five kilometres from Jiri with a flat tyre. Will it be fixable or will I have to run on and find them somewhere on that road beyond Jiri? Wherever they are I know I can make it, and then we can decide how to deal with the situation. Another chirrup, they have arrived: 'Storm passed. Now fresh in Jiri.' Great, that means that I'll soon run out of this incessant downpour. I run on through the wet village, across the bridge and onwards and upwards towards the last pass. The rain dries up and I'm getting close now, pulled onwards by the thought of Richard waiting, of cappuccino and banana bread.

I remember every twist and all the furrowed ruts of the trail here. I know where to expect to hear voices, where I will pass homesteads and empty lodges. Once this was the only way to get into the Khumbu but now with the airstrip in Lukla foreigners rarely make the effort and I have seen very few.

I'm focused on Jiri and don't really think about stopping to eat or drink something. The thought of that coffee, banana bread and fruit is far more enticing than anything I have left in my rucksack and it doesn't really seem worth wasting time to stop anywhere. I just want to get there. It's good to be out of the storm now and it's easy finding my way. At last I'm on the final descent through the woods; it is still light in the open but getting darker now under the cover of the trees. I'm so close.

Suddenly, the ground sways away from under my feet.

I'm still moving downwards, but it feels like the earth is tumbling, and no longer the solid, dependable trail it had been. I stop myself and put my hands to the ground. I hold myself still until the swaying stops. And I carry on.

It happens again.

And again.

What is this? I've not experienced anything like this before.

It worries me. I am so close now. Richard and Upendra are waiting for me right at the bottom of this trail. They can only be about ten or fifteen minutes further down. Can I get myself to them? If only I can reach them we can figure this out then.

I focus all my effort. The world stays the right way up just long enough for me to emerge out of the woods and onto the jeep track leading into Jiri. I see them there waiting. It is going to be OK. I feel like a spectre from a different world. I've been thirty-five hours or so on my feet by now and I've made it to Jiri. It's been just me and my tiny backpack.

They lead me up the track to the bus park, where our minibus and drivers are waiting. I dive inside the bus and grab a change of clothes from the bag that I'd hurriedly left with Richard all those days before. He points me to the upstairs of one of the tea shacks. I pull off all my wet layers, and change completely, it makes me feel so much better – almost human again. Food is laid out on the table: bread, cheese, olives, banana bread, fruit juice and there is a sinkful of grapes soaking. Richard has followed my requests to the letter and beyond. He hands me a beaker of hot, frothy, milky coffee and I look up, inordinately thankful that he is there.

I feel like lingering, I'm dry again now and after the hours of being alone it is just so nice to be in the company of friends. But that long road I know so well is waiting. I feel rude leaving Richard to pack up, re-organise everything and pay the tea lady, but time is ticking. My work is outside on the waiting road. From here our bus will follow and I have no need to carry my pack, so after a big hug goodbye I set off into the now-fallen night, water-proof on, and Upendra at my side.

❖ ❖ ❖

By August 2011 I'd done my then customary back-to-back training days on the UTMB route in both storms and 30°C heat. I felt fit, I felt ready.

Race day dawned. There was thunder in the morning. It wasn't conducive to rest, inducing all too many memories of the shenanigans of the previous year. All kinds of thoughts ran through my head. Eventually we were given word that the race start would be delayed by five hours until 11.30 p.m. Those extra hours were a challenge, but eventually we found ourselves on the start line and inevitably there was a great enthusiasm despite the steady and pouring rain.

Somewhere along the wet and slippy trail to Les Contamines I fell. It didn't bother me so much then. On my ascent to the first high col the rains stopped and the clouds parted. I was bowled over by the beauty; I was on the second high col when dawn came. Ice underfoot, fallen snow on the peaks above us and a beautiful light in the sky – it was a winter wonderland. Running swiftly off the col and down

Early days. Sports day in Upminster.
© Robert Hawker

With my brothers in the shadow of the Matterhorn.
© Robert Hawker

Ryder Bay, off Rothera Point on Adelaide Island, West Antarctic Peninsula.
© Lizzy Hawker

RRS *James Clark Ross* in the ice.
© Mark Brandon

left: Youth at play, during the 2005 UTMB. © Quim Farrero

right: With Rob Collister heading towards Kalanag (6,287m) in the Garwahl Himalaya. © Lizzy Hawker

below: Drinking chai after skiing Kalang. Garwahl Himalaya, 2008.
© Lizzy Hawker

above: Coming to the end.
UTMB, 2008.
© The North Face Archive

right: Pre-race reveries.
© Damiano Levati

left: Ever
upwards.
During the
UTMB,
2010.
© Damiano
Levati

above: Night running in 2010. © Damiano Levati

below: A foot in 2009. © Damiano Levati

Focused. In barley fields in Mustang, Nepal.
© Richard Bull

left: Contemplating the awesome landscape of Mustang, Nepal.
© Richard Bull

right: Happy days, happy women in Mustang.
© Natacha Giler

above: High in the Khumba, Nepal.
© Alex Treadway

left: Back in Kathmandu after the Great Himalaya Trail attempt, scratched but still smiling. © Richard Bull

Sky high in the Himalaya,
with Ama Dablam behind.
© Alex Treadway

Onwards and upwards. Heading towards the 5,100m Larkya La, Nepal.
© Richard Bull

Emerging from the woods to Jiri after thirty-five hours of running.
© Richard Bull

Dry again and refuelling in Jiri.
© Richard Bull

Searching for the old trail to Mudhe with Upendra Sunuwar, Nepal.
© Richard Bull

One foot during the third Everest Base Camp to Kathmandu run.
© Richard Bull

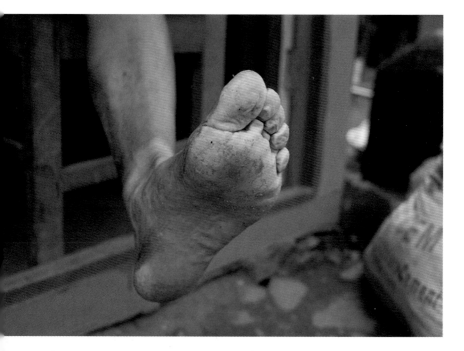

Hard times
during the
third Everest
Base Camp to
Kathmandu
run.
© Richard Bull

Colourful
back streets of
Boudha, Nepal.
© Alex Treadway

With Richard Bull and Upendra Sunuwar at the gates of the stadium at the end of the third Everest Base Camp to Kathmandu run. © Dennis Curry

Dream trail, above Zermatt, Switzerland.
© Alex Treadway

Trust: some trails are meant to be shared, Nepal.
© Richard Bull

towards Courmayeur I realised I was well ahead of time to finish in under twenty-four hours despite the conditions. But somewhere between Courmayeur and La Fouly the pain from my fall set in. I ate none of the food I'd taken in Courmayeur, I forced myself into a run, out of mistaken pride, behind Mike Foote when the helicopter flew over us between Rifugio Bonatti and Arnuva. But by the time we reached La Fouly on the Swiss side of the border I had lost Mike, I'd slowed to little more than a walk, and I couldn't see how to carry on.

In tears I entered the checkpoint. Keith Byrne, my friend and then marketing manager at The North Face, tried to figure out what was going on. He saw how little I'd eaten since last seeing him at Courmayeur. He asked me if I'd taken anything for the pain. I had, but it had been totally ineffective. He sat me down, and stopping for a while he was able to encourage me to eat something. Ten minutes later we had decided that I could just try to carry on to Champex, the next checkpoint. There we could reassess the situation. Despite how much I'd slowed I was still in first position and had a big margin. I had nothing to lose except the effort it would take me to get to Champex. Food, pain-killers and a ten-minute break helped. Running into Champex I was a different person.

I can't say it was easy from then on, but I wasn't going to let up. The night's foul weather had damaged the refreshment point at Bovine, so the organisation diverted the race down to Martigny. It lengthened the race to over 170km with considerably more climb and descent. Keith told me about the reroute to Martigny but omitted to mention that it would add both distance and metres of ascent and descent. It mattered not so much, I was on a mission to finish this race despite the pain, and conceivably could have run through anything. At the makeshift checkpoint some-where outside Martigny Keith was able to stop his van in listening range – he and my parents (in accompaniment) played me Queen's 'Don't Stop Me Now'. It was what I needed to hear, but at that stage of the race nothing short of broken bones would have stopped me.

It was a long, long ascent to the Col de la Forclaz from there. Never demanding, just relentless. I passed my team-mate Mike Wolfe and my stomach sank, knowing that it must be a tough race for him. Despite the latening hour people lined the final metres to the col as though we were in the Tour de France. Down to Trient and up the last big ascent. My gait became ever more lop-sided with every passing hour but I was determined not to be caught at that stage of the race after all the pain I had suffered. I finally ran into Chamonix, albeit with a decided lean.

I arrived at the finish line almost three hours ahead of the next woman. That was my fourth win.

Twenty-four hours. How can you even start thinking about racing on the road for that length of time? It had first been mentioned to me in 2006 as I ran around that cold and windy loop of an RAF base in Gloucester during my second 100km race. But it wasn't really something I seriously thought about. Then or later.

In 2011, in a bid to further establish mountain, trail and ultrarunning within the international athletics com-munity, a Commonwealth Championships was organised. The second of its kind, this time it included mountain running, a 53km trail race, and the 24-hour road race. I'd had a full summer of training and racing in the mountains

culminating in that lengthened UTMB. It was now just a
few weeks later and I had plans to head directly to Nepal for
my attempt of the Great Himalaya Trail. The Commonwealth
Championships was just one thing along the way, it was
almost one more job to be done before I could pack my
bags and head for the challenges of some wild and remote
Himalayan trails.

I'd been selected for both the Trail and 24-hour events
and, assured that I would not be preventing another woman
from taking up a place, I was able to leave my decision right
until the last moment.

Most people would have expected me to choose to race
the Trail event. In good form after a summer of mountain
racing, well rested (three weeks) after winning the lengthened UTMB, I would have had a good chance to race well
and place on the podium.

But I felt like trying something new. It was a curiosity, a
desire to challenge myself in the unknown. I had absolutely
no expectations of myself. How could I? The longest road
race I'd done had been seven and a half hours. I'd been
running all summer on mountain trails – a far cry from the
typical training most of my competitors would have been
focused on. I had no idea how my body would react to the
impact of running on the road for so many hours. In all
honesty I had no real emotional or mental investment in
this Championships. I had the opportunity to race. That
was it. My effort and concern was totally focused on what
to me was both a far more exciting and far scarier challenge
awaiting in Nepal. Everything else paled in comparison.
The race was simply one last commitment.

I had one night in London en route from the Alps before
catching the train to Llandudno in North Wales. It was a

journey I had made so many times in earlier years before heading into Snowdonia, or to visit Rob and his wife Netti in Conwy. Strange now to stay only in the town, but time was short and I was there just for the race. I walked from the station to the B&B that England Athletics had organised for us. Stopping at the supermarket I bought myself a picnic supper and some supplies for the next day's race.

I was given my kit to run in and briefly met the rest of the England 24-hour team. I had no one there of my own in support, but the husband of one of my teammates offered to look after us both. It was fortuitous for me.

A picnic supper in my room and a quiet night, I kept myself to myself. It's what I did before races, needing that time to focus inwards, too much talking or interaction dissipating the energy. Morning dawned, a slow breakfast . . . how to plan for a midday start? Morning-time races are easy – you sleep (even if fitfully), you wake up, you dress in race kit, eat breakfast (I like to eat two hours before the start of a race), travel to start and that's it. Job done. Midday is more tricky, with too much time on your hands it leaves you in no-man's land. I sat quietly on the only patch of grass by our bed and breakfast trying to gather my thoughts. It all felt a little surreal; it was hard to believe that we were about to compete in a Commonwealth Championships.

I walked down to the promenade and watched people going about their morning business. I found a supermarket and bought a litre of milky coffee to add to my supplies to see me through the race. I felt out of place there in that bustling shop, already dressed in my England kit, about to run for twenty-four hours, the people in the queue next to me having absolutely no idea a race was even about to start. I walked slowly down the high street through the morning shoppers in a bizarre collision of worlds. It put things in perspective. Yes, I was about to start a championship race that would entail running beyond the limits I had so far explored. And yet very few people in this town would even be aware of it, daily life was carrying on just as normal. Whatever happened during the course of the race would be insignificant, just one thing happening on an ordinary day, in an ordinary setting.

Slowly I made my way to the start of the race – an innocuous 500m stretch of a double-laned residential road. One lane in each direction was blocked off for us, the lanes giving access to the rows of houses remaining available for use by the local residents. Our race route was a simple clockwise loop – 500m up one side of the street, a turn over a bump containing the timing cables, 500m back down the other side, and over another bump. The grass strip separating the lanes of the road held a few Portaloos and the tables for the support – each nationality having their own.

It was a somehow incongruous and unexpected setting for a race, a championship race at that. It was a very ordinary road, and it was a very ordinary grey September day.

Twelve noon rolled forward and at last we were stood on the start line. It was an incredibly bizarre feeling. I'm perfectly comfortable with going off for a 24-hour (or longer) run to take me from A to B or even on a journey scribing a large circle to end up where I started. But this was something else entirely. Knowing that I would be running for twenty-four hours but staying within that one-kilometre loop made no sense. I wasn't sure I could do it.

The unknown lay ahead – physically and mentally. This was the first race where I had no finish line to aim for, simply a set amount of time to run for. It is a very different mental challenge. I wondered how difficult it would be to keep focused.

One of my teammates, Sharon Gayter, had won Gold at the previous 24-hour Commonwealth Championships two years earlier, and at our team briefing she warned us to take it slowly. It worried me though. I wasn't actually sure that I could run a slow enough pace, slower than even 10km per hour.

The start was almost painfully slow, so slow as to be uncomfortable. It felt as though we were simply heading off for an easy weekend jog. After a lap or two I realised I had to set myself free from the 'sensible' or recommended pace. If running slightly faster was more comfortable then surely that would make it easier.

Time passed.

I ran with this person and that person for short spells, falling into an easy conversation. I broke up the early hours asking for half a piece of banana bread or a cup of chocolate milk. I had no nutritional strategy, but unlike many ultrarunners I am rarely sick during racing, I prefer to go by feel and take what I need when I need it. So this time I just had a variety of food and was guided by what I felt I wanted and when. Early on during the race food was more for distraction, something to look forward to, something to mark the time. A race like this was so easy logistically, each country had a table set up with all our personal provisions, and since we passed by every kilometre I would think for a while about what I'd like to ask for, then ask, then (usually) be given it on the following lap or two. Easy. No need to carry food or think ahead like on long mountain runs or expeditions.

The hours started to slip past, my feet kept a gentle and steady rhythm, the world started to shrink down to this

500m stretch of road – up one side, back the other, loop after loop.

Onlookers came and went. Afternoon turned into night. Darkness fell. My parents had driven up that day, they appeared somewhere in the evening time, stayed a while before going to find food in the town. They would have a night's sleep and then come back sometime the next morning. The evening got later. The few onlookers became fewer still. And we were still gently running loop after loop. It struck me how bizarre it must be for the residents – perhaps returning home after a long day's work, eating, drawing curtains shut, having a night of sleep, then waking to the spectacle of these strange people still there running loop after loop.

I had lapped people again and again but I kept no track of how many loops I had run, or the distance, and had no idea of my overall placing. It was impossible to keep track, and of no concern to me in fact. I was totally focused on the running. Step by step by step. No need to think further than one step at a time.

Thoughts about Nepal and all that still needed to be pre-pared and organised were almost on hold. The long and busy summer behind me was of no consequence. I was right there inside the experience of the race and all of me was focused simply on moving forwards until the time came to stop.

Loop after loop. Loop after loop.

I kept myself going continuously for twelve hours, at which point I decided to have a treat – a two-minute stop. I kept to my self-imposed time limit, but it was good just to stop moving completely for even that brief time, to give the internal organs a break from being shaken around as much as for the legs or head. Then I pushed myself onwards again. Back into the night and the relentless monotony of loop after loop.

Loop after loop.

Somewhere in the depths of night, or in the early hours of the morning to be more precise, I was given word that if I made the next four laps in a certain time I could set a new world record for 100 miles. What do you do when told something like that? Having had absolutely no idea even of what such a record was, I went from a state of blissful ignorance to suddenly realising I was within probable reach. Curiosity impelled me to try. I picked up my pace from my gentle fairly pedestrian jog to something more recognisable as a run. Probably still slow, but more than 14 hours into a 24-hour race it felt like a fairly decent effort. It took some metres before the legs started to turn over more quickly, and then it was actually a relief to be moving faster. I can only imagine what my fellow competitors must have been thinking as I suddenly came past them at an unadvisable speed. But word filtered through the field and they slowly realised the reason for my inexplicable behaviour. Race officials had been woken from sleep, I made the time comfortably, only then to be told they had got it wrong – not a world record, just a UK and Commonwealth record. It had been an effort. It was interesting to see how it took me some time to settle back into a gentle rhythm again. I tried to get some food back in me, but it was difficult, some melon and some smashed-up Weetabix was the best I could manage.

In the later stages of the race stops were limited to infrequent dives into the Portaloo, trying hard not to knock it over. It felt somehow unstable, but that could also have been me swaying with the unusual cessation of movement.

Sometimes I had been pausing for thirty seconds at our support table to take on food, but towards the end of the race it hurt more to get the limbs and joints moving again after a stop than it did to simply keep moving, so I kept moving. Similarly, since it hurt a fair bit by then to move at any pace I figured I may as well move more quickly than slowly. The logic of this would have been obvious had there been a finish line to reach. But mentally this was the strange thing about this race – the objective being simply to run as hard and as fast as possible for the twenty-four hours. Hard and fast being relative terms in a situation like this.

Loop after loop.

Graham, the husband of my teammate, who was so generously also supporting me later remarked that watching me perform was an extraordinary experience: 'The running, of course – but, as a meditation teacher, I was absolutely astonished by the level of Lizzy's concentration and focus, and for how long she was able to maintain it.'

A grey dawn dawned on that very ordinary street on another very ordinary day. It brought no great uplifting renewal of spirit or energy, too dull and grey for that. But the arrival of morning did mean that this strange experiment was in its closing stages, just a few hours to go. The field had thinned, losing casualties to the night. My feet carried me forwards, still beating their regular rhythm. I was right there somewhere within my effort. Not really thinking, just there.

Somewhere in the last hour I passed the distance that marked the current world record. It was a distance that had stood for eighteen years. There was some quiet applause and I carried on running. That was the anticlimax, but there was still time to go before noon marked the end of our twenty-four hours. I had to keep my focus and just concentrate on moving forwards. Twenty-four hours was the goal, not some arbitrary distance. The minutes ticked by. Eventually each runner was handed a beanbag – when we heard the gun marking the end of the twenty-four hours we were to stop and drop the beanbag right there where we were. From that they could record our final distance for the official results. I also had an official jog a step behind me, verification (I presume) that I wouldn't hurl my beanbag metres from where I stopped.

The long-awaited moment came. The gun stopped us in our tracks. I dropped my beanbag. I have it still. I won the race outright with my 247km. It was the strangest end to a race. It looked a bit like a battlefield – some runners had dropped to their knees, others lay down there on the road, their bodies unable to cope with the sudden cessation of movement, others were helped away as though a casualty from some terrible accident scene. I probably exaggerate, that is just the imprint of the memory that remains.

I walked slowly over to our supporters table. What to do now?

There was a brief ceremony at the roadside, I gave my parents a hug, and pretty quickly people seemed to disperse. I had one last job to do – drugs test. As I sat by the mobile first-aid vehicle I watched the evidence of the race dismantled. By the time I left it had been returned to its normal guise as that very ordinary residential road.

Sometimes something almost extraordinary does happen on the most ordinary of days in the most ordinary of settings.

I walked slowly back to the B&B and had a warm shower.

It was all fairly unremarkable. We had a slightly longer awards ceremony that evening, I went out to support the trail event the following morning and then, shopping list for Nepal in my hand, I drove back to London with my parents.

Job done. It was time to get back to the Alps, organise, pack for Nepal and prepare for the challenges that awaited me there.

Whatever my inner feeling when I am running it is sometimes enlightening to step back and listen to what others actually observe. I have often been told that it is beautiful to watch me run. It is probably something to do with running being a natural movement for me, and when it feels comfortable then it must also look graceful to the onlooker – somehow effortless despite the work that is being put in.

Returning to Graham's remarks after my world record 24-hour run, that grace must also be something to do with a focused harmony of body and mind. Perhaps we don't reach this point in every run, but the potential is there, particularly when the challenge, the preparation and the performance are all in synchrony – sometimes within the setting of a race, often not. And that potential is probably reason enough to run.

One of the practices in Buddhist monasticism is the training of the mind, often for years, in order to be able to hold focus on an object of choice for a period of time. It is said that to observe Lamas meditating can be to observe a complete and focused harmony of body and mind.

Graham claimed that to observe me running during that 24-hour race was to see something akin to that complete and focused harmony of body and mind, saying,

'There is a Buddhist sudhana or daily practice that involves running in order to enhance focus: Lizzy reverses that – she uses her extraordinary concentration and focus to enhance her running. It is wonderful to witness.' The sudhanas of which Graham speaks are something which have long fascinated me.

One such practice is the Kaihōgyō set of ascetic spiritual trainings for the Buddhist 'marathon monks'[1] of Mount Hiei, near Kyoto in Japan. Kaihōgyō, meaning circling the mountain, is literally what they do and it is seen as the ultimate expression of a desire to attain enlightenment in the current life. The training takes a thousand days over a period of seven years to complete in its entirety – progressing from almost a marathon a day for 100 days in the first year, to 84km for 100 days, followed by another near marathon a day for a further 100 days in the seventh year. Only 46 men have completed the 1,000-day challenge since 1885, and of those three people have completed the circuit twice. It is an incredible feat of endurance, mental and physical.

There was another such esoteric practice in Tibet, known as *Lung-gom-pa*. Lama Anagarika Govinda, a German-born Buddhist monk who travelled through Tibet in 1947, defines the term in his book *The Way of the White Clouds*. *Lung* denotes both a physical and mental phenomenon (an illusory distinction in Buddhism) referring both to air and vital energy (prana in the yogic tradition). *Gom* signifies meditation or focused concentration. So a *lung-gom-pa* would be someone who has mastered the art of harnessing their spiritual energy through focused meditation and conscious breathing, and in doing so has transcended the perceived physical limits of the body. Legend has it they could run 48 hours without stopping and over 200 miles in one day.

The French explorer Alexandra David-Neel in her book *Magic and Mystery in Tibet* described witnessing a monk 'fleeter than a horse' who 'seemed to lift himself from the ground . . . his steps had the regularity of a pendulum . . . the traveller seemed to be in a trance'.[2] She also describes how almost a thousand years ago Milarepa, one of Tibet's most famous yogis and poets, told of having 'crossed in a few days, a distance which, before his training in black magic, had taken him more than a month. He ascribes his gift to the clever control of "internal air".' These bodily practices (yoga included) are, of course, nothing to do with bodily performance and everything to do with spiritual discipline.

I can lay no claim to an extraordinary focus; meditation still leaves me at the mercy of my monkey mind and wandering thoughts. And more often than not I am lost somewhere in the perplexing tension between my hopes, dreams and passions and the reality of my thoughts, actions and emotions. It can be easier to 'know' something intellectually and to write about it than to 'know' with the feelings and to live it. But then, as the Buddhist teacher Pema Chödrön says, 'in that awkward ambiguous moment . . . in the uncertainty of everyday chaos is our wisdom'.[3]

If I can harness my concentration and focus when I run then my challenge is to learn how to direct it to good effect in my daily life. Therein being the value in my daily run – apart from bringing me to physical health and a point of balance – it presents me with an opportunity to learn, to grow, to change in my every day.

Chapter Eleven

You do not need to seek freedom in a different land,
for it exists with your own body, heart, mind and soul.

B.K.S. Iyengar, *Light on Life*

We leave Jiri behind us. It is great to have company now, a double set of footsteps doing time on the road. The coffee and cake
seem to have done the trick. There are no more episodes of the
world falling away from me. I feel I can carry on. We keep up
a good pace during these night hours and it goes easily, despite
the pouring rain. The bus plays leapfrog with us, first driving
ahead a few kilometres and then waiting; we make it all the way
to the Tama Koshi river like this. And then Upendra and I decide
to weave together some assortment of tiny trails, to short-cut
the long zigzags of the road. We are back on trail and climbing
steeply now, it is a relief to be able to push hand on knees and
not run. I can't remember exactly the way I took last time so
we just do our best to piece together bits of trail, it is fun, a
welcome break from the monotony of the road. Periodically
we cross the road, each time Richard somehow intuits where
we will pop out and is there waiting with the bus. We make it
up like this until the spot where Upendra and I know we need
to leave the road and re-find the old trails to Mudhe.

It is difficult though. Neither of us can quite remember exactly which cluster of shacks marks the way we took last time, and now in the depths of night there is no one to ask. It's going to take us some hours from here so I shoulder my pack again, taking some water and two pieces of banana bread. Upendra does the same. That will have to do us until we reach Mudhe, hopefully around breakfast time. Richard should be there waiting by then – it is going to take him and the bus a while to get there themselves, the road winds a long way round here. We will cut hours with our short cut, if we can get it right. But I am learning the sense of the short cuts now. If you know your direction and where you are headed, you can piece things together.

We find a workable way down to the river and the light comes back into the sky. It takes longer than I expect and the last part of the ascent to Mudhe stretches out further than ever. Tiredness is creeping over me now. I know just how far there is to go, it is a long way, I am going to have to hold fast to every shred of strength I have left.

We reach the village and it is a relief to sit for a while, to eat something and down more frothy, milky coffee. I briefly expose my shrivelled feet to the air and try to gather some enthusiasm to get running again. I set off alone. Upendra needs some sleep and to rest a while now. The road feels hard beneath my tired feet. Can I get myself into a rhythm; how can I distract myself? I tell myself that it is all downhill to Lamosangu. It has to be easy, right? But I know the descent is still kilometres of running, on an unforgiving surface. The bus passes me and, having tidied up our food stop and reorganised everything, Richard jumps out ready to join me and run. I hadn't realised he was going to, it is a huge relief and I'm happy to have his company, I'm feeling tired and daunted by the distance still to go.

We run sometimes side by side and then I sometimes drop behind, falling into his rhythm and drawing on his strength. We make progress, our tempo periodically disrupted as we give space to the passing buses. The road here descends in a series of long winding turns, in places we can short-cut between the long zigzags and each time we do I have a huge sense of relief. The trail is softer underfoot and gives rest from the relentless sameness of our footsteps on the road.

Eventually we reach the valley floor and the bridge across the river to Lamosangu. The boys stop for dal bhat.[1] I snack and change into a fresh T-shirt hoping that it will also put some freshness in my stride. It seems to work for a while. Richard carries on with me for some more kilometres; we are on the Arniko Highway now, the road that will lead us home. When he takes a break in the bus, I start to pick off the kilometres, marked by the white posts at the side of the road. Sometimes I miss one and happily find myself a couple of kilometres further on than I thought. I break it down, I argue myself through one kilometre, then the next, then the next. Deep in focus, I am suddenly startled by Richard sitting on a rock just ahead – his camera captures the surprised smile on my face. Then the last long sweep down across the bridge and through the town. We take a break at a tea place, we are making good progress.

The road climbs continuously for thirty kilometres here. I gather all remaining shreds of motivation into one stream of focus. Upendra and I set off and settle into the relentless climb. It seems to flow, we aren't running fast, but we keep an even pace and the kilometres drift away beneath our feet. I am almost surprised when we reach the halfway point. Is it really going to be this easy? Richard and Upendra swap roles and I fall in behind Richard. Again I catch his rhythm, focusing hard on not letting myself drop further than a few steps behind him. We cross the flat section and then it is back to a relentless winding climb. The ease of that first half has disappeared and I'm sure I don't remember it being this long. Like a petulant child I keep asking Richard, 'are we nearly there yet?', desperately hoping for him to reply, 'nearly'. It is a long while before he does say it. This section I had run only at night, and now in the harsh light of day I realise just how long it is. I should be able to remember from my many bus journeys to Jiri but I am beyond rational thought. I stupidly bargain with myself that I can make this in one go, not stopping until we reach the hilltop town. I mumble to Richard words to the effect, 'I think I might fall over if I stop now.' The body is a curious thing, it can go so much further than you think, but sometimes when it stops it realises that it has been making an uncommon effort, and things fall apart. I don't want that to happen halfway up the hill. But Richard takes no notice of my mumbled theories between my repeated questioning of how much further we have to go, and makes me stop when we next catch our bus parked on a bend. He hands me an apple pastry, all that is left of the bag of goodies he had brought. The rush of sugar feels good. We set off again and I realise how much more comfortable I feel now; he was right, it had been worth stopping. A few kilometres later and I am glad we did, this climb is endless. I keep up my sporadic questioning, 'are we surely nearly there yet?' He must be despairing but finally he can give me the answer that the hilltop town lies around just a couple more curves, we are going to make it. We coast into the ramshackle town.

A last pit stop. Our food supplies are rapidly dwindling, but this should be good now – just thirty kilometres to go on a descending road. My lower back is screaming out in pain. It is just like the pain I had last year with my lower-back/psoas/hamstring tangle. I ask Richard to dig his elbow hard into where the pain is coming from and it seems to help. Night is approaching now and the air is cooling, it is time to don a warmer layer and head onwards. Upendra with me, we keep a swift (relatively speaking) pace. I forget my tiredness of the relentless ascent, can it be this easy? We coast onwards.

❖ ❖ ❖

Imagine finding a trail winding a way through the highest summits of the Himalaya. A 'Shangri-la' for those who love moving on foot through the mountains. With vision, passion and dedication, this dream became a concept and this concept became a reality. The Great Himalaya Trail (GHT)[2] was born – one of the highest and longest 'trails' in the world, linking ancient trading routes and pilgrimage trails through remote and rugged mountain districts. The route was pioneered by Robin Boustead, and others, over a period of six months with a meticulous recording of GPS and detailed specifics, following years of research.

After that first run from Everest Base Camp back to Kathmandu I yearned to make another journey, but longer and keeping in the high mountains. I had no idea what shape a journey like this could take, although thinking back to the Crane brothers' crossing of the Himalayas from before Kanchenjunga to Nanga Parbat[3] I wondered if another such journey was possible, but staying higher, threading a route through all the base camps of the fourteen 8,000m mountains. I knew nothing then about the Great Himalaya Trail, but it was in fact the embodiment of the kind of journey I had been thinking about.

It became a dream of mine after receiving an email from Richard early in 2010. He was then working on a marketing project for the organisation involved in developing the trail and thought it would be a 'beautiful, rough, hard and unforgettable journey'. Emails had continued backwards and forwards between us until finally, resting on my bed the afternoon before 2011 UTMB, clearly not entirely focused on the race, I wrote to him and Roger to say that I was definitely coming to attempt the Great Himalaya Trail, and could they help? This project, my 'Sky Dance', was the challenge that awaited me after those twenty-four hours of running up and down that residential road in North Wales.

With Richard's help I made it out of Kathmandu and up to Kanchenjunga Base Camp. But just days into my attempt I lost the way in a remote forest between the villages of Thudam and Chyamtang between the Kanchenjunga and Makalu regions. That didn't matter so much, I found myself again, and it was just lost time. But I also lost all my means of communication and my hard-won permits for the entire journey. There was no choice but to stop.[4] I'd known that the journey would need all my humility, courage and passion, but also the sensitivity and willingness to adapt with a calm patience. It did.

It is a story still to be continued and so yet to be told, and elsewhere.

After my abandoned attempt I found myself at a loss in Kathmandu with a thousand mixed emotions, humbled, scratched and sad to have stopped, but with a real joy for life and immensely thankful for the support of friends and family, and for the precious connections that I'd had with complete strangers. I wasn't yet ready to return directly to Europe, and I was longing to be back in the mountains, running again on those sky-high trails. Bruno Poirier, a French journalist and veteran Himalayan runner, had for many years been organising some incredible stage races in Nepal. I had a standing invitation. His Everest Sky Race was starting a week after my return to Kathmandu. Richard was going as a journalist, I could go too. There lay my chance to get back to the mountains.

It was a beautiful and demanding journey – through the wild Rolwaling, over the 5,760m always-to-be-respected Tashi Labsta (a non-race stage), over the Renjo La (5,300m) and Cho La (5,420m) up to Kalar Patthar (5,643m) and a great descent to Pangboche, the village at the foot of Ama Dablam. I led the race overall until we reached Gokyo but, already weakened from my Sky Dance efforts, I had fallen victim to the Khumbu cough, and I was eventually beaten by Jorbir Rai and Deepak Rai. It was a wonderful adventure, treading new trails, treading old trails already familiar from previous adventures, crossing between two wildly different mountain areas, sitting in sunshine sheltered from the wind at the end of the day's stage and sharing experiences, deepening friendships.

The race ended, and we bade farewell to our friends; some were headed downwards to Lukla and their flight back to Kathmandu, some were headed upwards for their ascent of Lobuche. Richard and I stayed in Pangboche – we hiked up to visit friends at Ama Dablam base camp for our daily exercise and sat by the stove of the lodge I had stayed in four years before with Mark and Spyke. Two days was all we had, I can't remember what I was racing – incoming weather, my flight home? You see, the idea had come up while talking with Roger back in Kathmandu that since our race would finish back in the Khumbu, why not try that record again. That first time I arrived back at the stadium in Kathmandu I'd had no intention of repeating the attempt.

But the opportunity was just there, and running would save the cost of the flight back. So why not? It was more the appeal of days of running, of reaching Kathmandu by my own efforts, than any real desire to better our previous time. I had written to Mark and Spyke, but 'of course' they didn't mind if I had another try. And so some simple plans had been laid, I would keep in touch with Roger by mobile (when I could get a signal) and he would meet me at Jiri with some Nepalese friends. All I had to do was make it back to Jiri. From there they could support me. All? I barely remembered some sections. It was a daunting prospect to make that journey alone.

A morning dawned. Richard and I shared a last breakfast, and then we hugged goodbye on that trail passing through Pangboche. Richard was headed downwards, on his own journey back to Kathmandu and waiting work obligations – jogging to Jiri and bus from there. I was headed upwards towards Everest Base Camp. I caught up to the climbing fragment of our race group at Pheriche and enjoyed some coffee, cake and an evening meal with them. We walked together up to Dhugla, from where our ways parted. Mr T was still there, and remembered me, promising me tea on my way down again. I spent a cold night at Gorak Shep, and again the lodge there remembered me from our previous attempt. I had an early start to walk up to EBC, just as before, and that was it. It was time to head downwards. It was strange to be there completely alone this time, no one to give witness to my effort or to share it with.

It was easy that first part. The trails I knew so well, the cough was bearable, I could just run and enjoy. I had no splits, I never take much note of things like that, not even in races, and I couldn't remember our timing from before.

All I had to guide me was a vague recollection of where we were when night fell and dawn came. Somewhere in that afternoon below Namche the rain began. I found the turn-off to avoid Lukla, but in the darkness of the falling night and pouring rain I missed the main trail and ended up on a side trail back up to Lukla. Realising my mistake I reached the far edge of the village. Knocking on a shack door I was pointed to the right trail leading onwards and downwards, but not before I had seen the lights, and heard the merriment. Lukla was full – rain had put paid to all flights out. What was I doing turning my back on that distant cocoon of comforts for the uncertain pleasures of running alone through a long, wet and muddy night? Even on that trail downwards from Lukla there are plenty of 'ups', hardly surprising when the Nepali 'flat' is up, down, up, down, and this trail had never even been described as flat. After the village of Surkhe where I had stopped for tomato soup and chapatis with Mark and Spyke all those years before, the trail grew strangely unfamiliar. I wondered if I had really taken in anything at all when I had run it before. I recognised nothing.

It is like that sometimes when I return to a race, I will find some sections that are burned into my memory so intently that I can remember every step, and other sections where absolutely nothing is familiar and I wonder if I had been there at all.

The rain grew heavier and the night grew darker. The trails were becoming rivers of mud and yak shit and my lightweight waterproof jacket didn't seem to be helping all that much. I was slowly becoming wetter and colder, and I was slowly becoming slower. I started to get worried. Hours like this would be asking for trouble. With the mud and the rocks I couldn't keep up a pace swift enough to keep any kind of warmth. *Ke garne*, what to do? It was late already. I'd run past lodges with lights still burning. Had I run myself out of any choices but to continue?

I finally reached the outskirts of the village of Bupsa, there was one flickering light. I knocked on the door, a young girl was just putting the fire to bed; she let me in. It was a very simple porters' shelter but she made me welcome, bedraggled and dripping as I was. She rekindled the fire, and put on a pan of sweet milk tea. Her parents rose from their bed and made it clear I was welcome to stay as long as I needed. I thought I would sit there an hour, let the rain abate, let the sweet tea revive me, dry out a little. The one hour became two, the deluge continued, two hours became three. I kept a lonely vigil until dawn, half-dozing, thankful to be sheltered, guilty to not be moving, worried about the time lost. The sleeping porters stirred, the incessant downpour had become just a little lighter, and after a few more cups of tea there was no more excuse to linger. Just as before with Mark and Spyke, now I had no idea whether the record would be within reach. But that was almost insignificant. I had at least to get myself to Jiri to my friends waiting at the road-head. And from there? Well, I suspected by that point I would just want to get back to Kathmandu under my own effort, record or not. And so I thanked my new friends for their utter generosity and joined the schoolchildren running downwards towards Kharikhola.

The clouds lingered but the rain had stopped. I reached Jubing Bridge, the point where with Mark and Spyke we had crossed the river to the accompaniment of barking dogs in the middle of the night. I'd lost about eight hours sitting out that downpour. I pushed that out of my mind as best I could and headed up the long ascent to the Taksindu La. This time in the light of day, it felt so different to the vague memories of before that I was unsure if I was even on the right trail. Eventually I reached the pass and as it opened out the memories flooded back. Onwards. Then a swift descent on the beautifully runnable trail around to Junbesi, this time breaking at the Everest View Lodge for tsampa porridge and tea, the aged proprietor worriedly giving me second helpings. Up towards the Lamjura La and here the rains had poured snow. Shivering and barely remembering the way from before, I finally got a signal on my phone and sent a text to Roger to let him know my delay. It is a long, long descent from there – it took me from winter to the heat of the summer.

I reached the floor of the valley, bought some biscuits and continued along the valley to the long ascent to the Deurali Pass where Upendra Sunuwar,[5] a Nepali friend of ours, would meet me. Darkness fell somewhere along the way, I got desperately confused between the old trail and the new still-being-built road. This time I could perfectly picture our ascent from before, but under darkness the old-trail/new-road confusion led me to unrecognisable meanderings. I lost time. It felt hopeless. This part had been so simple last time, I was getting tired now and just wanted to reach Jiri. Eventually I was pointed in the right direction and finally, close to the pass, I heard a shout from Upendra. I didn't know him so well then but I was more than thankful to finally meet with him, we could be company for each other; more accurately he would be great company for me. He knew the trails from here to Jiri well. I could finally just focus on the effort of moving myself as quickly as possible and have a rest from thinking about the 'how' of getting to where we needed to be. We stopped for a Coca-Cola in the lodge where Upendra had been waiting those hours for me. The unaccustomed rush of sugar (Coke being something I avoid until the later stages of a race situation) and caffeine gave us both a boost. Our descent to Shivalaya, and the subsequent ascent and descent to Jiri, seemed almost simple. Following behind someone who knew where they were took all the worry away, all I had to do was to follow and keep moving.

We reached Jiri somewhere around midnight, again. Just like before with Mark and Spyke. For hours now, I'd been putting my hopes on some food at Jiri. A pit stop of sorts. But it was that same seedy and unwelcoming place in the middle of the night, the tea shops and lodges all boarded up and in darkness. And all those weeks before, discussing things with Roger in the comfort of Kathmandu, I hadn't been specific enough in asking him to bring food supplies. So it was a few quick hellos, some nuts and raisins, and onwards into the night.

From there, one or other of them ran with me, it gave me a distraction, it broke the monotony, it took me back outside of myself to have a companion to be concerned about. Running with Raj through the town of Maina Pokhari just as the first light was coming into the sky we found lights flickering in one of the roadside tea shops. The ubiquitous pan of milk tea was already on the fire. A bemused lady served us a couple of glasses each. Nepali tea is served hot, but I have a strange ability to drink things at almost boiling temperature. At times it is a useful habit.

Dawn broke, morning established itself, and there were several of us piecing together the bits of old trail left between the zigs and zags of descending road. We broke for breakfast. More bread, more sweet tea. Hitting the bridge across the Tama Koshi we made our way up the ascent towards Kirantichap, patching together another hotchpotch of tiny trails leading between homesteads to the accompaniment of horns from the buses crawling their way up the twisting road. Eventually the incline eased and we hit the road. Some metres ahead Roger had stopped with the bus and a small crowd had gathered. He had been asking directions for the best descent to find the old trail to Mudhe. I remembered too well the efforts Spyke and I had made, but if we could find the right way it would save kilometres and hours, compared to staying on the road. Again fuelled by tea, I set off with Upendra and Narayan. We picked together a route, asking anyone we came across for confirmation of the way. Eventually we crossed the bridge and began the long ascent up to Mudhe.

It was completely different to the way Spyke and I had found before. That didn't matter, but I had the strangest feeling of being followed, as though in a race, only it was Spyke and a four-years-younger-me who were chasing. I could almost feel us behind me, getting ever closer, and I almost wouldn't have been surprised to be passed by *us*. Reaching Mudhe, I realised we had made up a lot of time – it was now the middle of the day, Spyke and I had previously reached there only as darkness was falling. The record could still be possible. I was fed some bread and hard yak cheese and it was Roger's turn to run with me for a while. The road from here descends in a series of long winding turns to the valley floor and the village of Lamosangu where we would join the main road, the Arniko Highway, leading from Kathmandu to the Sino-Nepal Friendship Bridge which crosses the Tibetan border. I remember him remarking with incredulity on my form, still landing on the front of my foot despite the tiredness that comes with well over fifty hours of effort.

The day wore on and turned to night somewhere on that long road. I managed pretty well until Dolalghat. But then started the long and winding ascent to Dhulikel and under the cover of darkness I started to feel a strange and horrible tiredness. I hadn't felt like this the previous time. But then before we had slept for four hours – this was now the longest I had ever been without sleep. I started to weave across the road, my eyes wouldn't focus. However much effort I made I couldn't pull myself together to keep a straight line. Every so often the others would ask me if I was OK, steer me away from the middle of the road to avoid the sporadic traffic, or pull me away from falling into the drainage at the side of the road. We carried on like this for a while. And then I gave in. I simply lay myself down on the hard road. I would lie there some minutes, before being able to pull myself back onto my feet and break into a stumbling jog. This happened a few times. Then we finally caught up to our waiting bus. I had to stop for a while and see if I could shake this overwhelming and dreadful tiredness. Roger gave me forty minutes. I'm not sure I slept, but the rest must have worked, I could keep moving forwards. It was slow progress, but the others were kind and patient in their relative freshness. We got through the rest of the night and the coming of day made things easier.

The long descent to Kathmandu had changed over the intervening years, it was no longer a dirt roadside gradually getting busier, noisier, smellier – it was now a seemingly endless major and tarmacked road. The moment came when we finally reached the gates of the stadium. This time it was full of morning activity with local clubs making their daily training. They had no idea where I'd come from but I had some laughing company for my final lap. And then it was over. A new record.

Roger had promised me a room back at the Summit Hotel, I sat there waiting a while and Richard appeared with a paper bag of bread, cheese and chocolate. He gave me a hug, promising to make it back later to join us for dinner, and telling me to eat, as he could feel my bones. It was a strange anticlimactic feeling. I fully intended to put myself straight under the cascade of hopefully warm water and clean up a bit. But it was then that the tiredness hit. It took me some hours to get myself to the point of cleanliness, to email family, to get myself into clean clothes, all between bouts of lying back on the bed to doze. The smallest chore was an effort. I joined Richard, Roger and Roger's family for a welcome-back dinner. For weeks now I'd been longing for a Greek salad, some naan and a large glass of red wine. This was my chance. But the effort of eating was too much, and even the glass of wine was beyond me. Richard had to help me out – I hate leaving anything to waste. And I let myself just enjoy being there, back in the company of my friends.

Chapter Twelve

When I let go of what I am, I become what I might be.

Lao Tzu

Oblivion. Darkness. Stillness. Total rest. The tarmac is hard and cold underneath my outstretched body. It was a few minutes at most. Awareness slowly floods back into every part of my body. I sense Rich standing near, watching over me. I open my eyes. He is a dark shadow, sporadically illuminated by the lights of the trucks passing on the road behind, unsure what he can do to help other than to watch and to wait. Without Richard, and without Upendra, I wouldn't have made it this far. But, neither of them can run for me. Despite their support, despite their companionship, I feel completely alone. I have to fight the tiredness, the urge to stay lying down, the overwhelming need just to shut my eyes. It is time to lever myself back onto my feet, to force my limbs to move, and head onwards into the darkness of the night.

Over sixty hours have passed since I started my journey from Everest Base Camp, high in the wild beauty of the Khumbu. Less than fifteen kilometres remain until I reach the gates of the stadium in Kathmandu. A distance less than that I typically run every day. And yet it feels almost an impossibility. We are so near, yet still so far away. I draw slowly further from the protective comfort of our bus, knowing that they will be watching as my figure fades into the distance.

I start to turn inwards, withdrawing my senses, blocking out all the external stimuli, blind to everything but the narrow stretch of road immediately ahead within my gaze. I focus on moving forwards, riding on the rhythm of my breath.

Why? Why, already hours into the third night, am I still asking my body to run?

It's not so much the physical tiredness. That is almost an old friend. We know how to work together, I know how to use it, to ride it through, to go beyond it. No, it's more this almost primal need just to shut my eyes. It is instinctive, unrelenting and refuses to be ignored.

I give in. For moments at a time. My feet and legs relentlessly carrying me blindly onwards.

The world and all of time has been distilled down into this one moment. Now. Nothing else exists. Nothing else matters. All that there ever was, and all that there ever will be, is embraced by this one moment and my struggle to keep moving through it.

The focus is absolute. It dissociates me from the rest of my journey.

I have no memory now of where it all began. I have no memory now of the seed that was sown in that long conversation with Richard one evening weeks before, or of the underlying impetus already contained within the effort of my two previous attempts. I have no memory now of the calm that settled over me as I felt the freedom of finally starting to run, having overcome the odds even to arrive at Base Camp, with no further need to question myself over preparations made or unmade. I have no memory now of the joy of having only one remaining demand, simply to sink into the experience, to let the journey unfold, the challenge lying therein – just to be present in the unfolding and its call for action or inaction. I have no memory now of the light dusting of snow which had turned the rocky boulders of the glacial moraine into a magical wonderland, or of the ease of those first kilometres, before hunger, thirst, tiredness could lay claim to my attention. I have no memory now of enjoying the fluidity of my physical movement despite the thin air of altitude, simply allowing my thoughts to come and to go, dancing on the shafts of light.

I have no concept yet either of the finish that will come. I have no concept yet of how the remaining kilometres could be subsumed one by one into the darkness of the night, washed away by the rain pouring down on us, as we run through the near-deserted roads emptied of their daytime traffic and incessant buzz of life. I have no concept yet of the relief that will come upon touching the locked gate of the stadium, or of the strange anticlimax that will accompany the loss of purpose, the realisation that there is nowhere to go, no need to keep moving forwards. I have no concept yet of that tiny group waiting to greet us, a couple of journalists with their cameras flashing, a couple of stalwart friends. I have no concept yet of the depth of my gratitude towards Richard and Upendra, for caring for me, for their companionship through such a large part of the journey, for giving up their time and effort to look after me and support me with no reward other than simply to be there for me. I have no concept yet of my realisation that without Rich's support I may not have taken the gamble to try again, or had the courage to keep going in a seemingly pointless endeavour when body, mind and emotions are screaming 'Why?'

No, all I have is this one moment. The entirety of what exists and doesn't exist, of what has gone before and what is yet to come, is comprised of this one moment. It is all-knowing, all-encompassing, pure effort. I am that I am. It is the energy of something so much greater than myself that runs through me. Simply that.

❖   ❖   ❖

The day of the 2012 UTMB dawned. I knew that if the weather allowed us to run the actual route rather than a shortened or lengthened version then I would have a chance to run within twenty-four hours. I was in good form, there was no reason why not. Thunder again reverberated around the valley the morning of the race. Eventually news came to us that the race was to be shortened to 100km and would keep to French territory. I was desperately disappointed, as I imagine were a lot of other people. To make the Ultra-Trail du Mont-Blanc then you have to encircle that immense massif of Mont Blanc – to do anything else is not the UTMB. That is how it felt to me then and is how it feels to me now.

My choice would be to have the possibility of a sliding start window – bringing forward or delaying the start by up to twenty-four hours. Weather systems at that time of year tend to be relatively swift-moving. In my opinion, such a window of opportunity would allow the best chance for the route to be run in its original form. With the cost of travel, taking time off work – not to mention the sacrifices made during the year in training – I would much prefer to plan for one extra day of leave, to pay for one more night of accommodation than to lose the chance to race the race I have trained for, that I have planned for, that I have sacrificed time, money, effort and goodwill to prepare for. But the race organisation made other decisions.

As it stood we raced a revised 104km route with over

6,000m ascent. Again I was in pain, having battled with some unresolved lower-back/psoas/hamstring tangle since the springtime. I set it aside and again, according to iRunFar, I was playing a game of chase with the boys all night, knifing out an almost fifty-minute lead over any other woman.

That was my sixth podium at the UTMB, and my fifth win.

An interviewer post-race remarked that I appeared to keep calm and collected throughout all of the excitement and concern about weather conditions and route changes before the start. They asked if I ever got angry, and if so then why. My answer was simple – to get angry in a situation like that would simply waste energy. In any endurance event part of the challenge is to be able to deal with whatever the mountains, the environment, your body, your mind, throw at you. In this situation we were stood at the start of a completely different race, so it became ever more important just to try to stay in the moment. Keeping that inner calm and equanimity is part of the challenge.

Frustrated by the shortened route of the 2012 UTMB and running better than I had earlier in the season with that back/psoas/hamstring tangle I was eager to race again.

I was already entered for the 250km Spartathlon four weeks later but the thought of a new 100-mile race in Colorado (USA), Run Rabbit Run, had been rattling around in my head. It was a thought that wouldn't go away. Would I really dare to try a 100km mountain race, a 100-mile mountain race and a 250km road race within the period of a month? I was renowned for racing often and recovering well but this would be asking a lot. Even for me.

I sent off an email to the organisers of RRR100. They were enthusiastically welcoming and ·in answer to my question as to whether I could camp near the start line immediately offered me some accommodation, sharing a condo with Mike Wolfe – there was no way they were going to have me fly halfway round the world and bring my tent. I finally figured out the logistics of getting to Steamboat Springs, Colorado, involving a long flight and a shuttle bus – racing in the USA always poses logistical challenges for me as a non-car driver, but in effect serves well to distract me from pre-race tension – and arrived to the glorious autumnal colours of the Aspens. This was the inaugural edition and the race organisers, Paul Sachs and Fred Abramowitz, had a novel idea to divide entrants into Hares and Tortoises depending on how long they expected to take to complete the race. Each would be eligible for a larger or smaller part of the prize money, and a divided start would allow some interaction as the Hares overtook the Tortoises and would allow everyone to finish as close together as possible and enjoy the party together.

I loved the tone in which they'd written their website:[1] 'The Run Rabbit Run courses are very much like life, in that there are many, many little and not so little ups and downs in between the obvious highs and lows. Be prepared.' This was going to be fun.

It was. But five miles into that hundred miles I fell. Hard. No knee scrape this time. Just an almighty bang to the bone. I was a while just lying there dazed on the trail before I could lever myself back to a standing position, let alone to break back into a run.

People who saw me at various checkpoints were convinced I was going to have to drop. The pain led me to vomit at the feet of the ever-gracious Krissy Moehl who was there supporting me, and leaving her to deal with the mess I ran off into the night with five or six hours of running still ahead of me. Running on empty, I reached the finish line as first woman (and fourth overall) in the beauty of the morning sunshine.

Spartathlon then: it is a historic 246km ultra distance foot race from Athens to Sparta, in Greece. It traces the footsteps of Pheidippides, an ancient Athenian long-distance runner, who in 490 BC, before the Battle of Marathon, was sent to Sparta to seek help in the war between the Greeks and the Persians. According to the ancient Greek historian Herodotus, Pheidippides arrived in Sparta the day after his departure from Athens.

To turn up at this iconic race after the previous efforts that month seemed deeply irreverent. Either that or I'd be in great form. The swelling of my knee had thankfully just been due to the blow to the bone, no damage done, and the intervening ten days had given the swelling time to subside. So a series of flights and train journeys later I was in Athens.

The race began at the Acropolis; it was an imposing start line. I stood there already tired, I'd slept badly for nights now, the hotel room being directly on a dual carriageway with an incessant and unrelenting hum from the passing cars. Lesson learned, more research needed in future. Graham, who had so generously supported me during that 24-hour race, had offered his help again.

The route is just a long, monotonous road run. The road stays open to traffic, so while the quiet country lanes were a pleasure to run there were also less than pleasurable moments dodging thundering lorries in the dead of night on the main road. There is one short off-road section cross-ing over a mountain pass, and at the checkpoint just before heading onto the upward trail the kindly volunteers warned me to take care. For me, it was a relief to be off the road, the hours of pounding had again kicked off that pain from the lower-back/psoas/hamstring tangle. I made short work of the climb and my enthusiasm for the race (nearly lost in the pain) was renewed as I crossed the windy pass. I overtook the first man on the descent, he admonished me to be careful; I wondered how long I could have held my lead had the mountain section been longer.

Morning dawned and the hours on tarmac were taking their toll. I thought back to that pavement run on the Upminster streets I had done as a child. Whenever back there now I run a longer six-mile loop. I remembered how it is a measurable amount of effort. I started to break down the remaining distance. Just four times that six miles left, then three, then two, then just six miles left to go. Surely I could urge tired legs, body and mind to complete that short distance that I had run so many times just one more time. It is like that. It is a game of deception.

Running into Sparta surrounded by the children on their bicycles, with so many people out in support, was a moving experience. And finally, after the last stretch of road lined with a cheering crowd, I could touch the statue of King Leonidas – the finish of the race. I was third overall – the first time in the history of the race that a woman had reached the overall podium.

It was special – not so much for me, but when I realised what it meant for the women of Sparta. A group came up to me in the street to thank me, it was a touching and humbling gesture. It still overwhelms me to realise that my own personal achievement and effort does in fact sometimes have a wider significance.

The ceremonies were amusing – the organisers weren't

quite sure how to deal with me. They called the first man up, then the second, then the third – but had to rethink their ordering when protests from the audience of runners clamoured for me to be presented in third.

A man came up to me afterwards wanting to touch my arm to feel my power. People have remarked that I have a strong presence, but that was a first.

Never mind that power, and ceremonies aside, there can be a distinctively unglamorous side to ultra distance running. It was a while before I could walk comfortably after Spartathlon. Not aching muscles as you might imagine, I rarely feel soreness, they have become all too well adapted to what I have subjected them to over the years. No, I was just rubbed raw from chafing. In the unusually hot conditions I had thrown as much water over myself as possible during those twenty-seven hours. Those last hours hurt.

Another time I found myself stripped naked and shivering in the bathroom of my hotel room not quite sure where to begin. I'd just walked back from the finish line of Transgrancanaria, I'd won the race, I'd been on my feet for nearly sixteen hours and I'd been awake for more than double that (the race starts at an uncivilised midnight hour). I was desperate for a crap, had feet that stank after running kilometres through a riverbed, bloody knees from an early fall, dried sweat from the effort put in and a back and hips rubbed raw by my rucksack. I was longing to put myself under a comforting cascade of water but I knew it was going to hurt. A lot. I wrapped myself in a towel and postponed the agony, hoping a short nap would give me more enthusiasm to deal with the mess.

And once, instead of enjoying post-race celebrations I was

whisked away to the Emergency Room (this was the US). I had fallen about five miles in during the inaugural North Face Endurance 50-mile in San Francisco. In the early morning darkness I hadn't stopped to inspect my knee, but the pain told me it was more than just a graze, as did the concerned questioning from first-aiders as I passed through the aid stations: 'Can we help?' Adrenaline pushed me onwards, this was the first race I had ever entered with a considerable sum of prize money – $10,000, it was all or nothing (the winner took all). And besides, I had a finish line to reach. Around halfway I stopped to pee, and crouching had a better look at my knee. It didn't look good. As the hours wore on the adrenaline wore off and I started to slow, it was becoming hard to force myself to bend the knee, and I couldn't understand why I hadn't yet been caught by the second woman. I wasn't. And later, sat there in the Emergency Room, I made the doctor's day. He had never treated someone who had run fifty miles before, let alone someone who had run that far with a puncture wound and won. I was lucky, no permanent damage, but he could see down the hole to the bone. Stitches and two courses of antibiotics ensued – it was three weeks before I could bend the knee again.

After that glorious month of September 2012 what I needed, or wanted, was something different. It was perhaps inevitable that I would turn back to Nepal. I needed a dose of the Himalaya and what it was I found there. Richard was organising a multi-stage race around the 8,156m Manaslu, the eighth-highest mountain in the world. He had invited me months earlier, back in the springtime, and the idea had been taking hold. Finally doing my sums I said, 'yes, please'. I would find a hook and a crook and scrape together the cost of the flight. It would be my release, my indulgence, my treat at the end of a long and hard year, a place to gain strength, a time to feed my soul before the final race of the year, another edition of The North Face Endurance Challenge in San Francisco. I shut my (borrowed) door, zipped up my duffel bag and looked forward to the month of training, racing and travelling that lay ahead.

As my postbus crossed the San Bernardino Pass en route from the mountains to Milan airport I had the strangest feeling of excitement tinged with trepidation. Travelling to races had become normal over the years. But this felt very different, I had no idea then but I had somehow intuited that the experiences ahead were going to mark a shift in my life.

Happy days. I left some blood, sweat, tears, laughs and smiles out on those trails in the sky around Manaslu. Its Nepali name, meaning 'Mountain of the Spirit', comes from the Sanskrit word *Manasa*, meaning 'soul'. It is without doubt a soulful place. Nepal never fails to shake me up and rub some corners off. But this time it was as though the winds had scoured me from the inside and completely emptied me out. I was refilled with the beautiful energy of the sun, of the deep-blue skies, of the thin air, and the awe-someness of the mountains. But thrown back into the very core of myself something had irrevocably changed.

We shared some great company on those miles of high mountain trails. It was indeed food for the soul.

Shooting stars scudding across the canopy of the night sky; icy torrents; bubbling hot springs; deeply forested gorge valleys; mountain ridges etched against a sky of deepest blue; trails strewn with chortens and stupas; the sweat and honesty of a long, steep ascent; the controlled joyful abandon of a fast descent; gompas, those ancient bastions of Tibetan Buddhism; living, vibrant, welcoming monasteries; changing, clashing cultures; laughing children, smiling faces; precious moments shared in the thin air.

I felt my vulnerability and weakness in the face of such immensity of landscape, I again realised my insignificance. There was a rawness of emotion, and yet I felt a beautiful power and strength in body, mind and spirit.

Injury intervened but I went back again then to Nepal.

I wanted this time to stay a while. So I had time now to train, to race, to work on some projects and to make some running expeditions, doing what I love doing, running lightly from lodge to lodge, moving fast.

Soon after arriving in Kathmandu I took the bus to Jiri and set off to run to the park gates (of the Sagarmārthā National Park) at Monjo. This was my last longer training for the Annapurna 100. It was my third time treading these trails, but the first time in that direction and in springtime. Travelling under the light of day I saw the mountains I had never seen before, and moving in the unfamiliar direction gave me new perspective. I made friends with the policeman at the gates, and he was to greet me several times more that season as I was to pass again four times (twice in each direction). I explored some way up the side valley from Monjo towards Kusum Kanguru base camp. It was beautiful, there was peace there in that quiet valley, I had found my own *beyul* (a sacred, hidden valley in the Buddhist tradition). I spent a simple night, and left early. Too early in the season, there were very few people on the trails, but stopping in the villages I made friends, and this time I absorbed every nuance of every part of the trail. I really learned to know it. Back to Jiri for the long bus ride to Kathmandu, I was quite happy this time not to be running that long road out. A return trip to Pokhara followed for the Annapurna 100 and then another running journey right out of the city of Kathmandu and into Langtang.

I had the luxury of time now to learn to know and love Kathmandu's riot of colour, smells, sights and sounds. I felt happy there.

During those spring weeks Richard and I had evenings full of long conversation. One night talk turned to the concept of endurance and the question of why. That is when the idea was born: I would make a third attempt at running from Everest Base Camp back to Kathmandu, Richard would come to support me at Jiri, and we would try to ask those questions.

❖ ❖ ❖

Then darkness falls.

My whole system is suddenly thrown into confusion. It is as though some primal instinct is refusing to believe that there is any actual need to keep running. I have to shut my eyes.

I lie down on the hard and cold tarmac.

There are a few minutes of oblivion, darkness, stillness. I'm in a state of total rest. It is close to what I have experienced in shavasana, the yogic pose of rest. My awareness has turned inwards and my senses have withdrawn.

I rouse myself.

I sense Richard standing there, watching and waiting to see if I can continue. I haul myself back onto my feet and move forwards, my feet and legs relentlessly carrying me blindly onwards.

I am locked deep within my effort, right there in my moment of struggle.

The remaining kilometres are subsumed one by one into the darkness of the night, as though washed away by the pouring rain. The roads are empty of their daytime traffic and incessant buzz of life, but I start to recognise familiar landmarks.

We reach the locked gates of the stadium. It is the end of the journey. I feel a strange relief to be able to stop moving but at the same time I'm disconcerted by the sudden loss of purpose. It is disorientating. There are a few flashes from cameras, I am handed some flowers, a garland is hung around my neck and I ask for a photo with Richard and Upendra. Our friend Dennis has brought a couple of beers, and we share a cupful each standing here in the pouring rain by these locked gates. The small crowd disperses, Upendra is given a lift home by a friend, and our bus delivers Richard and me back to Lazimpat. We have a small sandwich of leftovers and a cup of tea. He hugs me goodbye, I scoop up my belongings, take my keys I'd left with him days earlier and walk slowly back to my borrowed bed the other side of Lazimpat Road. I attempt to shower but it is a half-hearted effort only under the cold water. I give up and bury myself in my sleeping bag.

Tomorrow will be a busy day. I want to help Richard as much as I can, the first edition of his Mustang Mountain Trail Race is just days away and there is a lot still to do.

Everest Base Camp to Kathmandu in just over sixty-three hours. Is that the end of that story, I wonder to myself? But before sleep can overtake me, I realise I know what the real challenge of this journey would be – to run there and back again. Kathmandu–Everest-Base-Camp–Kathmandu with the threefold challenge of altitude, distance and time. Bonkers.

I wonder if I will ever try. And if I do, then why?

Part III

A Journey of Rediscovery and Realisation

Chapter Thirteen

There are only two mistakes one can make along the road to truth;
not going all the way, and not starting.

Buddha (attrib.)

'Tell it how it is,' you said. 'Everything is possible.'

There is a time for everything. There is a time to keep silent, and a time to speak.

I am at Boudha,[1] circling and circling, just one small part of this flowing mass of humanity. Kora after kora around the stupa. Loop after loop. The prayer flags are blowing gently in the wind. The sun has just dropped over the hills of the valley rim, they are clear against the winter sky. You are up there somewhere. Running.

Loop after loop. Kora after kora.

Darkness falls. And I am just part of this flow of movement, circling and circling. I think back to all the nights I have run through. The nights where clouds have obscured any route markings, the nights where there just haven't been any route markings. The nights I have been hungry, cold, soaked to the skin, despondent. The night where I reached a horrible tired-ness that forced me to lie down right there on the ground beneath me and you wondered if I would be able to get up and continue. The nights where I have felt like I can't take another step. And the nights when I have realised I can't not, or there will be no end to the night.

That is what it feels like now. The way forward is uncertain and the darkness thicker than any night I have run through. But I'm moving forwards, I can't not. So it goes, step by step.

Everything that came before had to happen for me to be the person I am now. All that is now has to happen for me to become the person I am. The greatest moments of clarity come when I look back and I realise that it was and is all necessary and all beautiful. This is a journey of rediscovery and a realisation. It is a rediscovery of what running really means to me. And it is a realisation of who I am as a woman.

❖   ❖   ❖

Injury is a hard master, a hard teacher. One that we don't always like to listen to. And yet in the dark places it can take us there is also a wonderful depth of opportunity. The delicate dance between injury and health gives us a space rich in opportunity to learn and to change. Life is shaped by our attitude, by our perception of what it is that is happening, and that is our choice. That is always our choice.

If the Ultra-Trail du Mont-Blanc and everything that went before that led me to stand on that start line was a journey of discovery, and running from Everest Base Camp to Kathmandu and the athletic career that my three attempts spanned were a journey of exploration, then injury and what it is teaching me now is a journey of rediscovery and realisation.

I know the importance of stepping outside of my comfort zone. As a runner I do it in every run, I do it in every race. But if the running itself has become my comfort zone, what then? Being out there alone and just outside what would be perceived to be my comfort zone, is my comfort zone. So what to do? Injury and life are hard taskmasters. Or rather, they are what they are, and I am my own antagonist in the way that I react to them. I am completely out of my depth. It is terrifying and it is fascinating and it is beautiful. This is the magic of life.

'Namaste, didi. Namaste.'

The cheerful greeting jolts me out of my morning ruminations and back to the beauty of now. It is early morning, and I'm sitting on dusty earth, my back against a stone wall in a remote village in a remote mountain valley in a remote corner of Nepal.

I am writing this from the riverside village of Kakkot in Dolpo, northern central Nepal. Tomorrow I head upwards to the base of the mountain I hope to climb – the 7,246m Putha Hiunchuli. This is where I have come to rest, to get perspective, to calm my mind, to soothe my emotions and to feed my soul. I am lucky that I have the luxury of time to make a long and wild journey. But I have also made sacrifices so that I can live this kind of existence. I didn't have to come so far, or leave so much behind. But this time I have.

This is my 'rest cure' as I recover from my sixth stress fracture in two years. No doctor can give a definite answer – as with anything there are a myriad of contributing factors – physical, emotional and mental stress all influence the physical body and will manifest in different ways. I do not want to discuss the specifics of injury. There are already too many experts, books and opinions for that. Instead I want to share the journey that injury has taken me on. I want to share the story of how this prolonged cycle of injury has shifted my perception of myself and the world around me; how it has forced me to explore in different ways and how it has clarified what is important to me about running and about life.

Our spirit, mind, heart and soul are inextricably linked to our physical body, at least in this life, and as we are living it at the moment. Our eyes might be our windows, but it is our feet that connect us to the earth we live on. Yes, that connection is all too often mediated through layers of concrete (pavements) or rubber and plastic (shoes). But what I say holds true. Our feet let us stand, they let us walk, run, jump, they give us motion and balance. They quite literally 'ground' us.

I have a very unbeautiful pair of feet. Of course, beauty is in the eye of the beholder. Still, no one, no one at all, would or could ever say I have nice feet.

I forget about them as much as I can. I ignore them. I hide them away. And yet, as a runner, these unloved, neglected, unappreciated parts of my anatomy are my 'workhorse'. Each foot hits the ground about 500 times per kilometre. They take the brunt of the impact. This repetitive pounding can take its toll.

We are back in Kathmandu now, after the freedom of running on those wild, beautiful sky-high trails around Manaslu. My post-race feet are scarcely visible under the deeply engrained layers of dirt and dust. You suggest a pedicure might be a good (possibly the only) solution. So, I take myself and my feet to a spa, hidden in the heart of Thamel. Almost too ashamed to even take my trainers off, I try to explain that I've been running, for a long way, and for many days. The lovely ladies assigned to help me do just that, and with smiles and laughter. They scrub, clip and massage my rather ugly appendages until they are finally at least clean and a little more presentable. My feet feel like they no longer belong to me. And I walk out feeling like I am walking on air. After all, the washing of feet is one of the kindest acts of service that you can be given.

My feet don't have very much time to rest. After a draining 52-hour door-to-door journey I am all too soon in San Francisco for The North Face Endurance Challenge 50-miler. The form and fitness from my days on the sky-high Nepalese trails is buried deep under the tiredness of the journey, the disorientation of changing, clashing cultures, and just too many nights of sleep lost.

I am drained standing here on this start line. I am physically tired from the travel, still empty from a stomach upset, and emotionally bereft. The driving rain, howling winds and mud aren't so unfriendly once I am completely soaked, buffeted and spattered. By this point I have sort of become rain, wind and mud. The distinction between 'I' and the elements has become a little blurred. Determined to persevere, I reach the finish line in my own sweet time. Somewhere in the sodden, murky, bespattered second half of the race I vaguely remember the start of a fair bit of foot pain. But, ignoring my feet is what I do, no?

Some days later, finally back to my (borrowed) home, I take these neglected feet to the doctor. Tendonitis (the doctor thinks). Great. Pacing the city streets of New York, visiting my younger brother, his wife and their baby twins on my roundabout trip home with my duffel (probably half my body weight) on my back probably hadn't helped. It's something I've had before (in various different places). Something I know will heal if I just give it some time. Bed rest. Well, almost. I give it a few days of no running and as little walking as I can stomach. It wouldn't matter but for the fact I decided I have one last big effort in me for 2012, an attempt at the 24-hour track world record. Time is getting close; should I or shouldn't I sort out the logistics to put myself on the start line? So, I make a test run. Well, two. Just four kilometres each, but there is my answer. After the second test I can barely put weight down on both feet. If I am hobbling around my room now, then it is highly improbable I'll be able to run for twenty-four hours in just a few days. The doctor was wrong. Not tendonitis. This is the first stress fracture.

I am stripped bare by the enforced stop. It takes me right back to scratch. Back to the point to where a ten-minute jog feels like an eternity and three kilometres is endless. It takes time, patience, diligence and hard work, but eventually the fitness, the confidence, the resilience returns.

I return to Nepal and progress to the point of being able to run that 320km or so from Everest Base Camp back to Kathmandu with only a few minutes of something vaguely akin to sleep at most. And follow that almost immediately with awesome racing in the wild beauty of Mustang.

My plan had always been to return to Europe for the summer racing season. But first I need the comfort of being back in the mountains. You get in touch with the organisers of the Everest Marathon on my behalf. And so it works out I can make one last jaunt to the mountains before leaving Kathmandu. It is the sixtieth anniversary of the first ascent of Everest and the Everest Marathon[2] has a 60km category in honour of the event. I decide to try it. I can then run back from Namche Bazaar to Jiri in two back-to-back long days – it will be my last training for my 100-mile race in Andorra. I see the moon full in Thame, have two glorious days crossing the Renjo La and the Cho La, and by the third evening I am back at Gorak Shep just below Everest Base Camp with a day in hand before the race itself.

The morning after the race I wake at 5 a.m. to the sound of incessant rain pattering on the corrugated tin roof of the lodge. The light has already been in the sky for a while, but it is very grey. Grey and very wet. The cobbled passageway is empty, save for one lady, early setting up her wares. I hesitate in the doorway, and then shrug myself into my jacket as though it can shelter me both from the elements and my fragile emotions. It doesn't. The pouring rain turns the trails into rivers of mud and shit. First yak (above about 3,000m), then mule (lower down). Even the mule drivers are in wellington boots. Hours down the trail, shortly before stopping for the night, I feel the first pain in my other foot. I have my suspicions. I sleep in a deserted lodge, eat soup and a chapati by the fire and leave before dawn. It is a full twelve-hour day on my feet again before I arrive at the road-head back in Jiri. After a short night I take the early bus back to Kathmandu. I am almost sure that I recognise this pain, and you persuade me to go and have an MRI. I have to know one way or the other. Planning depends on it. This is the second stress fracture.

Echoing the words of that famous rock band (Queen), who said it better than I ever could, I thought I'd paid my dues already for this year. Done my time. Lessons learned. I was wrong. A second enforced stop. Stress fractures are unequivocal in their demands: no running. Feeling like I am standing on shifting sands I decide to try to yield to the way things are, rather than to resist.

I have long wanted to do a yoga teacher training, Sivananda style. There is one training course with dates that fall exactly across the period that I need to rest from running, in Japan. Determined to turn injury into something positive

I immerse myself in the intense Sivananda training, ashram style, doing without all that had become my normal. I am suddenly stripped of everything; the companionship of friends who have actually become so much closer than just friends, from mountains, from running, from the chaotic beauty of Kathmandu, from language, from bread, from cheese, from sharing coffee or a beer. I am suddenly among a group of people whose lives are so distant from where I think mine belongs that we may never expect to meet again.

And yet, all that matters is right here in our actions and interactions, in the moments that we share.

Flexibility of body brings flexibility of mind. Or so they say? And doing without cultivates strength? Challenge lies in the unexpected corners. Life is a strange mixture of austerities (tapas) and luxury, probably very different things for me than for the other fifty-nine Japanese students. I learn to love the *onsen* (hot springs) with the decadence of full immersion in hot water after months of meagre showers in Nepal. It takes me some time to get used to the idea of constant electricity (no need to keep the headtorch handy), a washing machine instead of a bucket and a brush, and the provision of freshly ironed white sheets. No bread, cheese, cappuccinos or beer in sight. I finally become adept with chopsticks (it's that or go hungry) and try weird and wonderful food (some weird, some wonderful). No running. No mountains. I (re)learn to sit, and I learn to breathe. The day (starting at 5 a.m.) consists of a mixture of meditation, kirtan, asana, pranayama, karma yoga, swadhyaya, philosophy, anatomy, physiology, the list goes on. There are not many spaces in between, so we learn to make the most of the ones there are, just as the body learns to adapt to the new spaces it finds within.

The Japanese people are very nice, very kind, very studious, very quiet, very private, very diligent. Diligent even down to the tucking in of T-shirts for headstands and handstands, yet remarkably comfortable with washing in public (in the *sento*, the communal bathing places), and the concept that such physical proximity brings emotional intimacy. The roads (near our lodging) seem strangely empty, yet those vehicles that are moving do so with unfeasible speed. It is in stark contrast to the roads of Kathmandu which are jam-packed with pedestrians, bicycles, scooters, motorcycles, taxis, buses . . . but all mostly moving at a speed slow enough to stop for a moment's hesitation.

A month later I emerge as a qualified yoga teacher. It is a month rich in learning and experiencing all those things that are mirrored also in ultra distance running, and in life. The cultivation of concentration, focus, mental endurance, dispassion, equanimity of mind. That mindset so eloquently described in Kipling's *If*.

Or so I think.

Until I reach the day when I try running again. Ten minutes. Or maybe not that day, since the realisation doesn't set in during these first couple of preliminary jogs. I'm not asking much. And even finding opportunity during the long journey from Japan to Milan via Kathmandu is in and of itself a distraction. No, it hits a few days later when I am back in the mountains and eager to recreate the feeling of invincibility that had been mine during our days running on those incredible trails of Mustang.

I am wracked by doubt, by fear. All the words I had ever said seem to be coming back to haunt me. You are right, I should tell it how it is, not how I want it to be for other people. The magic isn't always there. And as the body fails, the strength of mind so carefully nurtured seems to fade as easily as haze on a summer morning. Nobody ever said it would be easy. But for a long time easy is how it felt. More or less. Give or take. But this is how it is. For *us* too, some of the time.

By *us* I mean those of us who sometimes find ourselves at the sharp end of a race, out in front, making the podium. Somehow, somewhere along the way, this became my normal, my ordinary. I'm not entirely sure how. Or even why. But I can't really question it, I just have to keep doing what I do, be grateful for the opportunities it gives me and try to use them to some effect.

It is strange though, to reach the point of suddenly realising that it has become normal to be giving interviews. Not only for the speciality press, those idiosyncratic websites and magazines targeting their select, dedicated audience, but no, now even for the broadsheets. To have people I have never met reading about me, knowing about me. Sometimes, even, so they say, being inspired by me. With the advent of social media it has become easy to realise that even though we are the smallest of pebbles thrown into a vast pond, the ripples we make reach further than we can ever imagine. I do mean 'small' though – ultra distance running doesn't (yet) send its ripples as far as those more celebrated sports of football, tennis, Formula One racing, to name but a few.

But still, when people write something, say something or reach back in some way, it is incredibly humbling. That is what gives motivation, or rather, hope that maybe somewhere in all of these seemingly pointless endeavours there is something of worth that extends beyond the 'I'.

To return to my point. Other people could be forgiven for imagining I somehow have it different. They see the good times, the strength, the power, the beauty. But the rawness of complete vulnerability is there for me too. You have seen it too often. The pain, the doubts. All that they feel. I feel it too.

I have rescinded all thoughts of serious racing except for this summer's UTMB. I am going to pour all the effort I can into preparing for that and regaining the fitness I need to be happy to stand on that start line. I'm scared witless by the prospect of the start just seven weeks away, I know how time to prepare is running in all the directions that I am not. Small runs. Very small. Uphill hikes. Also small. Aching legs.

Equanimity of mind? Muscle memory? Both seem to have faded like that haze on a summer morning. The learning and experience are, of course, always still there. But how easily, and how discouragingly quickly, they are buried by the layers and layers of normality beneath which I hide myself in my everyday.

So yes, I also have those days when I am simply too scared to step out the door. Those days when I am too scared to stare in the face of my fears. Those days when I am too scared to accept my weakness.

And then, when I do reach deep inside to find that one remaining sliver of courage and force myself to take a step out onto the trails, I have the answers to questions that I don't even want to ask. That yes, the foot still has that funny sensation in the bone, not exactly pain, but definitely a 'not completely healed' sort of a sensation, leaving the mind open to a deluge of wavering uncertainties of whether or not the foot is ready. That yes, therefore I have to question whether I should yet even be attempting to use it. That yes, the leanness of training has of course fled just at the time when the foot would appreciate as little weight to bear as possible. That yes, going up feels hard, coming down feels hard, and I am not entirely sure how to get through a full hour or two on my feet, even if it is a walk-run with less of the running than the walking.

So I take a day. I persuade myself the foot can't take the strain yet. But my mind doesn't believe me. So the rest turns out to be no rest at all.

And the next day I take all those wavering uncertainties back out on the trail with me.

And the day after, and the day after the day after. And the day after that.

Until, small glimmers of hope appear like the hairline fractures in the bone of the foot that caused the disturbance in the first place. Day by day. Marginal but noticeable differences. Incremental improvements.

I broke into a packet of my precious supply of Mustang (tsampa) biscuits today. And no, I wasn't running hard or fast. But I did run long. That is, longer than I thought I could. This morning I crossed a start line, and this afternoon I crossed a finish line. Less than twenty-four hours passed between deciding to race and reaching that finish. It felt so much longer with its kaleidoscopic medley of emotions, uncertainties, doubts, pain and effort.

The Swiss Alpine K78 (78km) is a race I have won three times already. From the outside it might have appeared to be an off day, well over an hour slower than I would expect to run, all things being equal.

But all things were not equal.

I had tears in my eyes crossing that finish line in fifth place, and probably felt more emotion than when I set the course record back in 2006. This was one start line I wasn't sure I should be on. I was uncertain if the foot would hold. Or if the legs could carry me. Or if the mind would be strong enough. Or if I'd even make it through those fast early kilometres of tarmac and out of town, let alone the rest. The healing of that stress fracture that was so unequivocal in its demands has remained a little too tenuous for comfort.

My plan was, at your suggestion, to imagine I'd written on the back of my T-shirt 'recovering from a stress fracture, please pass me to the right', to take photos, to talk a lot at the refreshment points, to have fun, to walk a lot, to enjoy having company around me. I wasn't sure I knew how not to race, but taking away my own expectations got me to the start line.

The reality? I felt the foot. Caution, and lack of training, dictated a slower than normal pace. But, the legs could still carry me. And the head and the heart wanted to pull on towards that finish line. So it went. Step by step, by step.

It hurt. It wasn't easy. But I ran harder than I thought I would be able to.

Just one short week before, my broken ribs (yoga teacher training not being quite so gentle as I'd imagined) were still giving enough pain to wake me from sleep, my legs were aching from two-hour uphill hikes, and I probably hadn't run even eight kilometres at a stretch. Three days before the race I'd tested myself with a walk-run of 50km. With considerably less of the running than the walking, it has to be said, and taking an unmentionable number of hours, due in part to copious amounts of very necessary 'rock sitting' and 'crumpled heap staring at the sky lying'. Not exactly confidence building. Neither was it adhering to conventional ideas of tapering. But after all, you can't really taper from near to nothing? And, at that point, racing was the furthest thing from my mind.

So, I'm not entirely sure how I managed to finish 78km of mountain racing. But somehow I went beyond what I thought was possible for my body and mind today. I drew so much strength from the words of support, the encouragement from fellow runners, the volunteers, the supporters.

My example is not to be followed. The 10 per cent rule of increasing intensity or volume is (probably) sensible. It does, however, refer to by the week, not by the day, or by the hour. From the very beginning I seemed to flout conventional wisdom, so I have long since abandoned the rule book, and go by feel. This time, even I knew I am asking the improbable, but with the UTMB so fast approaching, I am willing (within reason) to risk throwing some caution to the wind.

Time is marching. I swallow my pride again, and again. I put myself on the start line of another race, another two to be more precise.

So, is this what it means to be an ultrarunner? When my legs feel fresher on the second day of two consecutive mountain marathons (each roughly 2,000m ascent and descent), and that rounding off a 100-mile week. This following a 120-mile week including that 78km race and on two weeks of running after an almost two-month layoff.

And, is this what it means to be a little bit 'crazy', when instead of being thankful to be running at all, and improving day by day, I berate myself for being slower than in the past, for not winning? It's a strange world.

* * *

It is time to forget the doubts and try to turn things around.

So, I forget about the feeling heavy on my feet, I forget my fear. And I remember back to the many times I have done this before. Two long days on the route of the UTMB breaking the journey at the Bonatti hut. It is over halfway, but it always seems to work out OK. They know me there now, they don't seem to mind me turning up at 9 p.m. and begging a bed. The English/French family I am staying with now in Chamonix have been unfailing in their support since that very first year in 2005 when, watching the Internet, they noticed this English girl creeping up the overall placings, and they came out into that dark and rainy evening to see me coming in. The children have grown, but they have become used to my annual pilgrimage and were asking where I was, why so late this summer? Yes, why so late? It's not ideal. After weeks of mostly settled, sunny, clear, hot weather I have chosen the two days with the worst forecast. But time isn't on my side. It is now or never, or there won't be time to make another 'round'.

In the inky dark of pre-dawn I pack my sack. Taking a little more than I like to, just to be prepared in case the weather is as bad as they say. Pouring rain, thunderstorms. Well, I heard the thunder in the night, not the greatest motivation for turning myself out of bed. Tea, bread, jam and a coffee. A last chat with you on Gmail. I shut the laptop. No more excuses. No more reason to delay opening the door. I head out into the murky dawn.

It's not raining though. So I am happy. There is a strange pain in the leg as I start off down the road leading out of Chamonix. But, it passes. I think nothing more of it. I take my time. Cautious to push too much too soon, I am aware still of the foot, aware of the lack of time on my feet, aware of the lack of form. But I am moving, and the familiar landmarks come and go. Along the wooded path that leads me to Les Houches further down the valley. Up and over the Col de Voza, dropping steeply back down to the town of St Gervais. Slower than I'd like, but I am on the way. I pause for a compote, and eat the second too. An hour along, the feet know the way, and Les Contamines makes good its promise of a fresh croissant.

Onwards . . .

My plan this summer has been to give some focus to the great mountain race of Sierre-Zinal, to prepare, to give myself a chance. The fortieth anniversary was an invitation I couldn't refuse. But with the injury and the UTMB training I arrive with just one day of rest after that 168km. I really do know how to do it to myself, don't I? Trying to mix it up with a hugely talented pool of runners in a short, speedy race. Knowing I have no chance, not in all honesty. In a strange way it takes the pressure right off. And I stand on that start line expecting nothing. It is always a fast start this one, I know that from experience. But I forget how slowly my legs move right now and I lose count of the women that are in front of me. I reach the turn that leads off the road and onto the steep path. Upwards, and ever upwards, through the wooded hillside. But the road feels longer than it ever has before. My legs are heavy, I feel like lead. The thought passes through my mind that maybe this is not such a great idea, am I going to have to stop after just a few kilometres? The path steepens even more and I can stop running. Everyone has. Hands on knees I push, and just focus inwards, trying to make the best effort I can. I pass a few women. I start to have fun and decide just to enjoy this part, to get as far as I can. The decision to stop will come or not. The legs somehow manage to pick up the pace on the flat runnable section before Chandolin. Amazingly, I pass a few more women. And I am still enjoying it. The last climb up to the Hotel Weisshorn, finally reaching above the tree line and the kind of mountain trail that I float up. And I do, passing more women. A sip of Coke at the refreshment point, and this is it, that beautiful path heading towards the five 4,000m summits at the head of the Zinal valley. It is a gem, a superbly runnable trail, traversing the length of the valley before dropping steeply down to the village. I pass more women, and feel like I could go quicker. This is good! I remember well. The feet know what to do. I am cautious over the few rocky sections. Still landing on the wrong part of the foot hurts. But it is OK. I can do this. I am nowhere near spent and hitting the road I push, oh so nearly catching that one ahead of me. Slower than previous years but not by too much. I feel a world better than during last weekend's double marathon, despite the 168km in my legs. Improvements. And I didn't feel the foot. Or that strange pain in the leg that had appeared three days earlier.

Another day on the train back to Chamonix. A rest day in the form of an interview and a photoshoot. But, that pain is back. Just a little worrying. Just there.

Dawn breaks again. This time the skies are clear. I make the same preparations, squeezing as much food as I can carry into my smaller sack; then tea, bread, jam and a coffee. No chatting on Gmail this time, but I send you a quick message, shut the laptop, and again the door is waiting to be opened.

This time already feels a little different. I already feel a little lighter on the feet. Just a little.

On this second 'round' I meet many people. It gives me a boost. I realise just how much goodwill there is out there for me. If I could get round on that alone then I would fly. I have asked you to come and support me. I visualise you waiting. I remember how I could draw on the support even from strangers at Davos. I know that you being there will give me extra strength when I have to dig deep. It will make all the difference. I can see myself reaching the finish line in Chamonix after all.

There are just two weeks now until the start of the UTMB and I have left the bustle of Chamonix behind. I am back on the quiet side of the Alps. A rest day to let the 168km drain out of my legs. And then I try again. Fifteen kilometres – up a dirt track and directly back down. The legs feel good. Apart from that one point. The pain is pretty bad. I run through it. I put in the effort. Feeling better than I have all summer on this run. The last excessive week of training has done me good. Except for this damn pain. A mountain biker works flat out to catch me, I am keeping a good tempo and he congratulates me on being in good shape. He keeps me company until my turning point, saying that if he passed me he would only be caught back. I thank him, I smile. But inside I am crying. If only he knew. I should be in good shape (look what the body has to be able to do in just two weeks). But, I should be in better. And, whatever it looks like, it hurts badly. I pause for a moment, turn, ready to fly back down. But I don't quite fly, I pull back a bit, scared of the pain. I feel how I am favouring the leg, the muscles on the other tightening.

I take a day. You tell me, 'Go swimming.'

I take another day. Go swimming again. I know it, I know really, I know what this pain is. But it's OK, I am seeing the doctor today. Nothing shows on x-ray, nothing shows on ultrasound. He gives me painkillers for the race. It will all be OK. Except that I know it isn't.

Another day. The same fifteen-kilometre run. It is hurting pretty bad and I know I am limping. I imagine myself running out of Chamonix, limping, it's laughable. Do I really think I can do it?

I don't run for a day. Again. This could be the one time I really taper. I swim. I think. My mind won't stop thinking.

Another day. I take one of those painkillers and head for that two-hour uphill hike. It is as though the last six weeks of progress haven't happened. I am back to walking out of the village, scared to start, scared of what the pain will tell me. But when I do persuade myself to pick the legs up into a run, purposely at the bottom of the hill so that small steps are excusable, the pain is bearable. I run my way up the runnable part, I push myself through the steeper parts, I gain the summit, the pain is bearable, I am feeling OK. What kind of a miracle is this? I sit for a moment on a rock. The light is incredible. The ridgeline is etched against the deep summer sky. I breathe. I believe again. Maybe, just maybe, I can still make that start line. My spirits lift. I take it easy on the downhill, but I am actually running downhill. I keep believing. There is just one week left until the start of the UTMB.

I am lying flat on my back. Stripped of everything except the blue hospital gown. The inside of the MRI machine has become an all-too-familiar place. Listening to bad radio that doesn't mask the loud reverberations. Nothing to do but to wait, and to think. How many more times will I have to do this? Not really the place to be just days before my race. Better to know? Perhaps? I get the train home. I take another painkiller and head out on that fifteen-kilometre training run again. It feels remarkably good. Relatively speaking. Compared to the last time. What kind of miracles do these painkillers work? Will it be enough? I start visualising myself in the race again. I start running through the different sections in my mind. Possible? Is it still possible?

Back home, I lift the lid of the laptop, it comes back to life. I scan emails and see one with subject 'MRI'. I turn my back, shower, yoga. I am feeling good. I am feeling positive. I am going to make that start line. I turn back to the laptop and read . . .

Oh, it's OK. It's only what I thought. Stress fracture. I feel calm. Nothing has changed. I am feeling good. That place on the start line is waiting.

Then sometime later something clicks. The tears are running down my face. I remember the painkillers. I remember the words stress fracture. Femur. Written down in black and white. Not a feeling. Not a suspicion. Reality.

This is the third stress fracture.

I tried. I really tried. I was patient that first time in the winter. It worked. I came back as strong as ever. I was patient at the beginning of the summer. I gave it as much time as I dared. But in the end I must have pushed too hard too soon. It is hard to know when you cross the line, but that line has been crossed. I know what this means. The femur takes longer than a foot to heal. It could be ten or twelve weeks. No running.

Could I race, still? The pain I can deal with. I have before. And those painkillers help. Could I postpone the 'not running' just for one week? Surely, surely that wouldn't make too much of a difference. I visualised running in pain during those training rounds. I have run through pain before. I know I can do it. Yes, it will be hard. But possible.

Should I? Could I?

Would I really take the risk?

Chapter Fourteen

Anyone who has not seen her inferno, has not seen its cure.

paraphrased from C.G. Jung by Dhir Lalit Priya

Competition and extreme endurance: these were and are a beautiful and vital part of my life – as was the journey of discovery to reach them. But I am a woman. And this means that we are carried forwards on a tide of life that ebbs and flows. Always changing. In the words of Anne Lindbergh: 'The only continuity possible, in life as in love, is in growth, in fluidity – in freedom.'[1]

I am still circling the stupa. Loop after loop. Carried along in this gently moving mass of people. It is darker now.

I told you that my mind has too much control over my body. For a while that was OK. It was how it had to be. It let me do the things that were there for me to do at the time. But it couldn't stay that way, and now my body is talking back. It is soft and heavy. It is disconcerting to be literally inside the physically unknown, but I have to hope it is only time before it reaches a new balance point.

But just as my body has been buffeted by injury, my heart and mind have been exposed to the howling winds of the passions. They will also come back to stillness. Desire, intention, detachment. The acknowledgement and acceptance of desire, the setting of intention, the surrender into detachment.

I told you I was terrified. You asked, 'Terrified of what though? Change from comfort zone?' My answer was that I was more terrified of falling back into that comfort zone. As you said, there are many kinds. This period of injury has forced a shift, turfed me out of what had become my normal. Perhaps it had to be so long and so hard because I was so focused on using my running to explore my limits, to bring me to balance. There are many, many other ways too.

I have had to let go of the storyline. I have had to slow down enough just to be present, to let go of my multitude of judgements, preconceptions, expectations, plans. I'm still struggling. But as you once said, 'The Sufi poets counselled "this too shall pass".'

You said, 'Sometimes things take years to learn, or to discover as true, but still it always comes back, in my opinion, to an active choice about how I want to see the world and my place in it. And it is growing the self-awareness to be able to keep doing that.'

Awareness: running has sometimes been for me an exploration in the art of being, the art of looking, the art of seeking, the art of becoming more aware. It has sometimes been the way I have become more self-aware and at other times it has let me hide behind myself.

I may still compete, I may still go to far-off mountains, I may still make long and wild journeys. I hope I do. But I won't need to. Because there are other ways to explore also – the beauty of *that* run, sitting still, sharing, conversing, creating, loving. Just being there with the raw and tender energy of the moment is enough. You showed me that.

You were there once waiting for me when I arrived back bewildered, scratched and humbled after being lost. I am lost again. This time the scratches aren't from the jungle forest, they are from my habit of taking things to the extreme. I'm being forced to realise this now, I am rediscovering who I am, stripped of all illusions. There is nothing to wait for. Life is only now.

As you said, 'You control your reality and how you look at things.'

Reality: running or a prolonged period in the mountains can give me an experience of this – it heightens my senses and focuses my attention, so expanding the frame within which I explore, leaving me free to experience a deeper reality beyond where I thought those limits were. But other things can too.

How I look at things: yes, I am trying to hold on to faith and let go of belief. A faith that is an unreserved opening of the mind to the truth, whatever it may turn out to be; a plunge into the unknown, without preconceptions – rather than belief with its insistence that the truth is what we want it to be. As Alan Watts says, 'belief clings, faith lets go'.[2]

The choices that we make define who we are. And it is always our choice.

As you said, pointing me towards Andreas Fransson's blog on The Beauty of Choice and the Depth of Now, 'You can choose an answer and make it real! Yay!' Andreas Fransson was a Swedish extreme skier. In this blog he was writing about the death of a friend; he has himself died since we first read these words.

Word after word, situation after situation and feeling after feeling – life goes on like a continuous wave that we can be on top of, under or behind. Whatever happens we will deal with it. And usually how we deal with it, how we feel and what we think about it is a choice we can learn to make (although the cause and effect is in the reverse order). Where we are at this moment is the deepest and most sophisticated, beautiful and incredible place where we can be. And if it isn't, then change the opinion or the situation, both are most often extremely doable. You can choose to create whichever reality you *like*. So then create a reality that *you* like! Life goes on and how we want it to go on is a choice . . . so we might as well make right now awesome. [3]

I'm still circling and circling. Making loop after loop. It is later now. The shops are all shut up. The bustle has died down. The flowing mass of humanity has thinned out. The dogs have roused themselves from sleep and are wandering too. Candles have been lit. Just the flickers of light bear witness to our kora.

❖ ❖ ❖

I put it to you, 'Race anyway. Run through the pain. Is possible.' You tell me about omission bias and bluntly say to me, 'I and others around you can't really let you do that, can we?' Well, no.

I admit I'm thinking about walking at the back of the field, you point out that 'walking 168km is as near as dammit running, no?' and you ask me why I still want to. 'Could be fun,' I say, 'get to say thank you to the volunteers that I never usually have time with, eat blueberry pie, sit on a rock, talk to people and avoid the journalists in Chamonix.' You add, 'love of running, love of competing, feeling left out, envy as they disappear from the start line'. Well yes, all of this and more.

You tell me, 'There is a story in not doing it also, and lessons for others.' This is that story.

You suggest going for a short walk to think about my plans, and how I am going to continue to get my endorphin rushes and mountain views: 'maybe it will be watercolour painting and Houdini-style straitjacket escape artistism'. Both of those are still on my to-try list.

Races will come and races will go. Whether I am there or not. The chance may or may not come again. With the perspective of time nothing ever feels so crucial. But it is easy once we are beyond the situation. How we deal with it in the moment is what is important.

I had put emotional and mental investment into being there on that start line. I had been looking forward to it. Plans were still in place to go to Chamonix, so what could I do but go, to try to keep smiling, and to just experience the 'other' side of the race.

However strongly I am focused on a race, time passes, and I realise that, distressing as it is to me right then, my presence or absence is of course absolutely irrelevant in the long term. That is the strange and disconcerting contradiction of racing. If I really want to focus on a race, and try to get everything out of myself, then for a time, just for a time, I have to delude myself into believing that this race is all that matters. When I step back and use my logic and rationality then of course a race is utterly insignificant.

It is (probably) the same with anything – creating a new project, painting a picture, taking a photograph, writing a poem, making a cup of tea, having a conversation, making love – for that moment, longer or shorter – the rest of the world falls away, the focus is held and it *is* all that matters.

Injury, it is a place I have been before and no doubt it is a place I will be in again. The uncertainty, the waiting, the long slow road to get back to lean fitness has happened before. But each time is new. Each time I wonder 'what if?' What if I can't get back to the fitness that lets me move, to race, to run? And I start to question why I need it.

Running or, more precisely, 'moving on my own two feet' (walking, trekking, climbing, mountaineering etc.) has become part of the rhythm of my everyday. It is what is normal to me. It is what I do. Take that away, and I am like a rudderless boat on the ocean waves. Who am I? Where am I? What am I doing? For if the truth of my running is that in my moving I find myself, then running is the gift that lets me know myself more deeply. So without the running, without the moving, I come face to face with a person I'm not sure I know.

Sometimes this can be scary. But sometimes this is freedom.

It can mean peeling back those layers of self-expectation, of self-definition. Like peeling an onion, it can make me cry. But it lets me stand back from myself, to feel, to watch, to listen, to observe. To become aware.

Simple awareness.

But is that enough to keep me on the right side of the line that I dance between strength and vulnerability? Injury always has something to teach. Whenever and however it comes. But I have been injured just too many times already. I have reached the point where I simply don't want to have to do this again. I feel like I don't have the wherewithal to learn any more lessons. What else can there be left to know? I have nothing left to reach down and pick myself up again. Yet again.

But there is no choice. I have to.

Or rather, there is a choice, and I do.

* * *

The start of the 2013 UTMB comes and goes. I am here. On the sidelines. Cheering.

The hard work has been done. I have put the hours in, I have cried tears of frustration, I have felt hope, I have been forced to swallow my fears, I have raced unfit in training and pushed through to the other side to regain my form. I have reminded my body and mind of every step they will make during the long night and day of the race – they know what it will take. But I have fallen on the wrong side of the line, that fine line between strength and vulnerability. I am powerless. I feel raw.

I see a different side of the race.

Instead of running into the stillness of the night, I am at the Bonatti hut, 88km into the race, eating a meal, sharing wine and sleeping for a few hours. You are here with me, you have still come to support me. We see the entire field through that checkpoint, from first to last. I witness the inspirational and beautiful run of my team-mate from The North Face, Rory Bosio. She achieved what I always thought possible for a woman to achieve within the race of the UTMB. Her sub-23-hour finish in seventh position overall will be remembered as much for her happy disposition as for her absolute supremacy.

I witness people exceeding their own expectations, I witness terrible struggle. I witness smiles and laughter, I witness tears and sobbing. I witness strength and power, I witness utter and complete exhaustion. It is humbling. I encounter absolute generosity from so many who in the middle of their race take the moment to let me know they appreciate me being there.

It is an overwhelming experience.

Before, during and after the race I have to dig deep. Perhaps deeper than ever I needed to when running the race itself. I knew that you being here would give me a deeper strength. I hadn't envisaged that to stand still would need more courage than to race. But it has.

I thought that would be it, just two months of no running, keeping strictly to my self-imposed constraints. I try to be patient. I tread dusty summits in Morocco and, resisting the urge to run, I walk in the breaking waves on an empty beach. I watch waves crashing against the rocks, I hear their song, I feel their power. I wander in souks and feel their vibrancy. I go back to the quiet side of the Alps and try to immerse myself in work.

But I miss the colours of Kathmandu, I miss its gentle dusty chaos, the crying cats, the barking dogs, the thieving monkeys, the red ball of a sun that rises in the morning. It is a city that assaults our senses with its multitude of sights and sounds and smells. It is a city full of poverty, a city full of riches, a city of contrasts and contradictions, but a city where life has a beauty of its own, played out in front of us on the street with a 'namaste' and a smile. I miss it all. I feel the pull back, to that country that never fails to strip me bare and yet fill me to the brim with life. It is time to return to the place that has captured my curiosity and holds my passion.

I arrive back and let myself fall back into the gentle familiarity of life here. And then the morning comes when I finally bend down to lace up my trainers, and take some gentle steps. I feel as though I am starting again at the very beginning. But I have to trust that I will tread the trails step by step by step until I find my feet again. I have a simple pleasure in my return to gentle morning runnings, exploring the trails out of Kathmandu, hearing again the cries of 'hi', 'hello', 'how are you' from laughing village children and dodging dogs, cows, goats and chickens.

Sometimes we find ourselves coming back to running after a time away. And when we do we find it is there waiting for us like a good friend.

There might be a myriad of reasons behind our not running – injury, illness, work, family, absence, discouragement or simply a winding down of effort during a long hot summer or a cold snowy winter. But the running doesn't care about the reason for our infidelity. It is just there, patiently waiting for us.

We may procrastinate, we may give ourselves a thousand reasons why we cannot run, we may try to forget what it is we love about running, we may try to ignore its pull. But there will come the morning when we finally decide that this is the morning; the injury is healed, the commitments have eased, the heat has passed, the snow has melted, or our motivation has simply returned, and we will bend down to lace up our trainers and take some gentle steps.

Whether our time away has been longer or shorter, or even if we have never been entirely absent but just less present, we feel like we are starting again at the very beginning. It is disconcerting, it is bewildering, it is scary. How can something once so familiar feel so strange? The steps have to be gentle ones. We need to have a simple trust that all we need to do is to tread the trails step by step by step until we find our feet again. One step at a time.

It is easy to expect too much too soon. We forget our infidelity. We ignore our absence, our neglect. We think we can pick up exactly where we left off. We imagine that our conversation had no pause. But life isn't like that. Everything needs time. Everything needs a period of readjustment. Even learning to live with or without a good friend, the friend who is always there waiting for us. Running is like that good friend. It is always there waiting for us. But just as we needed time to learn to live without it for a while, so we need time to learn to live together again.

The return has to be slow, it has to be forgiving, it has to be understanding. It needs some give and some take. We need time to become reacquainted. We need to learn to keep each other company again. Us and our running. We need to swallow our pride, we need to dig deep inside to find our remaining sliver of courage. And we need to go back out on *that* run. It is the run we can go to now because it is waiting to enfold us back into its familiar embrace. It is the run that we can go to now in our vulnerability, stripped of all expectations.

We may get dejected, we may get discouraged. We may be daunted by the amount of work to do. We may even absent ourselves for a day or two, uncertain what it is that we are doing. And then we will return and take all those wavering uncertainties back out with us on *that* run.

We have to keep our focus, we have to keep our commitment.

Just as on the yoga mat we have to learn to be fully present, there on that mat, our mat, not anyone else's, so too when we go out on *that* run. Our gaze has to turn into ourselves. It doesn't matter how far into a pose the person next to us can go. It doesn't matter how far into a pose we went yesterday. We have to find our edge in our today. So too on *that* run. It will feel different to before. We cannot compare ourselves to anyone else, or to our before-that-time-away self. We have to find our edge in our today. And then the next day. And the next.

And then the morning will come when a small glimmer of hope will appear. Day by day there will be marginal but noticeable differences. Incremental improvements. The strange will become familiar once again. We will briefly taste the promise of that feeling of euphoria we used to know so well, induced by the endorphins released after having run a long way.

The morning will eventually come when, our infidelity forgotten, we know that the land remembers the rhythm of our feet again, and we can resume our beautiful conversation.

I feel strangely nervous as I return to the Manaslu Mountain Trail Race. This is a first for me, to join a race with the intention of not running as hard as I can. It is a step outside of my ordinary, but there is no better place to take gentle steps back to form after injury. There is no better place to share some tears and fears, some laughs and smiles. There is no better place to explore off the beaten track with few distractions and to just spend time in the mountains and with good friends, old and new. I am happy to be back here on these sky-high trails under these deep-blue skies and fluttering prayer flags.

I am loitering in the in-between – running but not racing. It is a beautiful place to be, just surrendering to the happiness of being able to run and walk back in a place that had changed me more than I realised it could.

Our part-circumambulation around Manaslu draws to its natural conclusion and, with a brief respite in Kathmandu, we leave immediately for the wilds of Mustang and a small, intimate winter edition of the Mustang Mountain Trail Race. I run harder, my feet learn again to beat a happy rhythm. I hurl myself down steep descents through indescribably awesome canyons. Magnificent running in an incredible landscape in great company – dusty legs, happy days. I become aware once more of that feeling of strength, tempered by the inevitable realisation of just how insignificant I am, and what I am doing is.

For me Mustang is the place where there are no limits, real or perceived. It is a place where my soul expands to fill the space between earth and sky. There is no place like it. Just as you told me.

I gain enough strength and fitness to feel I am on my way 'back'. I start to look forward to 2014 and the challenge of racing again.

Back in Europe, I read some words written by our friend Roger about trends on the trail. It makes me think. It has been a year where injury has time, after time, after time, forced me to consider what it is that I do when I run. And 'run-walk-hike-jog-trek-and-occasionally-sit-for-a-few-minutes' has certainly had its place.

While the competitiveness will always be there when the occasion calls, I have learned also the value of the social side of running, which is not necessarily just running with people. Rather it is the talking, the sharing, the exploring of our mindset and our world. Whether that is during, before or after running. I (re)learned the importance of that. Sharing a physical activity such as running encourages people to open up and be accepting of those with whom we are sharing. This is the first requirement for real discussion. I realise the gratitude I have towards all of those who have shared the trails with me. And I realise an even deeper gratitude towards those who have gone on from the trails to spend hours of life discussing everything and nothing with me.

A new year brings new hope and, for the runner, new lines to cross.

There is a saying here in Nepal that says it how it is. *Ke garne?* A beautiful Nepali phrase that translates literally to 'what to do?' but really represents an attitude, a mindset, a philosophy.

What to do? – because sometimes we just don't know. And when we don't know what to do; then what do we do? We just go on doing what we do. We go on trying, we go on failing, we go on trusting, we go on loving, we go on living.

Ke garne? It is something we would say when we are faced with a difficult, frustrating or challenging situation. It is what we would say if we had a pain in our leg that worsened on steep inclines; but when rest would be out of the question because our daily chores involved walking long distances up and down hills to collect wood and leaves; and those leaves and pieces of wood that we gather would be what allow us to cook and heat our home.

Ke garne? What to do? It is a saying that doesn't ask for an answer but simply describes that feeling of being between a rock and a hard place. It is a saying that accepts and surrenders to how things are. Because only then can we decide how to react or not react to a situation.

I start the new year with hope. I race fifty kilometres on the rim of the Kathmandu valley, slowly, not full out. It is lovely. I have fun, and stupidly I start to look forwards.

Then pain. In the tibia. A long spell of no running, again. *Ke garne?*

This is the fourth stress fracture.

I'm lucky. I don't actually have to walk up and down hills to keep the wheels of life turning, to keep warm, to eat. I don't have to gather leaves and wood just to let me cook and to let me heat my home. When in Kathmandu, life has its own challenges, for sure, twelve- to eighteen-hour power cuts, intermittent Internet, sporadic hot water, the list goes on. But I have choices. I have a bed to sleep in, food to eat. So life is easy. I don't need all that much when I think about it. Or at least the things that I really need aren't of the material kind.

Why do I run? It is an expression of who I am. That is why I run. Simply that. But there are other expressions of whatever is 'me' also. And I can make the choice not to run for a while.

But there have been too many days when I have had to make that choice. I have gone for hours on a borrowed bike. Children have said hello. And when children say hello, it demands an answer with a smile. They don't need to know that I am crying inside. Because with every injury it gets that little bit harder to keep trusting, to keep believing. And so I smile.

Time passes. I heal. Again the morning comes when I finally bend down to lace up my trainers, and take some gentle steps. I go back to Mustang. I fall in love with pink dots and my new-found role starting at dawn to mark the route for the others. The initial hard work to regain some strength is done here on these wild, sky-high trails. The land here knows the rhythm of my feet now. My legs ache on the long uphill climbs, my heart learns to work again keeping a pace on these rolling, superbly runnable trails above 4,000m and I recover some of my natural proprioception as again I hurl myself down these steep descents through indescribably awesome canyons.

We come home and I start to find again the fragile peace that comes with the beautiful rhythm of a daily run. Rising quietly above the tumult of the city below, the hills of Shivapuri welcome me back as I make my longest run in four months. I know them well by now, I know them with the intensity of racing, the more benign pace of training and with an unhurried walk. I know them green and lush in the post-monsoon fecundity, I know them sparse and dry. The groundwork is in place. This is my turning point: the days, the months stretch ahead of me. I start to hope, I start to dream again, I start to believe I will race this summer.

I took care. As much care as I could. And then?

And then I find myself lying on my back. Staring into a blue sky. Dust catching in my throat. Dust catching in my eyes. Giving an excuse for the sob and the tears that are already there. But I am alone on the rooftop. There is no one to listen, no one to see. I can hear the sound of dogs barking in the alley far below and the low hum from the rumble of the road – with its fascinating mix of pedestrians, bicycles, scooters, motorcycles, taxis, buses, all punctuated by the sounds of horns hooting. Pain. In the ankle. No recollection of having twisted or turned it. The pain is simply there. An MRI, a physio appointment, and an orthopaedic doctor's appointment later. And I am here lying on my back. Staring into the blue sky. My foot strapped to half a cast, and crutches waiting.

This is the fifth stress fracture.

I can run more than a hundred miles. I have done so on countless occasions now. In training, in racing and for fun. So why does the prospect of two weeks on crutches scare me? Why does it feel an act of endurance that is beyond me? I have huge blisters on my hands. My arms are aching, my leg is tired from holding itself up with the added weight of the cast, my ribs are bruised, my whole body is sore from its uncommon effort. I have fallen off a chair and very nearly tumbled off the kerb. I can't carry my cup of morning coffee from kitchen to desk. And this is the first twen-ty-four hours.

Whether the crutches are strictly necessary is debatable. But if it speeds healing it has to be worth it.

I miss the running. But beyond that I miss the loss of freedom to jump on my bike to do my errands, the loss of mobility to the point where the easiest of tasks takes an unfamiliar effort. It reminds me just how precious a gift our movement is. And that loss reminds me how fine the line is that divides me from what I want to be able to do and what I can do.

I will run a hundred miles again, but lying on my back on this empty rooftop staring into the blue sky I know that every hundred metres is a reward for the effort it takes.

I endure, I have to. My body adapts, it learns quickly and my mind learns to surrender yet again to how things are. My world shrinks to the world I can move about in.

My arms grow stronger and my world grows bigger. I go to Bhutan, I support a marathon I had been invited to run and I meet some wonderfully interesting people, I give a talk. And still on crutches I haul myself up a mountain path to the iconic Taktsang Palphug (Tiger's Nest) Monastery, 900m above the valley floor.

I am humbled by the response I receive and to be thanked for my effort by the devotees who pass me. They don't perceive my effort to be limited to my own personal challenge, injury having been caused by my devotion to my habit of running, a habit of questionable use or significance to anyone beyond myself. Instead they perceive my effort to be also for them, for us all, for something beyond ourselves. In reality it is my innate stubbornness, and a severe form of self-reliance, that powers me up and down. But that response puts things into perspective for me; it is the same feeling I have when people thank me for inspiring them, for winning a race, giving a talk, sharing a piece of writing. Sometimes the effort that we make does go beyond the personal, it is instead somehow an offering.

I give away my crutches and get my freedom back in return, in the form of being able to go out to buy a packet of milk without need for major expedition, carry my morning coffee from kitchen to desk and to jump on my bicycle at a whim. The simple things of life have become very sweet. And then again the morning comes when I finally bend down to lace up my trainers, and take some gentle steps.

I return to Europe for the summer and gradually ease myself back into the running. I progress from not being able to run a few flat kilometres to making a decent effort on a fifteen-kilometre up-and-down, I progress from small power hikes to multi-day walk-runs around the Tour de Monte Rosa and from Zermatt to Chamonix.

Every day it takes courage to step out the door. Each day

is slightly better than the last. I wonder if I can dream of the Tor des Géants, that mammoth 330km Endurance Trail in the Val d'Aosta of Italy. The idea slowly takes a hold of me, so much so that I write to the organisers and am offered a wild-card entry. I even write asking if you would consider coming over to support in lieu of my did-not-start at the 2013 UTMB. Your response is that you will always consider Alpine follies, but that this sounds like 'driving Paris–Dakar when you're OK with the engine but not entirely sure of the suspension'. That is it in a nutshell: every day I go out fearing that this will be the run, this will be the day when a new pain will materialise.

That day comes. The suspension fails. This is the sixth stress fracture.

A six- to eight-month break from running seems preferable to uncertain intervention with drugs.

And so, this is how I find myself in this dusty, windy village of Kakkot in this remote valley, in this remote corner of Nepal.

What next? I don't know where the answer lies, or even what questions I should be asking. *Ke garne?*

As Samuel Beckett so wisely said in *Worstward Ho*: 'Ever tried. Ever failed. No matter. Try again. Fail again. Fail better.'[4]

Chapter Fifteen

You only are free when you realise you belong no place – you belong every place – no place at all.

Maya Angelou, *Conversations with Maya Angelou*

I'm still circling and circling. Loop after loop. It is deserted here now. Just the wandering dogs and me. I keep circling. It is getting colder. The stars are bright in the sky. I keep circling, not rushing, not dawdling, just here and present, surrendering into now.

Belonging. It is what I mean when I say the word home.

Home. It is defined as a place of residence, a congenial environment, the focus of our domestic attention, the place where we are at ease and in harmony with our surroundings. But you can reside in a place for a moment or a lifetime, it is nothing to do with where you live. Home is no place and every place.

We have talked over and over again about this. You still think that home for me is the answer that I give in interviews – the mountains. The truth is more complicated. Yes, I can feel at home in the mountains. I can also feel at home walking through the breaking waves. I can feel at home here circling this stupa at Boudha. Home is simply that feeling of being fully present, fully in my environment. And that sometimes happens more easily in nature than in the city. But, home isn't limited to this either. I've learned that now. I have come to realise that it doesn't have to be a place, it can be a person, or a feeling I have for a person, or the emotion within me that person evokes. It is love.

External circumstances are always going to change – whether by our choice or not. Everything can be taken from us except our attitude in a given set of circumstances.[1] So ultimately home and belonging has to be within ourselves or we will always be lost.

Belonging to no place, every place, no place at all. This is freedom. I have learned the truth of this time over again.

I learned the truth of this sitting on a stile on the South Downs Way, on that very first longer-than-marathon run, looking over the pastoral landscape before me, much of it owned, but that was irrelevant perhaps. I had made that landscape my own by running through it, by experiencing it, by feeling it, by being present in it. It didn't matter that I didn't have a garden to call my own; nature is our birthright, no one can give it to us, no one can take it from us. Mary Frye put it beautifully: 'I am a thousand winds that blow. I am the diamond glints on the snow. I am the sunlight on ripened grain. I am the gentle autumn rain.'[2]

I learned the same truth sitting high above a mountain tarn in Snowdonia. Cuddled by the mountain at my back, I could have been in a bird's nest. I looked out over what lay before me. It wasn't mine. It belonged to no one (or perhaps the Snowdonia National Park). But in that sense it belonged to us all. And I had found my bird's nest on my own two feet. No one could take that moment from me. That moment of knowing the land and I were one.

I felt its truth somewhere below the Rui La. Lying for a while there with you, the rough grass beneath us, staring into a deep-blue sky, an incredible wild mountainscape before us and with life feeling full of infinite possibility.

I've learned it many times since. Near to Zmutt (a tiny

hamlet above Zermatt) nestled into the rock behind me, staring up at my mountain of mountains, the Matterhorn. All of those places that belong to no one belong to us all. If we explore them we make them our own. I ran to where I know a patch of edelweiss grow, they were there waiting.

I can only go so long before I need to lie on the bare earth, feel its cold, feel its heat, feel it as it is. People sometimes find it hard to understand that I can prefer to lie there on the bare earth, nothing between it and me, nothing to cushion the hardness. It might mean my pants are ever dusty but I need that intimate connection, it is what I miss when I'm not running. Bleak nights in Kathmandu I have lain on the rooftop, even in the cold of winter, simply to see the stars above me and to feel the cold air on my face.

We belong to those places we reach under our own power, on our own two feet. And we belong to each other when our belonging is an undemanding offering of love, asking nothing, giving all. Freedom. When we are home we are free.

❖ ❖ ❖

'Namaste, didi. Namaste.'

The cheerful greeting again jolts me out of my morning ruminations as I walk back through this dusty, windy village of Kakkot in this remote mountain valley in this remote corner of Nepal. I left our 4,500m camp at dawn while the rest of our group were still sleeping; it will be a long day ahead so I was eager to get an early start.

Our attempt to climb the 7,246m Putha Hiunchuli has been thwarted by heavy snowfall during Cyclone Hudhud. So too have my hopes of walking home from Dolpo via the rarely crossed 5,700m Mu La into Mustang.

Eager still to return under my own efforts I have left the rest of our group to make their slower descent. I have ahead of me two long days following the Thuli Bheri river right to the 'road-head' – a walk usually completed in seven days (or more). From there I face a nine-hour local jeep ride on a half-made track and a twenty-four-hour bus journey. I'm not entirely sure why a longer walk and a long bus ride feel more appealing than a slower, shorter walk and a plane ride, but they do.

I have moments of abject regret during the long night hours of this awful bus journey, half-standing, half-sitting in the aisle, putting my uncertain trust into the unknown competency of our driver. There is a chirrup from my phone. 'Location update?' you ask. 'Hell,' my reply.

But my reward is making the journey under my own effort and the experiences that it gives me. I feel again the tiredness that comes with fourteen-hour days of walking, the feeling of space that comes with time to think alone. The reception I have from local people tells me that not many foreigners travel this valley, indeed I see no others until the end of my bus journey back in Kathmandu. But despite the obvious poverty I receive a humbling generosity – I am offered tea, fed dal, given a bed, people talk to me and they look after me – even on this desperately long and wretched bus journey. Where language fails us we talk in smiles and eye to eye.

Inevitably our expedition plans had to bow to circumstance. But I still made a long and wild journey, and I learned from it. I found no answers there, no startling new perspectives, but it gave my body the space to move and my mind some quiet time to think.

Thinking about perspective reminds me of an experience I had in the winter of 2013 training on skis instead of running during the period of recovery after that first stress fracture.

The mountains taught me a lesson this morning. I lesson that I've learned before, and will learn again. And again and again.

This morning I wanted to train on my skis. To skin up a route I have come to know so well. I know how long it will take, I know where to push, where to ease up. I know what I will see when I reach a certain rise. I know each turn, curve, undulation. I know how it will feel with almost every glide of my skis beneath me. I know how the river will fall away to my side. I know just when I will start to feel I have reached the sky as I come level with the summits around me.

But today the mountains had another idea. Snowfalls over the past few days meant that after a beautiful dawn it was time to start shooting down the avalanches. So, I was stopped in my tracks. I had to take a new route. Into the unknown. A way I hadn't skinned before. The way was gentler in places, it took longer to gain height. It gave me a different view and a new perspective.

And on that long skin up towards the sky I realised what I was being reminded of. The world is as it is, and I am as I am. It will snow when it snows. The wind will blow when it blows. The sun will shine when it shines. I cannot make things as I want them to be, need them to be, or wish them to be. They are as they are.

But that is the magic of life.

I have to learn to flow. To flow with the ups and the downs, around the twists and turns, into the corners, into the wide open, to turn myself inside out and stand on my head if need be. I'm not saying I shouldn't fight for the truth of what I believe. It is just that sometimes the truth isn't what I wish it was. I cannot bend, shape, fold the world into how I wish things were. Instead I have to bend, shape, fold myself to follow the course that life throws before me; when things feel harsh or difficult, as well as when they are gentle and easy. Being grateful for what is there, for what I have in that moment, rather than wishing for more, lest what I have in that moment is taken from me.

I have to fight for what I believe to be true, but I cannot let my will, my wish, my want, delude me. Nothing is permanent, life is in constant ebb and flow. I have to go with it. Things are as they are, and that is OK. It is always OK.

Henry Thoreau said, 'The question is not what you look at, but what you see.' And what we see is our choice. Perception is the act of apprehending by means of the senses or the mind, of understanding, of having insight, intuition and discernment. Perspective is a particular attitude towards or way of regarding something, a point of view. Perception and perspective. As they say, beauty is in the eye of the beholder. Nothing is good or bad in itself. It just is.

Snow: might be wonderful for me as a skier, terrible (or at least unwanted) for me as a runner looking for dry trails. But snow is neither good nor bad in itself. My experience of it depends entirely on what I make it. It depends entirely on my perception and perspective. This is an incredibly empowering thought, because that then means that I have the power to colour my experiences and so live the life that I choose. If I choose to. 'Your choice,' as you so often say.

'It was a beautiful run all in all,' you said. It was. But if beauty is in the eye of the beholder then finding it is also a choice and it can come in many guises. Sometimes I find it in the hidden corner or the most unexpected of situations: the compassion in the kindness of a touch, gesture or word from a good friend; sharing moments with friends who know the 'Lizzy' that the world doesn't always see; a piece of writing, some music, a work of art, a photo that so perfectly captures that fleeting emotion; the sight of a snow-covered ridge stark against a deep-blue sky in the fierce cold of the winter mountains; the first flower of springtime; stars in a clear night sky; a full moon; in creating community around; in the happy laughter of a child; in the smile of a stranger.

Watching somebody doing something well is a gift. Whether it is in the baking of a loaf of bread, the making of a cup of coffee, the playing of a piece of music, the writing of an article, the washing up of a cup. So yes, some might tend to inspire more than others. But witnessing anything done well, or with full attention or awareness, has the power to provoke me to also put my full effort into whatever it is that I have to do.

I see beauty when an athlete is an absolute master of their craft, and executes an elegant race with passion. But, I don't only see beauty there. I see it also in the middle-of-the-pack runner who sacrifices so much to get to the start line, and to finish. I see it also in the courage and determination of the back-of-the-pack runner who has to dig deep to make it to the end. I see it in the generosity and kindness of the volunteer. First, last or there in support is possibly irrelevant (particularly in ultrarunning where prize money is a rare reward). What matters is that search for the edge. For each of us our edges are in a different place, and those places are constantly changing. But the search to find them can teach us more about ourselves.

There is a time for everything. We know it but it is sometimes easier to remember than others. Inevitably. At different times during my life, beauty will have a different expression and I will find different edges to explore. The pursuit of excellence and of mastering my craft (whatever it is at that moment) will be realised in different ways. This will take me from passing exams, to being buried in work, to winning races, to climbing mountains, to nurturing relationships, to sustaining friendships, to creating community, to giving, to taking . . .

As a child I was fascinated by abstract concepts like infinity even while being rooted in the experience of running and feeling 'home' to be in the mountains. Both these seeds grew in my adolescent reading of popular science on the one hand and high-altitude mountaineering and polar exploration on the other. These strands carried over and ran parallel in adult life through my professional life as an environmental scientist exploring the polar world, and in my personal life – learning to climb, to explore, to wander the mountains, to run. An academic or professional concern for the environment was mirrored by my love of immersing myself in it, or vice versa. Worlds collided as I tried to explore physical, mental and conceptual limits. The emotional ones were to come some time later.

Older now, I still have few of the attachments that have become normal in much of the world. I have no house, no car, just that one bicycle in Kathmandu and that laptop that travels the world with me. It is a fairly Buddhist way of life. Or that's what I liked to think. Until I realised the attachment I have to certain situations, such as taking for granted a physical ability that will let me explore to my limits (even beyond the physical). Because of course exploring those limits is actually completely and utterly irrelevant. Talking with you made me realise that. The explorations themselves are, of course, not without value because they are what make me who I am, but the only thing that is important is that I find the way to share them, to use them to make a difference in someone else's life. Otherwise, then yes, they are completely and utterly irrelevant.

Running is, of course, a luxury. But it does give a context within which to cultivate physical, mental and emotional health. It gives me discipline and provides me with the motivation to question myself – to decide what among the myriad of obligations of daily life is most important. It allows me to put myself in situations in which I am challenged and forced to step outside of my comfort zone. As a runner I do it in every run, I do it in every race.

So what does happen when the running *is* my normal, my comfort zone? What then?

I thought I knew what humility was. But I realise now that it is something very different to modesty. I can afford to be modest about my achievements, I can be modest in the way that I live, I can be modest in my interactions with others. But it is a choice that I make. And a choice that I sometimes live with more grace than other times. I am human. But real humility is not a choice. It is what is left when I have been broken again and again. It is what is left when I am stripped bare. It is what is left when my dreams are in shattered pieces, it is what is left when all I have worked for is taken from me and I am forced to start over again. And then start over again, again. It is what allows me to try to believe that I'm not broken after all and that I can learn to dream new dreams. It is again what Kipling was talking about in his elegant masterpiece *If*.

If life is magical then language is the structure of magic.[3] Language has a fascinating power that we don't always appreciate. How we think affects the language that we use and the language that we use affects the patterns in which we think. Our use of grammar is essentially how we fit dictionary words into context, and that inevitably has implications for how we take responsibility for things, passively or actively.

We have had some heated discussions, you get frustrated by my almost pathological reluctance to accept the enormity of some of the things I have achieved. You have a point. At the far end of the spectrum modesty is destructive, a self-indulgent denigration. Take anything to the extreme and it is dangerous. I have a strange and probably unnecessary tendency to dismiss anything I have done. It comes of that inner drive of always wanting to do my best. You have this drive too, which means you recognise it (and other things) too clearly in me. But I never quite reach the point of doing my best, because what I do has become my normal and this then is the mark against which I judge everything that I try.

There is some representation of how we think about ourselves, how we see ourselves, how we want to present ourselves in the language that we use. It is only now, years later, talking at length with you that I realise my almost wilful misuse of language in the way I even thought about my running. It negated my taking responsibility for those good races, while feeling it so keenly for those races in which I felt I could or should have done better. It begs the question of what would have happened if I had been more accurate in my use of language then, even just in my thinking. Would anything have changed? Would it have made a difference if I could then have taken an active possession of those times when I did (despite what I thought I felt) perform well? Modesty is also a fault when taken too far. Everything in moderation, including moderation, as the saying goes.

Our exploration of reality is framed by the limitations of our attention and our sensory awareness. Most of us are guilty of deletions, omissions and generalisations in the language that we use. This diminishes the world that we know and constrains our perspectives. It can be hard to change habits in the way that we use language to communicate the world that we experience, but it is important at least to develop the self-awareness to recognise what we do and when we do it. It has implications for the choices that we make.

Fear is sometimes the harshest limit on our exploration of reality. It rocks our fragile equanimity. And we are all afraid. That fear is, more often than not, either a fear of the unknown, or a fear of failing, or a combination of both. Both the known and the unknown can be utterly terrifying.

As you said, 'Almost everything in the head comes down to fear of one thing or another, wouldn't you say? It's not easy to face up to your fears, to write them down, to take slow steps forward to get over them, or just open up to them whatever they may be. What fun!'

Well yes, because the biggest adventure in life can be to fail since it is then that we live and realise what it is to live. We are not our fears. If we can face them, let them pass through us and beyond, then they will simply come and go. We can watch them, be aware of them, but we start to understand that they don't define us.

Some of us are afraid to stand still. Some of us are afraid to climb mountains. Some of us are afraid to dive into the sea. Some of us are afraid to try something new. Some of us are afraid of the 9 to 5. Some of us are afraid of things most people would totally understand. I am afraid of things most people would laugh at, if only they knew.

Anxiety flourishes in the gap between what we fear might and what we hope could happen. If we have the courage to come to terms with the worst possibilities, then when we look at our fears we realise that we would cope even if they came to pass. We know ourselves and our small part of the world better than any other, so of course in our own minds we have an exaggerated importance and the small incidents of our lives loom large, with a significance out of all proportion. Necessarily so! But if we can keep some perspective then we can also hold on to our equanimity.

Once I went to the mountains to open up my world – literally and metaphorically – the higher I climbed the further to the horizon I could see and the wider my perspective. It put things in context, reminding me of my insignificance, of just how big the world is and how small my place in it. It still does, but I don't need to find that only there now. Instead it is the talking to people, the trying to understand how it is for other people that gives me new perspective and allows me to perceive things in a different way. I realise now that you have been showing me this. I'm still learning. It is the same but different – just two strands of the same thread . . .

For years, I thought I was happy to be alone, preferred it that way. Being, by nature, a person who never minded being alone or fending for myself, it was easy. And I rattled comfortably along in this world of my own making for a while. But life gives us a long rein for only so long. Life demands more of ourselves than we demand of ourselves. It strips us bare. It rips away all that we thought we knew. My self-sufficiency, my self-reliance, my independence, were illusory just as everything is.

They are traits of absolute necessity when you run. Any length of run. On any terrain. But it is only when body and mind are taken towards the edge of what they can cope with that we remember. And the edge is always in the unexpected – it is not in the race long trained for – it is in the unplanned-for illness, the mental turmoil, or the emotional anguish.

In the running I have these traits to a fault. But there is, perhaps, a tragic contradiction. We are born, alone. We die, alone. But from birth until death we are social beings.

I have always been comfortable in my own company. Being a runner this is just as well since inevitably I am alone with myself for long periods of time. And being alone is never the same as being lonely. I can be completely alone but not lonely when I feel the love of a good friend with me. I can be terrifyingly lonely in a crowd, with a few, or with one, if that precious connection has been lost even momentarily.

There is a strange and wonderful dichotomy in life; we absolutely need the support of each other but ultimately we can rely only on ourselves. No one is going to pick us up from the tarmac and run for us. Just as nobody can live for us.

Connection, whether with ourselves or with others, is all about being present. As Parker Palmer put it so well:

Solitude does not necessarily mean living apart from others; rather it means never living apart from one's self. It is not about the absence of other people – it is about being fully present to ourselves, whether or not we are with others. *Community* does not necessarily mean living face-to-face with others; rather, it means never losing the awareness that we are connected to each other. It is not about the presence of other people – it is about being fully open to the reality of relationship, whether or not we are alone.[4]

My time at sea in the Antarctic taught me how we do the best with what we have, from where we are, right now. Once we leave shore, our world dwindles to the size of the ship. No equipment, no personnel can join. We have to make things work with what we have. The people we live with become our world. There is an intensity that is diluted in our everyday where, ironically, we can easily lose ourselves in anonymity, detached from those closest to us. At sea we live in a forced proximity. We may have nothing in common. But we learn to care for and about each other. We have no choice. We live each other's ups and downs. We learn how to give space when there is no physical space to give. We observe the extremes of excitement, happiness, inadequacy, boredom, frustration. We experience them ourselves. It is humbling. Despite the immensity of the landscape (or seascape) surrounding us, we cannot escape the wonderful yet terrifying limitations of being human.

It is the same on a mountain expedition. It is the same on a multi-stage race.

It is the same during an ultra distance race or challenge.

Except then we also realise how alone we are. For despite

the strength that the support and goodwill those around us can give, we are in fact totally and absolutely reliant on ourselves. No one can run for us. No one can make the effort for us, we have to make our own way from start to finish. This is life.

All that matters, perhaps, is what we give each other, and what we allow others to give to us. Because that is all that is left.

'A hundred miles is a life in a day,' said the legendary ultrarunner, Ann Trason.

It can feel like this. And a long race certainly mirrors a life. It has its ups, its downs, the times when it feels almost easy, the times when it feels like I am fighting hard just to stand still, the times when I am sharing (with fellow competitors, volunteers, supporters present and absent), and the times when I feel entirely alone.

But a race is simple. It may not feel so at the time. But there are, if many, just a limited number of variables: our health, our fitness, our preparation, our mental state, our happiness, the weather, the route, the terrain. We could divide it further, but the variables can be defined by what the environment throws at us, and what our body and mind throw at us.

But, life? We have talked about this. Life is another matter. Life is complicated. Despite the independence that we congratulate ourselves on, despite our admirable self-reliance, we are social. And we interact with others. It can take different forms. And other people are the unknown. We have no power. We have no power over how they will react, interpret, behave, act, love, live. And so life is complicated. Magical. But complicated.

Chapter Sixteen

Lines. The lines that we cross and the lines that we don't cross.
The start line of the race we didn't plan to run.
The finish line that we never thought we'd reach.
The red line we came almost too close to.
The fine line between doing too much and not enough.
The line that dangles us precariously somewhere
between injury and being in the form of our life.
The line that marks the boundary of what we thought was possible.
The line that signifies the edge we are pushing towards.
The line that is our sutra, the thread that pulls all the
terrifyingly beautiful disparate parts of our life together
and takes us right back to where we started.

The light is coming back now. Dawn is breaking and colours are flooding the sky. I'm still turning around the stupa. Circling and circling. The wandering dogs are my only company. Day has followed night. The innate grace in these repeated refrains of nature is somehow reassuring. They are a mark of constancy in an uncertain world.

Modern physics tells us that nothing is solid, that the physical world is one large and ever-changing energy field. Our senses perceive this sea of energy from a limited standpoint and we create an image of our world from that. These wandering dogs are experiencing the world very differently to me, hearing a different range of sounds as they do. Neither they nor I have a complete or accurate picture of the world. Neither is right, neither is wrong. Mine is just one interpretation and based on the idea of reality that I have built up through all the experiences I have had throughout my life so far. You will have another and different interpretation.

Our experiences of running are probably also very different. I fret about how to tell others about what running means to me: 'but running doesn't feel normal to me at the moment, it is hard remembering how I feel about it and hard to know how I want to write about it.' You tell me, 'You can imagine it better than anyone though. You are always an authority on your own experiences, and no one can contradict what you experienced.'

I struggle over the prospect of trying to finish *Runner* with an unfinished story of injury: 'Wouldn't the message be stronger that I can go through a tough time and come out the other side, in whatever way that turns out to be?' You tell me bluntly, 'But the other side *is* the dealing with the tough time, not the eventual phoenix rising from the flames.'

Yes, this is the real story, the tough time. Life is not a race, there is no finish line, there is no ending, happy or unhappy. All that we have is the journey that we are making and the attitude with which we make it. There is a powerful opportunity in this chaos if I just have the courage to rest in its uncertainty.

The challenges we face only ever match what we can deal with at that moment. And these challenges are constantly changing. Nature is full of obstacles. On the trail we let our run be a beautiful flowing movement over the rocks and the roots. This is our lesson in our everyday too – not to struggle against the obstacles that come up, but to learn from them, to let them go, to surrender into life, because it is also a beautiful flowing movement when we stop resisting, when we stop struggling.

We have a choice how we to react to any situation. We always have that choice. And as you tell me, 'You don't have to wait for things to get better or change because they may or may not, or it may be quick and it may not, and things may get better and you might still feel pathetic.' We create our world by our attention and our intention. So we can choose to make our world how we want it to be. It is always our choice.

Loop after loop. The prayer flags are again blowing gently in the wind. The sun has risen over the hills of the valley rim, they are still clear against the winter sky. I make one last turn around the stupa. I am going now. It is time to say hello to the waiting morning. I'm going to cycle home through the streets still empty of their daytime bustle. And as I cycle I will be remembering *that* run. You know the one.

❖   ❖   ❖

If I am a runner, then who I am when I cannot run? It is a question I have been asking myself time and again during these months of injury after injury. Running is just one expression of who I am, but it is a fairly fundamental one. So when I'm not running, am I still a runner? I still wrestle with the answer. I say to you, 'That I'm not "Lizzy" at the moment doesn't help.' You ask, 'If you are not "Lizzy", who is? What is "Lizzy"?'

What is our concept of self, and can we trust it?

She slipped her small hand in mine. That simple gesture of trust reminded me of everything our race was about: confidence, hope, positivity. We were running across a footbridge high above the Budhi Gandaki river. We exchanged words and smiles with some village children walking home from school, but something made one small girl want to prolong our brief connection. Leaving her friends, we jog-trotted along the trail a little while, her small hand in mine. We were united for that moment in the very simple desire to run past you. Moments like that cannot be contrived. And far less forgotten. Some trails are meant to be shared. That is something that your races do; whatever personal challenges we face on those sky-high trails, we learn to trust in ourselves and each other. I still remember the feeling of that small hand in mine. Learning to trust is something that lasts far beyond the finish line.

But I lost the trust in myself, in my body and in my mind. Years ago after a long solo hike before that first UTMB I came to the realisation 'that I could trust both body and mind to carry me through a long journey alone and on my two feet. It was liberating.' I lost that trust when I realised there can sometimes be a wide gaping chasm between what I want to be able to do, and what I can do. But perhaps somewhere within that realisation is a deeper liberation.

So who are we? The psychologist David DeSteno asked, 'Can the present you trust the future you?'[1] It is a question that reminds me how our future self is fundamentally different from our present self – our emotions, beliefs and ideals are constantly evolving. Biologically most of the cells in my body will have been completely renewed in seven years, so am I then just a series of cells, sensations and moods in constant flux?

I can see myself as a runner now with dispassion, it is just one expression of who I am. A stranger will see a very different 'Lizzy' to the me that you know. But even you will know a different 'Lizzy' to the me that I know. And the me that I thought I knew is also an illusion. Detachment. We are beyond definition, so why do we try to limit ourselves? We are constantly learning, constantly changing. If we can detach from our preconceptions and expectations then we can go beyond what we thought was possible. As Lao Tzu put it so succinctly: 'When I let go of what I am, I become what I might be.'

The joy of running. What is it? It is possibly also beyond definition, but is something I have always felt. And to some extent it must be the reason why I run. My running has never been for the races or for the records. That is not to say that I'm not competitive, but rather that the competition is there inside. I have won races and not been happy when I felt I hadn't done my best. Running has always been for the feeling that it gives me. The sheer enjoyment I get from making a journey under my own effort at the most basic level – a way of exploring myself and the world around me – and the empowerment it gives me at a deeper level, realising that anything and everything can be possible.

It is partly the physical movement itself, the simple rhythmical beat of my feet striking the ground beneath me. It is partly the being outside and exposed to the elements, feeling the cold, the heat, the rain, the wind, the snow, the sunshine. It is partly the feeling it leaves me with after-wards, the satisfaction of something started and completed, the physical wellbeing, the mental clarity.

But it is more than that also, and I hadn't fully realised how much running gives me until this cycle of injury. I've tried (inadequately) to explain it to you. It gives a beautiful feeling of empowerment. Yes, running gives confidence in so many ways, but it goes far beyond that. Going for a run, any run, gives me a sense that anything is possible – it gives me a space in which I can dream and plan for the future, it gives me hope for the world – all while pulling me right there inside the moment, forcing me to live in the now. Empowerment: it is that feeling of infinite possibility, and it is how we manifest that potential as reality.

This kind of empowerment that I'm talking about doesn't necessarily have to come from running. Everyone will find it in a different place in their life, and that place might be different at different stages in life. But the finding of it is essential.

I try to tell you, 'Achievements don't count for anything, they are just another kind of possession, and it is who you are that really matters, right?'

'Fool,' you say, 'who you are led to those achievements, you have some power in a limited frame and you can use it or mock it. Help others before you think about yourself, then you won't have to think about yourself.'

That is what you do. Help others.

But it is true what you say, and the Bhagavad Gita says it in another way: 'You are only entitled to the action, never to its fruits. Do not let the fruits of action be your motive, but do not attach yourself to nonaction.' You've told me time and again, 'Reduce relying on being so doubtful and so unconfident, stick your neck out and say, "It is what it is – there you go!"' Apologising for, or not appreciating, achievement is also an attachment; we have to do the work that is there for us to do with dispassion, losing emotional attachment to the result or the outcome. Only then can we maintain some measure of equanimity.

'Use that power to inspire!' you tell me.

I ask you, 'How can I create a race[2] when I'm not running myself'? You say, 'You want to share the joy of running, so just create the situation that worked for you and hope it works for others.'

Injury or not, running or not, you make me realise the opportunity that I have. You say, 'It is what it is, and in the meantime you are organising a race in a place you love so that others can enjoy it too. You have an opportunity here to encourage more women into running, which in turn demonstrably changes the world for the better.'

You make me laugh: 'Well it could have been worse. You could have been a beauty queen, then started to wither too much for Photoshop and decided to start a beauty contest.'

You say it as it is. 'Happiness does not need definition – it is a by-product of other things,' you say, 'running; playing with children; taking a nice picture; feeling the breeze; helping someone; eating something new and tasty; jumping in the sea; climbing to the top of a hill; seeing an old friend; receiving a nice email; meeting a funny taxi driver; observing something funny in the street; taking someone to the lassi shop.'

Motivation and intention. We have to be doing what we do because we love it, simply that. In running, as in life, we have to learn to take the rough with the smooth, the ups with the downs. The Buddhist doctrine of impermanence teaches that one of the truths about life is that nothing lasts. Everything will pass. Everything indeed has to. It is in the nature of things. We cannot fight against the tide of life. In running, and in life, we have to reach deep within ourselves to find an equanimity that allows us to flow through the good and the not so good. Once more Kipling's *If* so eloquently describes that mindset:[3]

> If you can force your heart and nerve and sinew
> To serve your turn long after they are gone,
> And so hold on when there is nothing in you
> Except the Will which says to them: 'Hold on!'

We have to learn to live with how we think, to learn what can be changed, to learn to change what needs changing, to learn to live with what can't be changed, to enjoy what is good, to enjoy what is easy, to work for what is difficult, to work through what is upsetting. Life is a rich tapestry of what we do and don't know. It is a continual learning. It is a letting go and it is a holding in. It is a recognition of all that is absolutely necessary and a discarding of all that is extraneous. It can take us some time to find out what these things are.

The best things will happen in an unexpected corner of a very ordinary day. There is no end to the unexpectedness, to the pain or to the disappointment, or to the possible joy.

Running has often been the tool that I use as a way to explore, to learn, to live. It takes me to a place of balance – physical, mental, emotional. Running or not is irrelevant. It is the finding something that lets us delve deeper into our own story that matters.

I start to turn inwards, withdrawing my senses, blocking out all the external stimuli, blind to everything but the narrow stretch of road immediately ahead within my gaze. I focus on moving forwards, riding on the rhythm of my breath. The world and all of time has been distilled down into this one moment. Now. Nothing else exists. Nothing else matters. All that there ever was, and all that there ever will be, is embraced by this one moment and my struggle to keep moving through it. The focus is absolute. It dissociates me from the rest of my journey. I am locked deep within my effort, right there in my moment of struggle.

Somewhere on that last stretch of the long road back into Kathmandu I came close to an understanding of what running has come to mean to me. It is that overwhelming sense of presence, of being firmly rooted in the moment. And being in the *moment* is a freedom. Dogen Zenji, founder of the Sōtō School of Zen Buddhism, put it beautifully: 'There is a penetrating liberation in immediate actuality.' The *moment* is of course the space between the known and unknown, the point of infinite possibility. What we do with that possibility is our challenge.

Jeff Lowe, a legendary mountain climber, has said, 'Climbing can be like a meditation, where everything else falls away and you're so focused for a long period of time that when you come out of that, you usually have a better perspective.'[4]

Running can put me in a similar place. Sometimes I need something that will absorb all of my attention. It is there that I meet myself. It is there that I learn to know myself more deeply. It is there that I experience life beyond the limitations of time and space. It gives me a moment where I almost touch reality. A moment where everything seems to make sense. A moment where I think I understand. Fleeting, ephemeral, short-lived. But real. Is it one of the reasons why I run? I've felt it only infrequently. But I have felt it. And maybe the potential is enough to keep running.

We all find our own way to feel it. I've felt it other times too. Buried in the making of what will become a good piece of writing. Or when I've been able to give what it took to help someone go beyond what they thought was possible. We don't need to run. We just need to recognise it for what it is. It is when life is imbued with meaning without needing to look for the meaning of life. It is when it is enough just to be alive.

There are, evidently, a multitude of reasons why I run. But I still find myself wrestling with the question. I ask you, 'But what is the *why* behind why I run?' You say, 'Apart from endorphin release I don't know either. Ask a biochemist. You don't have to know the answer to this question. The not knowing makes it more interesting.'

It does.

❖ ❖ ❖

We all have one. It is *that* run. Its physical location may change as we move house, region, country, continent. But it is the run that is always with us. It is the run that we can trust ourselves to. It is the run that is waiting to enfold us back again after injury, absence or discouragement. It is where we go in the cool of the early morning, in the heat of the day, in the fading light of a setting sun. It is a place we go to in all seasons, observing and feeling the changes, until the rhythm of the earth becomes our own, a comforting reminder of the impermanence of all things. It is where we go to seek solace, to seek challenge. It is where we go when we need to push, to hold back. It is where we go when we need to find a fragile peace.

I step outside. Lock the door behind me. Legs feel heavy. I have that morning time post-sleep tiredness, despite the coffee. I lift myself onto my bicycle. It is my lifeline, the conduit that channels me between the chaotic streets of Kathmandu and the freedom of the hills. Kathmandu is a city that assaults our senses with its multitude of sights, sounds and smells. It is a city of poverty, a city of riches, a city of contrasts and contradictions, but a city where life has a beauty of its own, played out in front of us on the street, with a namaste and a smile. You know it too. The cycle jolts me out of morning inertia and the tide of life sweeps me along with it until the city has dwindled into the paddy fields at the foot of the Shivapuri hills.

Bike locked, I start slowly. The legs, the body, take their time to ease into movement. But even with the first step I'm shaken into a stillness. The turmoil of emotion that permeates my every day – the doubts, the fears, the hopes, the apprehensions, the joy – is held in suspension. There is a quiet within my move- ment. I think. But my thoughts are not my master. For the moment I am simply running. Identity and purpose are irrele- vant. To be running is enough. Because if I am running then I am alive. And to be alive is everything.

Today alone. Often with you. This run was once new enough that I would frequently lose myself, but with repetition I learned to know these paths and trails, until I could run them with ease, without need for concentration or effort. Until I would lose myself again, in a different sense, immersed simply in the pure effort of the run. I know how it will feel beneath my feet, I know where there will be mud even on the hottest day, I know which rocks I will slip on and which not, I know which branch to grab to break a descent or ease a step up. I know it green and lush in the post-monsoon fecundity, I know it sparse and dry. You know it too.

The beautiful contrast between the quiet of the hilly woods and the cries of 'hi', 'hello', 'how are you' from laughing village children, between the solitude and the dodging of dogs, cows, goats, chickens, soothes me. It reminds me of my own insignificance, and yet at the same time of the fundamental necessity of my existence.

It is *that* run. It is the run that sets me free and brings me back home; to that still place within the core of my being where I love with all that I am.

'Tell it how it is,' you said. 'Everything is possible.'

> *Time past and time future*
> *What might have been and what has been*
> *Point to one end, which is always present.*

T.S. Eliot, *Four Quartets*[5]

Epilogue

The core of a book is only reached through the act of writing itself. This in itself has taken me on a journey deep into myself and into my relationship with others and the world around me. This story has evolved into something very different to that simple story of a long race that I had envisaged years ago. As I wrote and my story took shape, it became a conversation between my head, my heart and my words. It became a meditation on love – a love of running and a love of life. These words are a snapshot in time for me, a blank canvas for you to draw your own understanding on.

It is the story of my journey of discovery, of exploration, and then of rediscovery and realisation.

Running became the way that I made that journey. The way is irrelevant, it is the *how* of how we make our journey and the *how* of how we share it with the people around us that is important.

I cannot give you a neat and tidy conclusion because my journey goes on . . . there is no destination, the journey *is* all. Whether you run or not, whether you race or not, you are also on a journey. This is your story too.

Race History

Editorial advice suggested that a full history of races and results might be interesting for the reader. I realise now that I have never actually kept a full record. Perhaps this was careless of me but there seemed to always be other things to be more concerned with.

Medals, certificates, trophies and cowbells are now haphazardly distributed between a box in London, a shelf in Switzerland and a window ledge in Kathmandu. Some never even made it that far and remained where they were given, thanks to an already too-full rucksack to be managed on my return bicycle or train journey. Bottles of wine and rounds of cheese were shared, the cut glass given away. A piece of gold remains in South Africa due to my reluctance to pay a significant customs charge for yet another medal (albeit one of gold).

Results are lost somewhere in the ethereal world of the Internet.

It was the running of the races that was important to me and where that running took me – geographically, physically, mentally, emotionally.

Probably I raced too much. But well, as Hunter S.

Thompson said: 'Life should not be a journey to the grave with the intention of arriving safely in a pretty and well-preserved body, but rather to skid in broadside in a cloud of smoke, thoroughly used up, totally worn out, and loudly proclaiming "Wow!" What a Ride!"'

It has been, and I hope not over yet.

For the purposes of clarity in the reading of *Runner* the following information is probably the most relevant.

The Ultra-Trail du Mont-Blanc – France, Italy, Switzerland

Year	Distance	Ascent	Position	Time
2005	158km	8,600m	1st woman, 24th overall	26:53:51
2008	166km	9,400m	1st woman, 14th overall	25:19:41
2009	166km	9,400m	2nd woman, 18th overall	25:04:42
2010	88km	5,100m	1st woman, 19th overall	11:47:30
2011	170km	9,700m	1st woman, 13th overall	25:02:00
2012	110km	5,600m	1st woman, 16th overall	12:32:13

Everest Base Camp to Kathmandu, Nepal

(about 320km with over 10,000m ascent and 14,000m descent)

Date	Time
October 2007	74 hours 36 minutes
November 2011	71 hours 25 minutes
April 2013	63 hours 8 minutes

Other relevant results

Date & location	Event	Position	Time/distance
October 2006, Korea	100km World Championships	1st woman, gold medal	07:28:46
October 2010, Gibraltar	100km World Championships	3rd woman, bronze medal	07:33:26
September 2011, UK	24hr Commonwealth Championships	1st woman, 1st overall	247.07km*
September 2012, Greece	Spartathlon	1st woman, 3rd overall	27:02:17**

* new women's world record for 24 hours on the road
** new women's course record

Further results (also incomplete) can be found at:
http://lizzyhawker.com/results-highlights/

Ultra Tour Monte Rosa

During the long alpine summers, my body and mind sometimes demanded a respite from my self-imposed two twelve-hour back-to-back training days over the route of the UTMB. It was probably inevitable that I would turn back to those mountains that had first held my curiosity and passion as a six-year-old child. So I would find myself making two far-longer-than-twelve-hour back-to-back training days running on the magnificent trails around the Monte Rosa on the Swiss–Italian border, anonymous and unrecognised, no other runner to be seen. These were the mountains that I had first looked up to as a child and then explored more intimately over the intervening years. As I learned to know and to love the trails of the Tour de Monte Rosa, the 150km footpath encircling the beautiful massif of the Monte Rosa, which passes beneath a multitude of other 4,000m summits including the iconic and awe-inspiring Matterhorn, I realised that *these* were the trails that I wanted to share with other runners. The idea of a new ultra marathon race was born.

The idea remained only that until, after hours of discussion with Richard, it started to take seed. He finally persuaded me to at least try to manifest the potential and make it a reality. Joined also by Richard's friend Jon, the idea germinated and now word is spreading.

Why another race? Our objective is simple – to share the joy that I have had from running. Over my years of running in the mountains I have explored incredible landscapes, experienced different cultures, shared great experiences and explored my own physical, mental and emotional limits. I have challenged myself in all sorts of ways and learned a huge amount about myself and others. It is all of these things that we hope to encourage people to experience for themselves – not only during the race, but during their journey to reach the start line, and their journey beyond the finish line.

Come and join us. Find out more about our Ultra Tour Monte Rosa at www.ultratourmonterosa.com.

Notes

Prologue

1 T. S. Eliot, *Four Quartets,* from 'Little Gidding', 1943.

Chapter One

1 The route evolved over the years; these are the figures for that third edition in 2005.

2 The list of obligatory kit is now far more extensive: mobile phone (that works in France, Italy, Switzerland), personal cup (15cl minimum), 1 litre water (minimum), two headtorches in good working order with replacement batteries, survival blanket (1.4m x 2m minimum), whistle, adhesive elastic bandage (100cm x 6cm), food reserve, waterproof jacket with hood, long running leggings or combination of leggings and long socks which cover the legs completely, additional warm midlayer, cap or bandana, warm hat, warm and waterproof gloves, waterproof overtrousers.

3 Robert Pirsig, *Zen and the Art of Motorcycle Maintenance: an Inquiry into Values*, Vintage, 2014.

Chapter Two

Opening quote: Do Hyun Choe

1 The booklet provided by the race organisers with all the relevant information, maps, profiles, timings – I was carrying the entire booklet unaware of just how well the route would be marked.

2 Wallisian: of the Wallis (Valais) canton of Switzerland.

Chapter Three

Opening quote: Edward Whymper, *Scrambles Amongst the Alps in the years 1860–69,* 2002

1 Sir Ernest Shackleton, *South: The Story of Shackleton's Last Expedition, 1914–1917,* 1999

2 We kept traditional ship watches for that cruise: 00:00 to 04:00 and 12:00 to 16:00, or 04:00 to 08:00 and 16:00 to 20:00, or 20:00 to 00:00 and 08:00 to 12:00. On later cruises I would work twelve-hour shifts, sometimes 20:00 to 08:00, or worse, 02:00 to 14:00.

3 A CTD is an oceanography instrument used to determine the conductivity, temperature and depth of the ocean.

Chapter Four

Opening quote: Apsley Cherry-Garrard, *The Worst Journey in the World.* The rest of this quote deserves expansion: 'And I tell you, if you have the desire for knowledge and the power to give it physical expression, go out and explore. If you are a brave man you will do nothing: if you are fearful you may do much, for none but cowards have need to prove their bravery. Some will tell you that you are mad, and nearly all will say, "What is the use?" For we are a nation of shopkeepers, and no shopkeeper will look at research which does not promise him a financial return within a year. And so you will sledge nearly alone, but those with whom you sledge will not be shopkeepers: that is worth a good deal. If you march your Winter Journeys you will have your rewards, so long as all you want is a penguin's egg.'

1 Skins are long strips made of nylon or mohair that can be attached to the bottom of a pair of skis allowing the user to slide the skis uphill without falling backwards.

2 Rob's collection of mountaineering essays, *Over the Hills and Far Away*, demonstrate both his love of quiet places and his inclination for raw adventure.

3 'Great things are done when men and mountains meet' – William Blake, c. 1793.

Chapter Six

1 As described, http://trailrunningnepal.org/running-for-records-across-nepal

2 See http://thegreathimalayatrail.org/the-ght/trail-history/

3 See www.everestmailrun.com

4 *Across the Top* by Sorrel Wilby, Pan Macmillan, 1992

5 The Bob Graham Round, http://www.bobgrahamclub.org.uk/

6 UK ultrarunning initiative, http://runfurther.com/

7 Mustang Mountain Trail Race, www.mustangtrailrace.com

Chapter Seven

Opening quote: William Blake, *Auguries of Innocence,* c. 1803

1 It is one of these photos that is now the cover of this book. See www.alextreadway.co.uk.

Chapter Eight

1 Himalayan Database: http://www.himalayandatabase.com/

2 Mihaly Csikszentmihalyi , *Finding Flow: The Psychology of Engagement with Everyday Life*, 1998

3 Alan Watts *Does It Matter? Essays on Man's Relation to Materiality*, 2007

Chapter Nine

Opening quote: Douglas Adams, *The Long Dark Teatime of the Soul*, William Heinemann, 1988

1 Laufschule Scuol: http://www.laufschule-scuol.ch/

2 Carl Sagan, *Cosmos*, Random House, 1980

3 Albert Mummery, *My Climbs in the Alps and Caucasus*, 1895

4 Manaslu Mountain Trail: manaslutrailrace.org; Mustang Mountain Trail Race: mustangtrailrace.com; Kathamandu Trail Race: ultratrailkathmandu.com

5 Trail Running Nepal: www.trailrunningnepal.org

6 irunfar.com: the most dedicated and comprehensive online portal for ultra distance running created by Bryon Powell and his partner Meghan Hicks.

7 98km sister race from Courmayeur to Chamonix.

8 *Does It Matter? Essays on Man's Relation to Materiality* by Alan Watts, 2007

9 Hong Kong 100 Ultra Trail Race: www.hk100-ultra.com

Chapter Ten

1 John Stevens, *The Marathon Monks of Mount Hiei*, 2013

2 Alexandra David-Neel, *Magic and Mystery in Tibet*, 2007

3 Pema Chödrön, *When Things Fall Apart*, Shambhala Publications, 2010

Chapter Eleven

Opening quote: B.K.S. Iyengar, *Light on Life: the Journey to Wholeness, Inner Peace and Ultimate Freedom*, Rodale, 2008

1 The traditional Nepali meal of steamed rice, lentil soup and vegetable curry.

2 Richard and Adrian Crane, *Running the Himalayas*, 1984

3 www.greathimalayatrail.com

4 http://www.thenorthfacejournal.com/still-dancing-on-these-paths-in-the-sky-by-lizzy-hawker/

5 Upendra Sunuwar: http://trailrunningnepal.org/about/about-trail-running-in-nepal/guide-service-for-running-fastpacking-in-nepal/

Chapter Twelve

Opening quote: Lao Tzu, reputed author of *Tao Te Ching*.

1 Run Rabbit Run: it is worth a look! http://runrabbitrunsteamboat.com/

Chapter Thirteen

1 Boudha: http://en.wikipedia.org/wiki/Boudhanath

2 Tenzing Hillary Everest Marathon: http://www.everestmarathon.com

Chapter Fourteen

Opening quote: The original quote is: 'A man who has not passed through the inferno of his passions has never overcome them'.
C.G.Jung

1 Anne Morrow Lindbergh, *Gift from the Sea*, Vintage Books, 1991
2 Alan Watts, *The Wisdom of Insecurity: A Message for an Age of Anxiety*, 2011
3 Andreas Fransson: http://andreasfransson.se/
4 Samuel Beckett, *Worstward Ho*, 1983

Chapter Fifteen

Opening quote: Maya Angelou, *Conversations with Maya Angelou*, ed. Jeffrey M Eliot, 1981

1 Viktor Frankl's classic tribute to hope, *Man's Search for Meaning*, 1946, is an example of this.
2 Mary Elizabeth Frye, 'Do Not Stand at My Grave and Weep', 1932
3 Richard Bandler and John Grinder, *The Structure of Magic*, Science and Behaviour Books Inc. 1975
4 Parker J. Palmer, *A Hidden Wholeness*, Wiley & Sons, 2004

Chapter Sixteen

1 David DeSteno, *The Truth about Trust*, Hudson Street Press, 2014
2 See: Ultra Tour Monte Rosa www.ultratourmonterosa.com
3 Please read Kipling's *If* in its entirety. It is worth it.
4 Jeff is now speechless through illness. These are his words as passed on by his partner Connie Self (http://www.denverpost.com/sports/ci_25739108/legendary-mountain-climber-jeff-lowe-slowly-dying-als).
5 T.S. Eliot, *Four Quartets*, 'Burnt Nerton'

Bibliography

Bandler, Richard and John Grinder, *The Structure of Magic*, Science and Behaviour Books Inc., 1975

Cherry-Garrard, Apsley, *The Worst Journey in the World*, Picador, 1994

Collister, Rob, *Over the Hills and Far Away*, Ernest Press, 1996

Crane, Nick, *Clear Waters Rising*, Penguin Books, 1997

Crane, Richard and Adrian, *Running the Himalayas*, Hodder & Stoughton Ltd, 1984

Csikszentmihalyi, Mihaly, *Finding Flow: The Psychology of Engagement with Everyday Life*, Basic Books, 1998

David-Neel, Alexandra, *Magic and Mystery in Tibet*, Souvenir Press Ltd, 2007

Frankl, Viktor E., *Man's Search for Meaning*, Rider, 2004

Govinda, Lama Anagarika, *The Way of the White Clouds*, Rider, 2006

Krabbé, Tim, *The Rider*, Bloomsbury Publishing, 2002

Mummery, Albert, *My Times in the Alps and Caucasus*, T. Fisher Unwin,1895

Palmer, Parker J., *A Hidden Wholeness*, Wiley & Sons, 2004

Pirsig, Robert, *Zen and the Art of Motorcycle Maintenance: an Inquiry into Values*, Vintage, 2014

Shackleton, Sir Ernest, *South: The Story of Shackleton's Last Expedition, 1914–1917*, Pimlico, 1999

Stevens, John, *The Marathon Monks of Mount Hiei*, Echo Point Books and Media, 2013

Watts, Alan, *Does It Matter? Essays on Man's Relation to Materiality*, New World Library, 2007

Watts, Alan, *The Wisdom of Insecurity: A Message for an Age of Anxiety*, Random House Inc., 2011

Whymper, Edward, *Scrambles Amongst the Alps in the Years 1860–69*, National Geographic Books, 2002

Wilby, Sorrel, *Across the Top*, Pan Macmillan, 1992

Acknowledgements

I am not entirely sure how I am supposed to write this. If I had little idea of how to write a book, I have even less about how to write an acknowledgements page. I have looked back into my PhD thesis, at the books on the shelf in front of me and searched on the Internet, but none seem to help very much.

How to give adequate thanks to all those who played some part in this story of a *long run* that has been part of a journey through a life? No chance.

Instead, here I simply give thanks due for the immediate task of writing this book. I'm terrified of leaving something or someone vital out (as, I think, all authors must be) so this will be mostly generic. Those of you who have helped me know who you are. You have been many and the help considerable. I will thank you personally.

So, this book. It is now, finally, a book. Thanks to all who had a part in getting it to this point, and in particular those who gave the editorial advice that provoked a complete restructuring, reworking and rewriting of the second two-thirds in the last two or three weeks. I did actually despair, but now, on the other side of all of that, this is as good as I can get this manuscript without many more months, editor by my side. So thank you. I hope I have salvaged something of the opportunity that was almost lost. For the subtitle also, thanks: the book became (eventually) what it said it would be.

If a picture is worth a thousand words I'd have to write another chapter or two to say thank you for the photos that capture those memories. I'm not even going to try. One word, thanks, will have to suffice.

To those who have read bits and pieces as I have gone along and given me the confidence that yes, I should really continue, whatever my head was telling me, heartfelt thanks. And thanks also to all who responded to my desperate eleventh-hour plea and read a particular chunk, some of you late at night (and some of you already in bed, I know), and told me it was, actually, OK. Be this on your heads. But thank you.

The last words have been written in Upminster, so thanks to my parents for patiently watching me drive myself nuts, and almost (but not quite, I think) resisting being driven nuts also. Thank you for being there now, as ever you have been.

And thanks also to you. Thank you for the hours of life spent discussing everything and nothing, as well as everything else. I didn't fully realise all that you were trying to say until I tried to write these words. I do now. Please forgive me for the ruthless borrowing. You told me, 'write whatever you feel'. I have done. Well, nearly. Not all. As you said, 'Like running, the book is now normal to you, never going to feel to you like a stranger reading for the first time.' All I hope is that this is of some small interest for that stranger reading for the first time. 'Send it,' you told me. I have now.

And to the reader, if you have made it this far then I thank you too. Please be gentle in your reading and please be harsh in your (self) reflections. I give to you a canvas upon which to reflect on your own journey. That is all. If you are reading this before rather than after then turn back the pages and I wish you the best of luck. A book needs a reader otherwise it has no point.

Namaste.